New Comparisons in World Literature

Series editors
Upamanyu Pablo Mukherjee
Department of English and Comparative Literary Studies
University of Warwick
Coventry, UK

Neil Lazarus
Department of English and Comparative Literary Studies
University of Warwick
Coventry, UK

New Comparisons in World Literature offers a fresh perspective on one of the most exciting current debates in humanities by approaching 'world literature' not in terms of particular kinds of reading but as a particular kind of writing. We take 'world literature' to be that body of writing that registers in various ways, at the levels of form and content, the historical experience of capitalist modernity. We aim to publish works that take up the challenge of understanding how literature registers both the global extension of 'modern' social forms and relations and the peculiar new modes of existence and experience that are engendered as a result. Our particular interest lies in studies that analyse the registration of this decisive historical process in literary consciousness and affect.

Editorial board
Dr. Nicholas Brown, University of Illinois, USA
Dr. Bo G. Ekelund, University of Stockholm, Sweden
Dr. Dorota Kolodziejczyk, Wroclaw University, Poland
Professor Paulo de Medeiros, University of Warwick, UK
Dr. Robert Spencer, University of Manchester, UK
Professor Imre Szeman, University of Alberta, Canada
Professor Peter Hitchcock, Baruch College, USA
Dr Ericka Beckman, University of Illinois at Urbana-Champaign, USA
Dr Sarah Brouillette, Carleton University, Canada
Professor Supriya Chaudhury, Jadavpur University, India
Professor Stephen Shapiro, University of Warwick, UK

More information about this series at
http://www.springer.com/series/15067

Melissa Kennedy

Narratives of Inequality

Postcolonial Literary Economics

Melissa Kennedy
University of Vienna
Vienna, Austria

New Comparisons in World Literature
ISBN 978-3-319-59956-4   ISBN 978-3-319-59957-1 (eBook)
DOI 10.1007/978-3-319-59957-1

Library of Congress Control Number: 2017944139

© The Editor(s) (if applicable) and The Author(s) 2017
This work is subject to copyright. All rights are solely and exclusively licensed by the Publisher, whether the whole or part of the material is concerned, specifically the rights of translation, reprinting, reuse of illustrations, recitation, broadcasting, reproduction on microfilms or in any other physical way, and transmission or information storage and retrieval, electronic adaptation, computer software, or by similar or dissimilar methodology now known or hereafter developed.
The use of general descriptive names, registered names, trademarks, service marks, etc. in this publication does not imply, even in the absence of a specific statement, that such names are exempt from the relevant protective laws and regulations and therefore free for general use.
The publisher, the authors and the editors are safe to assume that the advice and information in this book are believed to be true and accurate at the date of publication. Neither the publisher nor the authors or the editors give a warranty, express or implied, with respect to the material contained herein or for any errors or omissions that may have been made. The publisher remains neutral with regard to jurisdictional claims in published maps and institutional affiliations.

Cover illustration: Blackout Concepts/Alamy Stock Photo

Printed on acid-free paper

This Palgrave Macmillan imprint is published by Springer Nature
The registered company is Springer International Publishing AG
The registered company address is: Gewerbestrasse 11, 6330 Cham, Switzerland

For Bev, John, and Nicky

Acknowledgements

This book was made possible both intellectually and materially by my husband and globalisation debate partner extraordinaire, Jan Zaleski, whom I thank for constant support, unflagging interest, and unstinting geekiness.

Many thanks also to members of the English Department at the University of Vienna, especially Monika Seidl and Susi Reichl, for their generosity and good will in taking on a homeless foreign academic when I moved to Austria in 2012. A draft of this manuscript was submitted at Vienna for my *Habilitation* in 2016. I thank the members of the commission for the extraordinary amount of time they spent on this process, and especially the external readers, Chris Prentice, Neil Lazarus, and John McLeod, whose input improved this final version.

Thanks to encouraging friends, mentors, and helpful readers Janet Wilson, Helga Ramsey-Kurz, Ole Birk Laursen, members of the Warwick Research Collective, and the World Literature Network. To my postcolonial and world literature peers in New Zealand, Ireland, the UK, France, Austria, and Germany, I am proud to be part of a supportive group whose ethical engagement in world politics and humanity in discussions of global inequality and poverty inspire my research. If only we ran the world.

Arguments made in this manuscript have been published in the following articles and book chapters: 'How to Be Rich, Popular and Have It All: Conflicted Attitudes to Wealth and Poverty in Post-Crisis Fiction' in *Uncommon Wealths in Postcolonial Fiction*, ed., Helga Ramsey-Kurz and Melissa Kennedy (2017); 'Economic Inequality in Postcolonial

Fiction' in *The Bloomsbury Introduction to Postcolonial Writing: New Contexts, New Narratives, New Debates*, ed., Jenni Ramone (2017); 'Urban Poverty and Homelessness in the international Postcolonial World' in *Postcolonialism: Globalization, Labour, and Rights*, ed., Pavan Malreddy, Birte Heidemann, Ole Birk Laursen, and Janet Wilson (2015); 'The Postcolonial Slum' in *Re-Inventing the Postcolonial (in the) Metropolis*, eds., Cecile Sandten and Annika Bauer (2016); and 'The Māori Renaissance' in *A Cambridge History of New Zealand Literature*, ed., Mark Williams (2016). I am grateful to the publishers for permission to reuse this material.

WORKS CITED

Malreddy, Pavan Kumar, and Birte Heidemann, Ole Birk Laursen and Janet Wilson, eds. *Reworking Postcolonialism: Globalization, Labour and Rights*. London: Palgrave Macmillan, 2015.
Ramone, Jenni, ed. *The Bloomsbury Introduction to Postcolonial Writing: New Contexts, New Narratives, NewDebates*. London: Bloomsbury, 2017.
Ramsey-Kurz, Helga and Melissa Kennedy, eds. *Uncommon Wealths in Postcolonial Fiction*. Leiden and Boston: Brill, 2017.
Sandten, Cecile, and Annika Bauer, eds. *Re-Inventing the Postcolonial (in the) Metropolis*. Leiden &Boston: Brill, 2016.
Williams, Mark, ed. *A Cambridge History of New Zealand Literature*. Cambridge: Cambridge University Press, 2016.

Contents

1 Introduction 1

2 Colonial Capitalism 35

3 Neocolonialism 99

4 Global Neoliberalism 155

5 Conclusion 211

Index 221

CHAPTER 1

Introduction

POSTCOLONIAL ECONOMIC CRITICISM

The financial crisis of 2008 caused a global recession to rival that of the 1930s Great Depression. After the shock of the seemingly unexpected crash wore off, anger, protests, and strikes spread around the world in response to unemployment, welfare cuts, and austerity measures on the one hand and, on the other, large government spending on the banking sector and major corporations that had caused the meltdown. Within the broad range of protest, a recurring cluster of issues pointed to widespread and growing public awareness of the failure of market-led political economy to adequately and fairly care for the majority in each country. While a culture of protest against neoliberal capitalism is not new, the sharp increase in protest, media coverage, and mass public articulation since the 2008 crisis makes the inequalities of neoliberal globalisation difficult to ignore. The instability of the market in boom-and-bust cycles and the persistence of relative poverty even in the world's richest countries have alerted many to the contradictions of a system in which liberal economic values, such as free markets, low tariffs, competition, and mobility of capital, prove incompatible with a liberal philosophy of individual freedom, choice, and the equality guaranteed by the United Nations' Universal Declaration of Human Rights. The growing gap between rich and poor—today refocused on that between the ultra-rich 1% and the struggling middle and working classes which identify with the Occupy slogan 'we are the 99 per cent'—reveals the failure of capitalism to fulfil the expectations of neoliberalism as best suited to regulate, distribute, and promote economic and social advancement. The proliferation of protest movements speaks to an increasingly mainstream critique of progress and development as more and more people feel shut out of the riches and opportunities promised by neoliberalism. The extent of this public interest is most apparent in the appearance of discussions on economic inequality in mainstream media and popular culture which, by 2017, show no sign of letting up.

The crash and its aftermath catalysed a rush of pop-economics books which made accessible to the general public critiques of the current political economy by leading economists including academics, Nobel Prize winners, and representatives of financial institutions. This concerted public interest is best illustrated by the unprecedented success of French economist Thomas Piketty's 700-page bestseller *Capital in the Twenty-first Century* (2014). Following the author on a sell-out US tour of lectures, radio, and television talk shows, *New York Magazine* called Piketty a 'rock-star economist' (Kachka 2014, n.p.). While one *Guardian* reporter quipped that, in a film of the book, Piketty ought to be played by Colin Firth (Moore 2014), visual media has already taken up the narrativisation of the financial crash, in films *The Big Short* (2015) and *The Wolf of Wall Street* (2013), and in documentaries *Inside Job* (2010) and *Inequality for All* (2013). New versions of classics have also been reinterpreted in light of the financial crisis. In his 2013 film of F. Scott Fitzgerald's *The Great Gatsby* (1925), director Baz Luhrmann calls attention to what he calls the 'parallels of place, culture and mind set' of New York in the Roaring Twenties and Wall Street in the early 2000s (Levy 2013, n.p.). In particular, the 2008 crisis reactivated indictment of the greed and hubris embodied by Fitzgerald's Tom and Daisy: 'careless people' who 'smashed up things and creatures and then retreated back into their money or their vast carelessness, ... and let other people clean up the mess they had made' (179). Indeed, this oft-cited line from the novel is one of the few quoted verbatim in the film, prominently positioned at the close. In post-crash analyses, the famous quote has been variously interpreted as representing the irresponsible risk-taking of the US banking industry (Das 2011, 342–343), as illustrating the corruption and dirty money of the elite (Quirk 2012), and as indicative of the USA's overselling of real estate (Mertens 2012). The sudden recall of Fitzgerald's line illuminates the periodicity of the 1929 and 2008 financial crises, while the public interest in various forms of narrativisation of the financial crisis—in fiction, non-fiction, film, and documentary—indicates the importance of cultural expression in making sense of the economy's role in society. Suddenly, Fitzgerald's novel *matters* again, newly interpreted for its critique on wealth by both literary and economic analysts. Furthermore, to bring back into circulation Fitzgerald's famous line in a movie, in mainstream journalism, and in economic arguments stakes a claim that literary fiction *tout court* has a role to play in making sense of the 2008 crisis and its aftermath.

British responses to the financial crisis and ensuing recession include a similar turn to the national literary tradition, which offers the general public accessible narratives of historical, social, and cultural experiences of economic shock and inequality. George Orwell's journalism of the Great Depression, *Down and Out in Paris and London* (1933), was updated in an exposé on poverty in Paris and London in 2011 for the BBC (Kirby 2011), and Stephen Armstrong repeated Orwell's northward trajectory in *The Road to Wigan Pier Revisited* (2012). British cartoonist Kate Evans's graphic art biography of Rosa Luxemburg, *Red Rosa* (2015), which includes summaries of Karl Marx's *Capital* (1867) in comic form, was reprinted four times in its first year. Journalism invoking urban inequality portrayed in nineteenth-century writing has proliferated since the 2011 High Pay Commission findings that ever-concentrating wealth has led to a rise in inequality which, 'if it continues unchecked will take us back to Victorian levels of pay inequality in less than thirty years' (Hargreaves et al. 2012, 16). Urban geographer Danny Dorling claims, 'people last lived lives as unequal as today, as measured by wage inequality, in 1854, when Charles Dickens was writing *Hard Times*' (2011, 316), while for Tristram Hunt, Friedrich Engels's *The Condition of the Working Class in England* (1872) accurately portrays the pressing inequality issues of today: '[t]he chasm between rich and poor seen in London today resembles the Manchester that Engels described in the 1840s' (2007, n.p.). To cite Dickens alongside Orwell in relation to today is not to randomly select like themes: the 1840s, 1930s, and 2010s represent moments in the economic cycle when wages were at their lowest, when un- and underemployment were high, and when social instability was prevalent despite record rates of profit and high-end salaries. In each era, literary representations of inequality, in their various forms of fiction and documentary reporting, register these moments. Read superficially for plot and content, such literature provides valuable and accessible historical records, and acts as an ever-accessible reminder of repeating structures of inequality and damning critiques of the social repercussions of the gap between rich and poor. Reading across different historical times and spaces illuminates striking commonalities of narrative emphasis, mode, and tone which invite closer consideration of the role and function of narrative for socio-economic critique.

Certainly, economists are likely to contest the truth of Dorling's or Hunt's dramatic claims, and literary critics are likely to warn against reading Dickens and Orwell for factual fidelity. Nevertheless, such casual journalistic recourse to fiction registers an instinct that literary narrative has something to teach us about our current socio-economic predicament, narrating through story how the economy works and how people—and characters—live in and respond to it. By evoking historical fiction (Dickens, Fitzgerald) and documentary (Engels, Orwell), contemporary analysts of economic inequality suggest that the subjective intuitions and artistic interpretations of local and specific historical moments contain echoes of similar economic contexts that are familiar today. The structures of inequality, and the daily materiality of poverty and its impact on social opportunities and outcomes of the past resonate with those of the present. Following the 2008 financial crisis, fiction suddenly became relevant again in mainstream journalism and in ever-growing numbers of pop-economics publications. Used as expedient shortcuts to bring to life the complex contexts of historical times and places, fiction helps readers ground in an imaginable reality the obtuse, abstract non-sense of political economy that in 2008 burst out of its tidily compartmentalised, easily overlooked dedicated pages in the newspaper and spots on the evening news. More importantly, punctuating dry economic facts with literature's vivid, fully realised life-worlds asks the reader to engage personally and imaginatively in discussions of the contemporary economy on emotive and affective levels: to claim 'Victorian levels of pay inequality' means little to a young Millennial, but to claim a Dickensian level of poverty evokes the injustice suffered by Oliver Twist or Pip, to name two of Dickens's heroes still current in popular culture and education.

When Baz Luhrmann mixed hip hop with 1920s jazz music for the soundtrack of *The Great Gatsby*, he registered an aesthetic parallel between the Great Depression and the Great Recession. In their respective eras, both jazz and hip hop were forms of musical expression containing cultural critique of inequality by racially and economically marginalised African Americans. Intercalating hip hop artist Jay Z's syncopated beat with 1920s jazz reflects the gaps and bridges of this time conflation. Luhrmann states: 'to quote one of Jay's rhymes "history doesn't repeat itself, it rhymes." What I get from that is just that the universal truth moves through time and geography' (Ohneswere 2013, n.p.). The movie's music speaks to long-term and long-range structures of inequality that reveal not period but periodicity, the ups and downs of the capitalist world-system. Piketty similarly cites from literature to bridge past and present: '[Honoré de Balzac's] Père Goriot's pasta may have become Steve Jobs's tablet, and investments in the West Indies in 1800 [in Jane Austen's *Mansfield Park*] may have become investments in China or South Africa in 2010' (115). In using music and fiction to illustrate *longue durée* economic patterns, Luhrmann and Piketty point to the longevity of cultural expression that remains remembered in the public imaginary—listening to jazz and reading Jane Austen—long after the specificities of their historical contexts have been forgotten.

Piketty's own statistics of wealth and salary distribution corroborate the literary registration of similarities across time and space that Luhrmann intuits. Gatsby's investment wealth and that of Steve Jobs represent pinnacles of financial success between the crashes of 1929 and 2008, peaks of national wealth invested in the stock market at the apogee of the age of European empire and again in the early 2000s. As Piketty summarises, 'it was not until the coming of the twenty-first century that the wealthy countries regained the same level of stock-market capitalization relative to GDP [Gross Domestic Product] that Paris and London achieved in the early 1900s' (28). At the bottom end of the scale, overly represented by African Americans and ethnic minorities to whom jazz and hip hop speak, Piketty claims 'the poorer half of the population [in the UK and USA] are as poor today as they were in the past, with barely 5% of total wealth in 2010, just as in 1910' (261). When, in response to such poverty, Muhammad Yunus's Bangladeshi microcredit bank for the poor, Grameen, opened a branch in New York in 2008 (there are now 11 branches in the USA) and in Glasgow in 2013, the gap between 'First' and 'Third' Worlds, and between socio-economic experiences of the past and present, appeared to have dissolved. Instead of a linear trajectory of improvement and progress through development created by capitalism, the global world economy is now more accurately characterised as one world shaped by inequality and uneven development, both internal and external.

Disproving or severely undermining the validity of foundational principles of neoliberalism has shaken confidence in the ability of capitalism to adequately adjudicate and regulate the world economy. The crash challenged the discourses of modernity, progress, and development that were touted as the prerequisites for worldwide improvement in standards of living. The extensive fallout from the 2008 crisis in developed nations challenges popular conceptions of wealth and poverty, by revealing at once worrying immiseration in the world's richest countries and great fortunes held by the elite in some of the poorest countries. To speak again today of poverty challenges the neoliberal understanding of globalisation as a world split into categories by economic performance, commonly labelled the First and Third Worlds, developed and developing nations, the West and the Rest, the Global North and South, the capitalist core and periphery. As registered in the terminology, these labels conceive of the world as economically divided, split between the European centres and colonial outposts that even today follow the geopolitical contours of nineteenth-century European empire. The global financial crisis, however, challenged these neat binaries: no longer was poverty restricted to the 'dollar a day' relief programmes of the world's poorest nations but evoked in relation to First World poverty for those hardest hit by welfare austerity, job loss, and housing foreclosures. At the same time, a new spotlight on the finance brokers and company directors whose risk-taking caused the crisis and subsequent market contraction focused attention on extreme wealth and the ethically dubious ways of creating it and spending it. As a result, there has been a concerted shift of emphasis away from talking about poverty to focus instead on comparative measures of inequality. This reorientation, popularised by the Occupy movement's motto 'we are the 99 per cent,' which spread globally in response to the 2008 crisis, takes away the thorny issue of scales of immiseration that make First and Third World poverty seem so dissimilar. Analysis of wealth and income in terms of percentiles, popularised by the Occupy slogan and Piketty's long-range data sets, enables international and historical comparison without confronting categories such as class, merit, or education, all of which are problematically loaded with socio-cultural specificities and subjective values.

The recent public interest in inequality mirrors a return in the economics discipline to the more relational methodology of historical, social, and behavioural economics, a turn welcomed by many economists who encourage input from other fields in the social sciences and humanities. At the time of Marx's theorising of capitalism as social relations, the emerging new field of economics was primarily based on applying Enlightenment philosophy to ethics, social relations, and the role of government, such as in work by John Locke, David Hume, Alexis de

Tocqueville, Adam Smith, and John Stuart Mill. Since the mid- to late-twentieth century, however, the discipline's historical, sociological, and philosophical *raison d'être* diminished, as the social science cast itself as an objective field based on mathematical equations, computer simulations, and big data. With this change, the ethics of economics and the social life-world of human behaviour on which financial exchange is based largely disappeared from view, until the 2008 financial crisis challenged the hegemony of late capitalism, rendering visible and subject to challenge its political, social, and cultural mechanisms. The increasing narrativisation of economics since the crisis is an important symptom of a widespread shift in thinking, from academics, experts, the creative arts, journalism, and the general public, that once again understands economics as a shifting, subjective, and mediated terrain.

Arguing for centring the social and the relational in economic analysis, in *Economics of Good and Evil: The Quest for Economic Meaning from Gilgamesh to Wall Street* (2011) Czech economist Tomáš Sedláček claims that 'modern economic theories based on rigorous modelling are nothing more than ... metanarratives retold in different (mathematical?) language' (5). He continues:

> [T]here is at least as much wisdom to be learned from our own philosophers, myths, religions, and poets as from exact and strict mathematical models of economic behaviour. I argue that economics should seek, discover, and talk about its own values, although we have been taught that economics is a value-free science. I argue that none of this is true and that there is more religion, myth, and archetype in economics than there is mathematics. (9)

Symptomatic of the difficulty of breaking out of disciplinary conventions, Sedláček's thesis failed to earn him a PhD in economics in the pre-crisis era[1]; post-crisis, it became an internationally bestselling book. Similarly arguing for the need to anchor the economic in its socio-cultural environment, Nobel Prize-winning American economists George Akerlof and Robert Shiller take a behavioural approach against the 'rational man' fallacy to privilege instead John Maynard Keynes's concept of 'animal spirits' in their popular economics book *Animal Spirits: How Human Psychology Drives the Economy and Why It Matters for Global Capitalism* (2009). They argue that markets, finance, and political economy are largely motivated by the public's understanding of and confidence in capital, learnt predominantly through narratives of media and culture: '[t]he stories no longer merely *explain* the facts; they *are* the facts. To really explain ... the ups and downs of most economies, one must look at the driving stories' (54, italics in original). Economics, they remind readers, is not separate from but rather an integral part of social relations produced by and out of culture. At its root, *oikonomia* is etymologically the management of the household, indicating the smallest and closest unit of social connection. Recent sociological studies of the economy, such as David Graeber's *Debt: The First 5000 Years* (2011) and Nigel Dodd's *The Social Life of Money* (2014), bring back into contemporary economic discourse the inseparable nature of the economy from society and its cultural mores, reminding readers that financial transactions occur out of human interaction, exchange, and relationships. In this book, I predominantly use the term 'political economy' rather than 'the economy,' in order to signal that economic structures and mechanisms are shaped by national government and international geopolitical expectations and allegiances, and are inseparable from the social contexts that control and bind them.

The disciplinary shift that understands economics as a way of mapping human social relationships based on culturally subjective narratives shaped by desires, ethics, emotions and socially constructed behaviours brings economics closer to literature, which is at its base another such mode of imagining culture and society. Indeed, in discussing the relationship of literary fiction to reality, Rita Felski in *Uses of Literature* (2008) echoes the above-mentioned economists in her claim that, following Paul Ricoeur on mimesis, there *is* no fixed 'out there' (84). Rather, reality consists of the narratives we create to describe it: 'our conceptions of politics, literature, human relations, the interaction between social structures and human agency, remain deeply beholden to the logic of narrative' (85). Just as the economists struggle to convince their discipline of the importance of subjective knowledge to understanding the economy, Felski's chapter on what literature knows of the world rejects her discipline's elitism and exceptionalism, its insistence on limited or non-referentiality. 'That literary works yield limited perspectives,' she claims, 'does not prevent them from also serving as sources of epistemic insight' (84). *Narratives of Inequality* is motivated by my conviction that literature is not just the poor cousin of other (more serious?) subjects of humanities and social sciences, but that it harbours, as Felski puts it, 'truths ... in different guises' (103).

Mark Osteen and Martha Woodmansee's influential early collection on economic literary criticism established a precedent for investigating the fiction of economics and the economics of fiction. It took until the 2008 financial crisis, however, for there to be more mainstream awareness of imaginative banking practices, creative financial packages, and the fictional nature of several neoliberal tenets. Pop-economics titles such as *Zombie Economics* (2012), *23 Things They Don't Tell You about Capitalism* (2012), *The Myth of the Rational Market* (2011), and *Seventeen Contradictions and the End of Capitalism* (2014) expose metaphors and imagery such as 'the rising tide lifts all boats,' 'trickle-down economics,' and 'free trade' as constructed rather than natural, and often containing hidden biases and structural mechanisms that favour the rich. The turn within economic criticism to emphasise falsehoods, myths, tall tales, and contradictions, to pay attention to imaginative forms such as the zombie and animal spirits, and to study attitudes toward debt (Graeber), fiduciary money (Dodd), and good and evil (Sedláček), all expose the discipline's subjectivity. Economists' forays into literature serve to break the assumed disciplinary divide constructed by *both* fields: economics' mathematical focus assumes no role for the subjective, and literary studies' privileging of the aesthetic to detach fiction from reality assumes an at-best tenuous rootedness in the real.

Economists' frequent use of fiction insists that literature is a valid source of historical information on income, wealth, and attitudes toward them. Narrative is as old as writing itself, and oral storytelling is older still. Sedláček's *Economics of Good and Evil* analyses the 4000-year-old *Epic of Gilgamesh*, classic mythology, the Old Testament, the Torah, and the Bible to identify ideologies and values of money, debt, and wealth which reveal ingrained cultural and social judgements contained in modern Western economics. Amartya Sen in *The Argumentative Indian* (2005) draws from the *Vedas*, the *Mahab'harata*, and the *Ramayana* to claim the civic role of debate. Swiss economist Hans Christoph Binswanger's *Money and Magic* (1994) interprets Goethe's *Faust* as a critique of monetarism through the metaphor of alchemy. Ellen Hodgson Brown's pre-financial-crisis text *Web of Debt* (2007) critiques the power of financial institutions in the long history of US capitalism through the sustained allegory of L. Frank Baum's *The Wizard of Oz*, a children's book some economists believe was written as a moral tale about the Gold Standard. Piketty uses Balzac's fiction to understand nineteenth-century French attitudes to inherited wealth and the need to work for a living (238–240). Sylvia Nasar opens her history of modern economics, *Grand Pursuit* (2011), with a calculation of Jane Austen's financial status in comparison with her contemporary average worker (xi). Economic historian Ha-Joon Chang cites critiques of greed in the fiction of Daniel Defoe, Jonathan Swift, and John Gay, and their reverberations in parliamentary discourse (Chang 2007). Such work claims a value for literature as in some way reflecting, representing, and portraying aspects of the economy, often in a critical fashion. Economic rather than literary analyses of texts such as religious sacred books, Defoe's satirical pamphlets, and John Gay's operatic lampooning of Robert Walpole in *The Beggar's Opera* (1728) are further a reminder of historical times when literature directly impacted on the construction of social values and on policy.

Given economists' interest in literature, it is somewhat surprising that literary critics appear largely uninterested in the connections between the political economy and fiction. This speaks to a surprisingly unequal disciplinary weighting: literary critics appear to find less relevance for fiction in the world than lay readers or academics from other disciplines do. In a 2014 introduction to neoliberal economics intended for a general readership, *Economics: The User's Guide*, Chang suggests that the public is cowed into assuming that economics is too difficult: '95 per cent of economics is common sense—made to look difficult, with the use of jargons and mathematics' (2014, 1). This intuition is amplified among literary scholars, many of whose passion and talent for the arts is compounded by a corresponding lack of interest and incompetence in the hard sciences, of which the formula-heavy economics is fallaciously perceived to be a part. Piketty cogently describes both sides of the problem:

> To be useful, economists must above all learn to be more pragmatic in their methodological choices, to make use of whatever tools are available, and thus to work more closely with other social science disciplines.
>
> Conversely, social scientists in other disciplines should not leave the study of economic facts to economists and must not flee in horror the minute a number rears its head, or content themselves with saying that every statistic is a social construct, which of course is true but insufficient. At bottom, both responses are the same, because they abandon the terrain to others. (575)

His challenge not to 'abandon the terrain' is a call to literary critics, as academics and as citizens, to engage in the political economies in which they are involved: local, national, regional, and international.

This present study is my own response to Chang's reassurance that economics is not that difficult to understand, and to Piketty's challenge not to retreat: I am myself guilty of refusing to engage with economics, using as excuses that I am not good at mathematics; that all cultural expression is subjective and contingent; that as a white Western woman I ought not to critique or compare minority experiences; and that literature doesn't matter *in the real world* anyway. By presenting a literary-centred history of the economic inequality that is portrayed in postcolonial fiction, this present study aims to engage the interest of literary critics unsure of the relevance of economics to literature. It responds to my conviction that the economic history of colonialism and its aftermath is much more poorly understood by postcolonial critics than it is by those writers who fall under its label. This study offers a historical and global sketch of the economics of inequality as a way toward filling this gap, motivated by my belief that literature and its study has an important role to play in the current critique of capitalism and the exploration of other economic formations that might be more equitable, just, and sustainable.

Concomitantly responsible for the lack of literary study of economic inequality portrayed in many works of fiction is the dominant current in literary criticism to privilege form as the means through which the social encodes itself in literary works—that which Terry Eagleton termed *The Ideology of the Aesthetic* (1990). The problem with belletrism for my current purposes is not the argument that the fictional 'work' is separate from the 'world,' or that aesthetics renders literature apolitical—an argument that many theorists reject, such as Theodor Adorno in his *Aesthetic Theory* (2002). More problematic for a study of how fiction registers structures and mechanisms of economic inequality is the expectation that the literary critic ought to read differently and with more complexity than the economist and the lay reader. It is this introverted concentration on revealing hidden literary meaning for a restricted audience of fellow literary specialists that Felski critiques in her manifesto. Critical reading, she claims, 'assigns all value to the act of reading and none to the objects read. Are these objects really inert and indifferent, supine and submissive, entirely at the mercy of our critical maneuvers? Do we gain nothing in particular from what we read?' (3). Castigating the discipline for its concern with uncovering meanings and theorising them in dense language accessible only to other literary critics (4), she claims such reading practices have been so concerned with the *how* as to miss the *what*: the content of literature that the non-specialist reader finds in ample evidence. Rather, she argues, we have to attend to 'how and why particular texts matter to us. We are called on to honor our implication and involvement in the works we read, rather than serving as shame-faced bystanders to our own aesthetic response' (19). To this end, Felski offers a phenomenological response to literature, through the reader's affective and cognitive modes of textual engagement through recognition, knowledge, shock, and enchantment. Her approach is particularly fruitful for analysis of economic inequality in fiction because, in our affective responses—of anger, perhaps, or painful empathy, sadness, or shame—we join the writers' moral condemnation of the injustice of economic inequality.

Felski's call to honesty is partly a critique of the academic and publishing marketplace; it is also a call to find new relevance and new avenues for reading and teaching literature. As humanities faculties throughout the Western world buckle under the neoliberal logic of knowledge as a consumer good and education as a means to employment, English departments are under increasing pressure to justify their value and are expected to compete for students and funding. This current study, agreeing with Felski that 'our language of critique is far more sophisticated and substantial than our language of justification' (22), advocates for the importance of literature in the modern world by arguing for the relevance of narrative as a valuable medium for portraying and understanding the world economy and our responses to it.

Certainly, economists' surface readings of Austen and Balzac, or journalists' citing of Fitzgerald or Dickens in regard to contemporary inequality miss the analytical depth of these rich and complex texts. However, economists' use of literature is also a critique of their own discipline's esoteric internal discourse, a way of breaking out of the mould in order to better see its flaws and challenge its dominant truths. Several literary economists record strong criticism from their colleagues for their disciplinary breach of research focus.[2] It is in this spirit of challenging disciplinary expectations that this current study reads fiction in a diagnostic rather than an analytical manner, using literature to trace the untold history of capitalism in the colonies that has been overlooked in postcolonial studies. While my surface reading does not fully address the literariness of these texts, the technique reveals patterns and congruities of economic inequality between cultures and across historical moments that are lost in close attention to cultural specificity and aesthetic innovation.

Postcolonial studies has long been concerned with questioning the reader's and critic's legitimacy to interpret, critique, or compare unfamiliar cultural experiences and aesthetics from their outside, often Eurocentric and middle-class standpoint(s). Here, postmodern resistance to synthesis and the possibility of representation is compounded by the rise of minority rights discourse and subaltern studies in the 1980s, and of globalisation discourse in the 1990s. These trends have engendered considerable analysis of the cultural identity politics of plurality, hybridity, liminality, and all types of 'trans-' of self and space. By coupling deconstruction and subaltern studies' notions of the impossibility of the text's ability or the critic's right to representation, the discipline has embraced theoretical concepts of difference such as of language, culture, and identity, while ignoring the material conditions of lived reality on which that difference is based. In its now well-worn discourse of difference that makes the postcolonial reader wary if not sceptical of familiarity, the field conforms in its own way to Felski's diagnosis of a more general problem in literary criticism of 'smoothly rehearsed moves that add up to a hermeneutics of suspicion' (1). As the Warwick Research Collective summarises, '"post"-theory' emphasises 'not comparison but incommensurability, not commonality but difference, not system but untotalisable fragment, not the potential of translation but rather its relative impossibility, and not antagonism but agonism' (2015, 12). Incommensurability underpins the postcolonial emphasis on cultural difference as a rejection of universalism and Eurocentrism, but in doing so it overlooks the deeply similar structures of economic inequality portrayed in fictional representations of material lives. As the corpus of fiction in this book establishes, hunger, homelessness, and the humiliation of material lack have very similar vocabularies, no matter where or when they were written.

In his critique of the discipline's biases, Neil Lazarus in *The Postcolonial Unconscious* (2011) contributes 'to a bridging of the gap between "text" and "critic," on the grounds that the "world" has to date typically been more adequately registered, and rendered, in "postcolonial" *literature* than in postcolonial *criticism*' (36, italics in original). His title's play on Fredric Jameson's *The Political Unconscious* (1981) signals his text's Marxist political engagement and critique of the hold of postmodernism in the academy of Jameson's earlier work. Felski, arguing about a different kind of gap between text and reader, identifies two incommensurable reading publics in the expert critic and the general public. She argues for an opening up of literary criticism to pay more attention to what non-specialist readers find valuable: '[a] respect for everyday perceptions is entirely compatible with a commitment to theory; such perceptions give us questions to pursue, not answers' (15). Although their approaches are different, Lazarus and Felski upset ingrained ways of reading that they feel have foreclosed understanding of key aspects of the literary text, obscured by analytical biases. Postcolonial economics is one such overlooked area which requires for its elucidation new ways of reading the text and synthesising the information contained within.

Along with Felski and Lazarus, Edward Said's *Culture and Imperialism* (1993) is a key text underpinning this present study's methodology and ambition. While '[a] novel is neither a frigate nor a bank draft,' Said finds missing from literary critique 'adumbrations of the actual world in which the novels and narratives take place' (1993, 87). More precisely, by 'actual world' he means the geopolitical economy of military and financial imperialism that has shaped the capitalist world from nineteenth-century empire to its present form, dominated by the USA. Key to Said's interpretative strategy is his conviction that these world-level patterns can best be viewed comparatively, by reading a large body of work from different languages, times, and places. This, he claims in his last article published before his death in 2003, is the purpose of humanistic critique, to 'open up the fields of struggle, to introduce a longer sequence of thought and analysis ... sustained by a sense of community with other interpreters and other societies and periods' (2003, n.p.). His plea 'to speak about issues of injustice and suffering within a context that is amply situated in history, culture, and socio-economic reality' (2003, n.p.) sketches the terrain of study with which to answer Piketty's call not to back down at the first sight of a fact or figure. Said's humanist ethics are highly relevant for responding to economic inequality in literature: unlike the culture of suspicion that Felski identifies as the modus operandi of literary criticism, it is ethically undesirable for the reader to remain a neutral bystander to fiction's representations of poverty in the face of great wealth. In his last words, as in his life's work, Said calls on public intellectuals to engage with injustice.

Lazarus's attention to the world in the text, Felski's affective and cognitive reading tactics, and Said's touchstone term 'humanism' all recall the ethical foundations of postcolonial studies. The fiction emerged from and is grounded in material and social realities, often with a strong didactic social function not only to educate and inspire recognition and respect for marginalised groups, but potentially also to incite activism. This book extends the role of Rob Nixon's concept of the writer-activist (2011, 22–30) to also include the reader-activist as an active agent responsible for engaging with the slow violence of capitalism's tendency toward economic inequality that is so compellingly portrayed in the literary texts. Reading, like writing, can be a form of activism: as Felski asserts, '[t]he act of reading enacts an ethics and a politics in its own right, rather than being a displacement of something more essential that is taking place elsewhere' (20). The global scale of the 2008 financial crisis, its repercussions, and its protests—from Occupy and anti-austerity movements to those less clearly related, such as Black Lives Matter in the USA and student protests against fee hikes in the UK—revealed the systemic and global trend of widening inequality. The global level of this financial shock and responses to it render it difficult to argue that postcolonial experiences are unique, discrete, and interpretable only within their individual cultural paradigms. The socially engaged fiction analysed here asks the reader, critic, reviewer, and teacher not only to bear witness to the local and specific forms of injustice that make up the novel's terrain, but also to think about how to apply, interpret, and extend the fictional context to relevant contemporary sites and situations—not least of which is the dwindling importance placed on reading or studying literature, a discipline suffering from slow violence that also requires, following Nixon's schema, new ways of making it visible.

The contemporary era of post-crisis re-evaluation of the material conditions of developed-world precarity render it timely for postcolonial studies to similarly harness the shift in focus to economic inequality and capitalist critique for its own purposes. Two Australian novels analysed further in later chapters—Kim Scott's *That Dead Man Dance* (2010) and Alexis Wright's *Carpentaria* (2006)—offer examples of the ease with which the cultural biases of postcolonial studies encourage interpretations that ignore the economic and the material, which are, nonetheless, portrayed in great detail in the texts. *That Dead Man Dance* ends with a sustained focus on Aboriginal dance as a dying form of communication no longer understood by the white colonists to whose side the balance of power has shifted. At the end of the dance, the novel's final sentences describe offstage action, the meaning of which is left hanging: '[Bobby] heard gunshots. And another sound: a little dog yelping' (403). In *Carpentaria*, after a storm and flood that devastated their mining town, the Aboriginal elder and his grandchild walk away empty-handed to the sound of frogs singing: '[i]t was a mystery, but there was so much song wafting off the watery land, singing the country afresh as they walked hand in hand out of town, down the road, Westside, to home' (438). It is tempting yet misleading to analyse these passages as the Aboriginal writers' insistence on the primacy and continuity of cultural practices and values, without equally recognising the injustice and inequality of material loss experienced by the characters in both examples. The shots Bobby hears signal either the killing or the dispossession of the last of the tribal elders from his traditional land. The grandfather in *Carpentaria* is heading back to the land historically designated for Aboriginal settlement on the edge of the municipal rubbish dump to rebuild his shack and his livelihood, now with a dependent child to care for.

While the presence of ongoing traditions and uniquely indigenous value systems is heartening, Bobby's dance and *Carpentaria*'s frog song do not make up for losing family to separation and death, experiencing violence and imprisonment, mental and physical illness, or dispossession, forced new starts, and lost livelihoods. The latter are all common outcomes of capitalist inequality, repeated across time and space, and disproportionately affecting marginalised communities: the indigenous, minorities, the colonised, the elderly, women, and children. Like Dickens's and Fitzgerald's synchronicity with the contemporary economic slump, *That Dead Man Dance* and *Carpentaria* provide opposite bookends of capitalist violence on Aboriginal communities at the beginning of settlement (Scott) and in contemporary times (Wright). Both novels end with Aboriginal mobility not as an echo of traditional nomadism but as a sign of the dispossessed: chased out, harassed, and even hunted by the police. If one thinks past the end of *That Deadman Dance*, Bobby will be imprisoned and then move to the Aboriginal settlement at the edge of town, a waste zone of abject poverty where readers of Scott's *Benang* (1999) follow Aborigines throughout the twentieth century, finding their descendants still there in the twenty-first century, in *Carpentaria*, in self-made shacks alongside startling mining wealth.

While literary critics defend the function of literature as privileging the imaginary over the real, often with strong reactions against a perceived reductionism in any suggestion that fiction can describe the real world (or that readers may wish it to do so), many postcolonial writers themselves appear motivated by the opposite. A great number of postcolonial novels which portray cultural and social marginalisation, discrimination, subjection, domination, and exploitation also establish economic alienation within their first pages. Three examples from different historical settings illustrate the precision with which many writers detail the economic contexts that set the scene for their novels' unfolding action.[3] In *Shark Dialogues* (1995), Hawai'ian writer Kiana Davenport introduces nineteenth-century Honolulu, the setting for the epic: '[i]t was becoming the business center of the islands, gathering place of traders and merchants. ... In the early 1840s, wealth was being accumulated overnight in Honolulu—human cargo smuggled in from the Orient as cheap labour, opium packed in champagne bottles' (45). As foreigners establish their wealth, indigenous Hawai'ians are displaced into slums (51). Colonialism, here, is construed as a web of business transactions that winnow out the indigenous and migrant losers from the winners of capitalism. In mid-twentieth-century decolonising Nigeria, Chinua Achebe begins *A Man of the People* (1966) with the economic crisis that sets the scene for the political wrangling, corruption, and military coup that forms the story's narrative drive: '[t]hen came the slump in the international coffee market. Overnight (or so it seemed to us) the Government had a dangerous financial crisis on its hands. Coffee was the prop of our economy just as coffee farmers were the bulwark of the P.O.P. [Progressive Alliance Party]' (3). Achebe sketches the inflammatory political environment engendered by the catch-22 of dependence on Europe for cash-crop exports at a time of fierce rhetoric of national independence across decolonising African states. In *Minaret* (2006), a novel set predominantly in contemporary London, Leila Aboulela sketches economic theories of the development and underdevelopment of Sudan in *Minaret* (2006):

> The Economics class was good that evening – Rostow's Take-off ... We would become great, become normal like all the other rich Western countries; we would catch up with them. ... But then the professor pushed his glasses up his nose and said, 'And now for the Marxist criticism of Rostow's explanation for underdevelopment.' So it wasn't true after all. We were not going to take off. (42–43)

The extreme inequality and resultant unrest between the Sudanese elite who live Western lives and the general populace of the Third World nation sparks the revolutionary coup that sends the novel's protagonists fleeing to London. In these postcolonial texts, racial discrimination of indigenous Hawai'ians (in Davenport), class subjugation of the poor by the comprador elite (in Achebe), and marginalisation of Muslim migrants (in Aboulela) are entangled in opportunities provided or denied by access to wealth.

The above passages make clear the importance of economic contexts to character formation and plot development. They also carry latent or blatant critiques of the inequality contained within the capitalist structures they name. Davenport's scare quotes around her information that '[i]n 1848, King Kamehameha III ... let himself be persuaded by white merchants and ex-missionaries to "abolish feudalism and make land-rights equal"' (46) registers her scepticism of white-settler intentions of equality in their demand for access to land. Achebe's narrator reveals how the poor feel powerless to contest the well-known strategy of upward mobility through embezzlement: 'he gave instance after instance of how some of our leaders who were ash-mouthed paupers five years ago had become near-millionaires under our very eyes'; 'many in the audience laughed. But it was the laughter of resignation to misfortune' (123). In Aboulela's novel, Anwar the communist activist constantly confronts Najwa with reminders of her exceptionalism: while Sudan is one of the poorest countries in the world, her family has servants, and although they both become refugees in London, her money, contacts, property, and familiarity with the city spare her from the humiliation and rootlessness he suffers. The reader is placed in the awkward position of sympathising with Najwa, as narrator and protagonist, yet understanding Anwar's attacks on her: '[d]oes it not strike you that it is wrong for such wide discrepancies to exist between people?' (33); '[y]ou and your family must be the Home Office's ideal asylum seekers—a flat in London, back accounts filled with the money your father swindled' (163).

The above writers are all socially engaged writer-activists who pair authorial information about the structures and mechanisms of economic inequality in their countries with a critical narrative tone that emotionally aligns with the disenfranchised. These writers thus share, in Nixon's terms, 'a desire to give human definition to such outsourced suffering, a desire to lay bare the dissociational dynamics' (22–23) that typically hide the structures of gross inequality supported and maintained by their respective political economies. The above sketches of three novels that are very different in terms of time and place setting, from writers from three continents, written in very different narrative modes, reflect the broad corpus of this present study, which comprises fiction that overtly narrativises economic theories and facts encoded in a critique of the resultant inequality as a form of injustice.

To refocus on the economic causes and structures of poverty is to grapple with the problematic, as Ngũgĩ wa Thiong'o does in *Globalectics* (2012), that 'one does not want to give dignity to poverty by according it theory' (2). His concept of poor theory is an attempt to register the imprint of poverty on the word, the body, and the cultural expression that comes out of necessity and lack. He strives to give dignity to the poor but not to poverty itself, which is never aesthetic or metaphysical—the stuff of literary analysis—but rather concrete and experiential. In taking seriously the novelists' critiques of capitalist-driven inequality, this current study agrees with Nixon's warning in *Slow Violence* that studies of aesthetics, the imaginary, and formal modes such as myth, cyclical narrative, bricolage, and hybridity run the risk of 'locat[ing] agency in the internal fissures of discourse' (Anne McClintock qtd in Nixon, 31). Rather, Nixon continues, '[i]n cautioning against a narrowing of literary studies that pulls back from the wider world, we need to recognize the radical energies that traditions of postcolonial engagement at their best have encouraged' (37). Agency, like poverty, does not reside in textual dexterity but in the real world, in action, activism, and political engagement.

The motivation to expose and critique economic inequality is not confined to postcolonial writers. Rather, they merely update and extend to new contexts the same desire to express outrage over injustices and inequalities present throughout the history of capitalism, to which the emergence of the novel genre has itself been linked (Woodmansee and Osteen, 5–11). Daniel Defoe and Jonathan Swift are early examples of satirists of political and economic policies in pamphlets and highly allegorical fiction. Dickens claims in an early preface, 'In all my writings, I hope I have taken every available opportunity to show the want of sanitary improvements in the neglected dwellings of the poor' (Preface to *Martin Chuzzlewit*, 2012). Across the Channel, Victor Hugo similarly uses the preface of *Les Misérables* to state his position: 'so long as ignorance and poverty exist on earth, books of the nature of *Les Misérables* cannot fail to be of use' (Preface, *Les Misérables*, 2010). Particularly compelling is John Steinbeck's emotional remark on the plight of Okies he witnessed in labour camps in California, which later became *The Grapes of Wrath*: 'I want to put a tag of shame on the greedy bastards who are responsible for this' (Steinbeck qtd in Benson 1984, 370–371).

If readers of fiction or literary critics might be surprised by the insistence of some writers to expose injustices in the political economy, this is often consistent with the writers' own careers. Johann Wolfgang von Goethe was finance minister of the court of Weimar. Defoe was a businessman, tax collector, and essayist on Tudor industrial policy. Dickens worked in law to improve sanitary conditions in slums, a topic on which he wrote several newspaper articles. Hugo was an elected senator who campaigned for penal reform, secular education, and rights for the poor. Ezra Pound wrote prolifically on Depression-era economics.[4] Marx wrote poetry, fiction, and essays on art and literature (Eagleton 2011, 123–124). Postcolonial writers follow their literary predecessors: Abdul Rahman Munif had a PhD in economics and worked for the Iraqi ministry of oil, Leila Aboulela has an MPhil from the London School of Economics, Shashi Tharoor is a parliamentarian and long served in the

United Nations, Aravind Adiga and Gautam Malkani are financial journalists, Vikas Swarup is an Indian diplomat, Sanjay Bahadur is a high-level civil servant in Indian tax and mining, and Mohsin Hamid graduated from Harvard Law School and worked as a management consultant. These writers' impressive professional résumés lend their work important insider knowledge on the mechanics of the capitalist world-system. They are thus able to offer an economically inflected viewpoint of inequality in the societies they represent, even though their education and professional careers situate their own experiences as outside of the life-worlds of marginalisation and immiseration that most of their fiction relates.

While the argument that fiction may also *not* be about the world is certainly valid; for many postcolonial writers their fiction is only one of several fronts on which they advocate and address the issues with which they are most concerned. Although certainly fiction has unique formal qualities, it does not need to be interpreted as wholly divorced from other forms of writing, such as essays, journalism, and biography, nor separated from the often overtly activist, educational, or politically engaged activities of its creator. In their professional capacities, the causes they support, their speeches, academic positions, fiction, and non-fiction, these writers harness multiple and various narrative modes to address inequality and its injustice. Nixon allows himself to be impressed and inspired by the 'ambitious communicative intent' (31) of authors across the genres and disciplines, including non-fiction and journalism. He thus inscribes his analysis of literary texts, cultural studies, and theoretical positions rarely combined in literary critique in an attempt 'to keep alive a sense of the hugely varied public registers that writers can marshal to testify on issues of world urgency' (31). Also arguing for more interdisciplinary openness in literary studies in order to expose fiction's critiques of governance, John Marx, in a book on literary geopolitics, contends: '[b]y discovering common ground with social scientists, literary critics can equip themselves to keep up with the interdisciplinary research already being undertaken by novelists' (2012, 9). If the writers understand aspects of the economy enough to offer a critique of it through fiction, it ill behoves literary critics to ignore it.

The interest from a significant number of economists to draw from literature to illustrate aspects of the economy, and conversely writers' desire to grapple with economics in their work, points to the validity of fiction to add to social discourse on the political economy. Just as Graeber traces a 5000-year history of debt through anthropological sources, and Sedláček outlines attitudes to good and evil through myths, fables, and religious texts, this present study uses postcolonial fiction that openly describes economic processes of labour relations and wealth accumulation as base resources to write a history of capitalist inequality from colonisation to the present. My position takes seriously the proposition that literature matters to writers, readers, and critics, as well as to many social scientists, including economists, who cite fiction in their scholarship. In particular, this book argues that postcolonial fiction ought to be part of contemporary critiques of capitalism, as a valuable source of insider perspectives from under-represented cultures and communities whose histories, including their economic histories, are rarely or barely registered. In the unique forms of aesthetically mediated narrative, fiction illuminates hidden structures that underpin capitalism, reveals linkages of time and place more usually invisible, and embodies the ethical engagement that drives the critique of capitalism.

EMPIRE AND CAPITALISM

To insert the grand narrative of colonial imperialism—often labelled the first age of globalisation—within the wider history of capitalism requires a theory of historical and global interaction and interdependencies. Defining the timeline and history of globalisation is contested across the disciplines; however, the importance of European and particularly British colonial imperialism to the rise of global capitalism is integral to all definitions. Common across the different forms of imperial control, in extractive, trade, settlement, and strategic-position colonies, is the primary drive to profit from the encounter. Denis Judd summarises the base motivation of empire thus: 'the desire for profitable trade, plunder and enrichment was the primary force that led to the establishment of the imperial structure' (1996, 3). Situating financial interests as the heart of globalisation renders all political, social, and cultural structures of empire subservient to the primary aim of wealth creation and investment through productivity from land and labour. The culture-centred understanding of globalisation popular across the humanities has made such a claim difficult, something that the recent turn to materialism is slowly changing. Historian Bernard Porter sums up the pressures of academic fashion in the fifth (2005) revised edition of his primer from the 1970s, *The Lion's Share: A Short History of British Imperialism, 1850 to the Present*:

> A few years ago this materialist explanation of British imperialism used to be widely contested, because it was felt to be ignoble, and tarred with the

neo-Marxist theory that used imperialism's 'capitalist' origins to condemn it; with the result that in the Preface to the first edition of this book I had almost to apologise for it. Today that is no longer necessary. Capitalism is respectable again. Its association with British imperialism seems obvious, and no longer a Marxist smear. ... This needs to be reiterated today, I think, when the essential structure of British imperialism is in danger of being obscured by more 'cultural' approaches. (8)

Porter's awareness of the forces of academic pressure in shaping an entire discipline's interpretative perspective applies equally to the postcolonial field, in which background knowledge of the history and geopolitics of European colonialism is remarkably absent. The disciplinary compartmentalising of postcolonial studies into nation, region, and language group has led to a general lack of understanding of how each locality's colonial experiences fit into the larger flows of world history and its geopolitics.

Eighteenth- and nineteenth-century writers were not unaware of the role of the colonies in Britain's rise to world dominance. Many of Defoe's theories of international commerce and empire fictionalised in his novels appear in his economic treatises (Sherman 1996). Samuel Taylor Coleridge's utopian Pantisocracy movement, which struggled to envisage an egalitarian form of imperialism *not* based on theft of land, private property, and class relations, exemplifies Romanticism's significant engagement with colonialism (McKusick 1998). In *Moby Dick* (1851), Herman Melville describes the whale as a physical embodiment of 'the Bank of England' (334) and as a metaphor of the world as full of unclaimed territories, 'loose-fish' free for the taking by the 'fast-fish' of England, the USA, the Ottoman Empire, and Tsarist Russia (375). In Joseph Conrad's *Heart of Darkness* (1899), Marlow is quick to silence his aunt's civilisationalist moralising about '"weaning those ignorant millions from their horrid ways," ... she made me quite uncomfortable. I ventured to hint that the Company was run for profit' (2007, 12). These and other writers of the mainstream English literary canon clearly register capitalist aspects of colonial expansion and the socio-cultural causes and effects of it, an awareness that prompts Said to claim, 'the novel ... and imperialism are unthinkable without each other' (1993, 84). As he elaborates throughout his examples in *Culture and Imperialism*, English literature 'makes constant references to itself as somehow participating in Europe's overseas expansion' (14). In order to encapsulate the capitalist relations expressed in fiction from different times and locations, the postcolonial remit must stretch past the narrow geographical and historical period of colonial post-independence. The size and scope of Said's humanist reading technique is here instructive: '[i]f, for example, French and Algerian or Vietnamese history, Caribbean or African or Indian and British history are studied separately rather than together, then the experiences of domination and being dominated remain artificially, and falsely, separated' (313). Said's extensive reading allows him to grasp the hegemony of imperialism and the worlding of capitalism across geographical spaces, everywhere represented in literature.

Goods and revenues from the colonies both supplied and funded the industrialisation that fuelled Britain's rise to world financial dominance in the eighteenth and nineteenth centuries.[5] By 1900, London was the capital of world finance as well as sovereign of one-quarter of the world's land surface—to paraphrase Said in an economic rather than literary context, the Industrial Revolution and imperialism are unthinkable without each other. The imperial aspiration did not emerge out of a vacuum but as the natural extension of the capitalism established at home (then in Ireland) since the sixteenth-century emergence of commercial agriculture, wage labour, and associated attitudes toward productivity and competition (Wood 2003, 73–78). Linking together the internal and external, Ellen Meiksins Wood claims, 'it seems indisputable that the development of British capitalism at home in Britain determined the shape of British imperialism' (89). Economic historian Nuala Zahedieh is more specific about the common factors behind both national and international growth, arguing that the British Industrial Revolution could only have occurred due to international mercantilism. She opens her book *The Capital and the Colonies: London and the Atlantic Economy 1660–1700* (2010) on this hinge period by citing Adam Smith's claim that the discovery of the Americas and the route to the East Indies were the catalysts for the great increase in industrialisation (1). Zahedieh's statistics of the colonial-era British economy support her claims: by the American Revolution of 1783, up to three-quarters of British trade was trans-oceanic, and by 1870, three-fifths of Britain's GDP came from the colonies (2014, 395). In the expanding world-scale replication of the capitalist economic structure and the associated political, military, and socio-cultural ideology it relied upon, the British Empire was integral to developing the capitalist world-system. The way the colonies tend to be left out of the grand narrative of the history of modern economics as a discipline mirrors the similar marginalisation of literary voices from peripheral spaces in English literature. The intervention of postcolonial studies to correct the latter may thus extend to also provide a counter-narrative to the former.

Perhaps responding to Porter's complaint of historians' lack of attention to materialism, Zahedieh centres overseas expansion and quantifies colonialism's economic impact and the various forms of wealth it generated in relation to British industrialisation (2010, 2–4). Along with Zahedieh, who acknowledges the importance of the world-systems approach in encapsulating the dynamics between Britain's (more specifically, London's) core and the colonial peripheries, Wood delineates the two-way traffic of colonial resources brought to Europe's factories and of European capitalism brought to the colonies. Her term for today's global neoliberal hegemony as 'imperial capitalism' (129) overtly fixes the extensive contribution of European empire to the creation of today's capitalist formations. Wood is careful to specify that analysing capitalism in the colonies is not a simple equation of calculating profits of new resources and trade versus the costs of settlement, infrastructure, military, and so on. The more important function of colonisation was to force open the world to capitalism to establish a set of economic relations that were self-perpetuating after the withdrawal of colonial administration. She identifies in the British Empire:

> ... a conception of empire rooted in capitalist principles, in pursuit of profit derived not simply from exchange but from the creation of value in competitive production. This is a conception of empire that is not simply about establishing imperial rule or even commercial supremacy but about extending the logic and the imperatives of the domestic economy and drawing others into its orbit. (100)

This understanding of the self-perpetuating conditions of capitalism account for its insertion into colonial spaces, its continuation through the turbulent years of decolonisation, and its encrustation in the contemporary form of globalisation known as neoliberalism. The terminology of Immanuel Wallerstein's *Historical Capitalism* (2011) and Wood's *Empire of Capital* signals a *longue durée* approach useful for understanding the structures that connect colonial to neocolonial and neoliberal periods within a history of continuous capitalist relations. As the fact of empire lies at the heart of postcolonial studies—perhaps the only metanarrative the discipline accepts—and as capitalist motivations lie at the heart of empire, it is thus impossible for postcolonial studies to ignore the economics of empire and its aftermath.

Understanding the centrality of the economic motivation for profit intrinsic to globalisation creates a framework for theorising the inequality inherent in capitalism's uneven expansion. Leon Trotsky's term 'uneven and combined development,' and Ernst Bloch's phrasing of 'the non-simultaneity of the simultaneous,' both reflect the spatial and temporal discordance of entry into and profit from the capitalist world-system. Inserting the postcolonial into the history of capitalism reanimates earlier configurations of the Marxist tradition, including Vladimir Lenin and Rosa Luxemburg on imperialism, and leading mid-twentieth-century revolutionaries including Frantz Fanon, Amilcar Cabral, Patrice Lumumba, Kwame Nkrumah, W.E.B. Dubois, Ho Chi Minh, and Che Guevara, whose ideas all arose from their experiences of colonial marginalisation.[6] Several foundational theorists to postcolonial studies, including Fanon, Nkrumah, and Dubois, as well as Said, Jacques Derrida, and Jameson, were all in different ways indebted to Marxist thought. Vivek Chibber, in *Postcolonial Theory and the Specter of Capital* (2013)—the title updates Derrida's early analysis of Marx's legacy in *Specters of Marx* (1993)—unmasks Marxism as one of the 'specters' inherent but out of sight in postcolonial critique, even though postcolonial studies positions itself as Marxism's successor of radical anti-capital critique (284). The issue is perhaps partly generational. Certainly, for postcolonialists such as myself, born into the neoliberal era and the identity politics of difference, these earlier critiques of capitalism were not part of our social consciousness. Nonetheless, in light of the contemporary turn to the ethics of economic inequality, *Narratives of Inequality* is indebted to Marx's global economic theory in *Capital,* one of the earliest attempts to synthesise the patterns of capitalism's expression across world spaces. As Harry Harootunian summarises, '[t]he Marxian critique of political economy was historical, always referred to the world at large, and joined colonial expropriation to the expansion of capitalism as it became the lever in forming the world market' (2010, 39). That Marx's text is foundational to all three disciplines central to this study—modern economics, sociology, and postcolonial studies—makes the centrality of his work incontrovertible although often not explicit.

Since the 2008 crisis and the turn to a materialist focus on inequality across the academic disciplines, Marx's haunting may be turning into something altogether more solid. In his summary and review of post-2000 publications on 'Marxism and Cultural Materialism,' Stephen Shapiro claims renewed relevance for a Marxist regard since the financial crisis and Occupy movement (2012):

Left cultural theory may have been relegated to the academic margins throughout the 1990s and 2000s, but it has sprouted anew. Much as left perspectives magnetized the post war 'golden age' of theory, this new decade seems likewise to re-establish Marxist and cultural materialist criticism as a compass for literary and cultural studies. Beyond the singular achievements of specific critics, larger structural pressures have made unapologetic Marxism a key syntax for the current times. (82)

Shapiro, like Porter, finds Marxism no longer a dirty word, no longer connotative of a retrograde nostalgia for the failed experiment of political communism and socialism, but of a forward-looking anticipation of generative energies found in the foundational texts of leftist thought. Postcolonial studies is founded on a steady belief in its ever-changing, contemporary relevance: that colonialism is not over but transformed, contained, and embodied in present-day considerations of identity, nation, and global interaction and movement. As the issue of inequality replaces that of cultural identity as the driving concern of our times, the discipline must respond to this change to incorporate the economic into its remit.

Although Chibber takes a polemical line of argument against only a narrow component of postcolonial and particularly subaltern studies, his underlying critique of the discipline's lack of engagement with capitalism is highly valid. Capitalism *is* a metanarrative to which all colonies were subjected under imperialism and remain to differing extents implicated as members of the global world-system. In his usual terse language, Slavoj Žižek rejects what he calls 'the postcolonial common sense' belief that the differences of postcolonial cultures put paid to the Western discourse of universalism. On the contrary, 'at the level of economy, capitalism has triumphed worldwide.' He specifies: in 'capitalist universalism simply all these cultural differences are in some sense irrelevant. ... I find it paradoxical when people talk of the decline of the West, of Western universalism, when precisely Western capitalism effectively *is* universal' (2014, n.p.). Chibber is equally blunt: 'capital simply does not care about workers' local culture as long as it does not interfere with the accumulation process' (236), a sweeping claim he palliates by adding that capitalism's global history 'means nothing more than that in *some* of their practices, agents in Bombay, Nairobi, Detroit, and Cairo are all subjected to a common set of constraints' (248, italics in original). Terry Eagleton expresses a similar sentiment in *Why Marx Was Right*, underlining that '[i]t is in the nature of capitalism to confound distinctions, collapse hierarchies and mix the most diverse forms of life promiscuously together. No form of life is more hybrid and pluralistic' (162–163). It is the very flexibility of capitalism that has meant its success, its continuity defanging the frequent predictions of its demise—most recently following the 2008 financial crisis.

Indeed, it is difficult to imagine an alternative when capitalist relations are found and desired by the public even in communist regimes such as China, in authoritarian states such as Saudi Arabia and Iran, and in heretofore isolated communities in the Brazilian rainforest and Papua New Guinea. It is, however, exactly this ability to imagine, model, try out, and explore multiple options that makes fiction so powerful. In its experience rooted in pre-contact social formations and cultural practices, postcolonial literature is particularly well suited to the task. At this present historical juncture, when inequality, global warming, and geopolitical power shifts both illuminate and question capitalism's hegemony, the demand for creative alternatives is growing. This environment invests renewed valence in fiction as a socially useful form of commentary and experimentation.

To shift focus from identity politics to economic inequality combats the failure of postcolonial studies to comprehensively account for and condemn the fact that in almost all ex-colonies the impoverished today are the same groups as those marginalised under colonial rule: the indigenous, ethnic minorities, the elderly, women, and children. Certainly, the 2010s have seen a more concerted effort within the discipline to centre materialist concerns amid a more general impetus to evaluate the discipline's parameters.[7] Offering one of the very few sustained studies on poverty in fiction, Gavin Jones opens his *American Hungers: The Problem of Poverty in U.S. Literature 1840–1945* (2008) with two questions relevant also to postcolonial critique: '[w]hy has an overwhelming concern with the socially marginalized emerged without a sufficient framework in which to situate an explicit discussion of material deprivation?' (6), and:

> Current critical methodologies are finely geared to break down essences, to dissolve race, gender, nation, and class as stable absolutes, to emphasize instead that individuals are more complex and hybrid than the categories into which we want to place them. ... But in this effort to highlight instability and uncertainty, what happens to the specificity of socioeconomic need? (12)

Narratives of Inequality responds to these queries. The point is not, of course, to replace a culturalist interpretive framework with an economic one, but to argue for the inclusion of economic considerations in culture-specific and text-centred postcolonial literary analyses in order to demonstrate what literature knows of the political economy of global capitalism.

Centralising socio-economic patterns that underpin social relations of labour, class, gender, age, race, and ethnicity shifts the postcolonial focus from cultural to economic marginalisation, with the contemporary emphasis on inequality between rich and poor particularly pertinent to ex-colonial contexts. This book aims to first and foremost trace the intermeshing histories of European (principally British) colonialism and capitalism during colonial, neocolonial, and neoliberal eras; without this global and historical perspective, fiction's considerable engagement in and critique of deep and long-standing structural inequalities remains isolated rather than systemic. My corpus consists of postcolonial novels in which the writers explicitly use economic vocabulary or explain the political economy of their time and place settings. Quoting from such passages in chronological order from capitalism's irruption, in historical novels, to contemporary forms of social alienation, provides the book's structure as the history of capitalist inequality as told in literature. Analysis of these passages principally asks what the author hopes to reveal in such open recourse to economics, and how the writing encourages recognition of contemporary patterns of inequality. The value of this literary history of capitalism is supported with theory from primarily historical, critical, and behavioural economics that in each case corroborates the thrust of literature's economic information and its critique. The strength of this interdisciplinary method, as Woodmansee and Osteen put it, is 'to rediscover the contact points among literature, culture, and economics, … to use each discourse as a monitor or counterpractice that will expose the weakness, blind spots, and biases of the other' (12).

Placing capitalism at the centre of study—rather than period, nationality, language, ethnicity, or gender—reveals similarities in capitalism's structural inequality and common responses to it. Reading texts written and set across diverse colonial spaces, including the Dutch East Indies and Egypt, and from the beginnings of capitalism in the colonies until its contemporary manifestations in postcolonial nation-states and in the colonial and financial core of London itself, illuminates periodicity between times and places usually excluded from postcolonial studies. Focusing on the economics represented in the fiction brings to the fore the fiction of economics itself, reducing the latter to a malleable, ever-changing narrative built out of social interaction and subjective perception and perspectives. Understanding that the current expression of neoliberal capitalism is merely a subjective narrative, albeit quasi-hegemonic, is prerequisite to imagining as possible other forms of or alternatives to capitalism, a project in which the postcolonial imaginary has always been involved.

Chapter 2 focuses on the capitalist motivations of colonisation and their expression in the ideologies of colonialism. The study investigates the structures of inequality instituted in the new colonies to maximise profit through resource extraction, land privatisation, and labour exploitation of indigenous populations as well as of British settlers, thereby perpetuating in the colonies the unequal social relations of home. The chapter further demonstrates the economic motivation behind British discriminatory attitudes toward the colonised, expressed as racism and the criminalisation of poverty, which emerged at this time and continue today, ingrained in cultural practice.

The third chapter considers the first 30 years after independence of the decolonised new nation-states to trace the push-and-pull dynamics of a desire to reject capitalism and its related dependence on the Western colonial powers, and yet the concomitant rise to power of a native elite intent on propagating the structures of domination and control inherited from the British. Not only did neocolonialism continue the capitalism implemented by colonial regimes, it also formalised in international relations, agreements, and debt structures the systematic underdevelopment of these newly independent states in the global economy. The study of absurdity and satire in neocolonial-era fiction, which is repeated in contemporary responses to the 2008 financial crisis, illuminates the difficulty of responding to a system rent with irreconcilable contradictions, of which blatant inequality is a part.

Chapter 4 considers contemporary portrayals of poverty in the housing estates of developed-world centres alongside postcolonial narratives of slums and homelessness, in each case analysing the economic causes of marginalisation, domination, exploitation, and impoverishment, and characters' reactions to this inequality. The chapter considers the emotions and behaviour behind the life choices made by low socio-economic members of society in order to understand the narrow range of options available within capitalism's neoliberal form that imagines 'there is no alternative,' embedded in all levels of social relations.

The three chapters on colonial, neocolonial, and neoliberal eras of capitalism give an overview of the history of colonialism during specific and identifiable phases of capitalism. More narrowly, each chapter concentrates on the same three aspects of economic inequality: wealth accumulation and material ownership; structures of internal inequality between the rich and the poor within homogenous cultural communities; and the psychology of capitalism that engenders particular emotions and behaviour. These foci reveal across time and space repeating patterns and trends in the mechanics of capitalism that create and maintain economic inequality, as well as the social and cultural beliefs and practices that justify and support it, and which equally resist and condemn it. Commonalities include: similarities of material existence living at the bottom of the economic scale (job precarity, inadequate housing, hunger, lack of access to public facilities and education); the trajectory into and conditions of the poverty trap (unemployment, broken families, unforeseen disasters, victimisation); and patterns of emotions (fear, anger, despondency, hopelessness) and behaviour (giving up, addiction, violence, learned helplessness) in response to an inability to participate in social norms and expectations. This study's focus on material living conditions, emotions, and behaviour across postcolonial literature reveals strikingly similar responses to poverty and inequality, regardless of time and place.

Notes

1. Sedláček was finally awarded a PhD from Charles University, Prague, in 2013, following the publication of his book in the Czech Republic in 2009 and its international success in several translated versions, including prizes in Germany and the USA.
2. For several examples about them and their colleagues, see Jack Amariglio and David F. Ruccio, 'Literary/Cultural "Economies," Economic Discourse, and the Question of Marxism,' in Woodmansee and Osteen, *The New Economic Criticism* (1999, 381–384).
3. The following three texts are analysed in greater length in later chapters.
4. Christopher Nealon argues that twentieth-century American poets were preoccupied with capitalism and its social impacts. See Nealon, *The Matter of Capital: Poetry and Crisis in the American Century* (2011).
5. For a postcolonial study of one example of this interdependence, see Michael Niblett's study of the Caribbean sugar industry: 'World-Economy, World-Ecology, World Literature (2012).'
6. The list refers only to thinkers within colonised spaces and the capitalist Western sphere of influence. Of course, Marxism also underpinned revolutionaries on the communist side of the Cold War split, notably Ho Chi Minh and Fidel Castro, but this lies outside the scope of this present study.
7. Notable examples as well as those already cited (Chibber, Lazarus, The Warwick Research Collective) include: Sharae Deckard, James Graham and Michael Niblett (eds.), *Postcolonial Studies and World Literature* (2012); Benita Parry, 'What is Left in Postcolonial Studies?'; Janet Wilson, Cristina Sandru and Sarah Lawson Welsh (eds.), *Rerouting the Postcolonial: New Directions for the New Millennium*; Pavan Malreddy, Birte Heidemann, Ole Birk Laursen and Janet Wilson (eds.), *Postcolonialism: Globalization, Labour, and Rights* (2010).

Works Cited

Primary

Aboulela, Leila. *Minaret*. London: Bloomsbury, 2006.
Achebe, Chinua. *A Man of the People*. Oxford: Heinemann Educational, 1988 [1966].
Conrad, Joseph. *Heart of Darkness*. Harmondsworth: Penguin, 2007 [1899].
Davenport, Kiana. *Shark Dialogues*. New York: Plume, 1995.
Dickens, Charles. *Martin Chuzzlewit*. Public Domain Books, 2012 [1849], Kindle Edition.
Evans, Kate. *Red Rosa: A Graphic Biography of Rosa Luxemburg*. London and New York: Verso, 2015.
Fitzgerald, F. Scott. *The Great Gatsby*. New York: Scribner, 2004 [1925].
Gay, John. *The Beggar's Opera and Polly*. Oxford, UK: Oxford World's Classics, 2013 [1728, 1729].
Hugo, Victor. *Les Misérables*. Trans. Isabel F. Hapgood. Public Domain Books, 2010 [1887].
Levy, Emanuel. 'Great Gatsby: Interview with Director Luhrmann,' 27 April, 2013, http://emanuellevy.com/comment/great-gatsby-interview-with-baz-luhrmann/. 3 January, 2017.
Marx, John. *Geopolitics and the Anglophone Novel, 1890–2011*. Cambridge: Cambridge University Press, 2012.
Melville, Herman. *Moby Dick: Or, The White Whale*. Public Domain Books, 2011 [1851], Kindle Edition.
Orwell, George. *Down and Out in Paris and London*. London: Penguin Classics, 2001 [1933].
Scott, Kim. *Benang: From the Heart*. Freemantle: Freemantle Arts Centre Press, 1999.
———. *That Dead Man Dance*. London: Bloomsbury, 2012 [2010].
Wright, Alexis. *Carpentaria*. London: Constable, 2008 [2006].

Films and Documentaries

Kornbluth, Jacob, dir. *Inequality for All*. 2013.
Luhrmann, Baz, dir. *The Great Gatsby*. Warner Brothers, 2013.
McKay, Adam, dir. *The Big Short*. Paramount, 2015.
Scorsese, Martin, dir. *The Wolf of Wall Street*. Red Granit Pictures, 2013.

Secondary

Adorno, Theodor. *Aesthetic Theory.* Eds. Gretel Adorno and Rolf Tiedemann. Trans. Robert Hullot-Kentor. London: Continuum, 2002 [1997].

Akerlof, George A., and Robert J. Shiller. *Animal Spirits: How Human Psychology Drives the Economy and Why It Matters for Global Capitalism.* Princeton: Princeton University Press, 2009.

Amariglio, Jack, and David F. Ruccio. 'Literary/Cultural "Economies,"Economic Discourse, and the Question of Marxism,' in Woodmansee andOsteen, *The New Economic Criticism,* 381–400.

Armstrong, Stephen. *The Road to Wigan Pier Revisited.* London: Constable, 2012.

Benson, Jackson J. *John Steinbeck, Writer: A Biography.* New York: Penguin, 1984.

Binswanger, Hans Christoph. *Money and Magic: A Crtique ofthe Modern Economy in the Light of Goethe's Faust.* Trans. J.E. Harrison. Chicago and London: Universityof Chicago Press, 1994 [1985].

Chang, Ha-Joon. *Bad Samaritans: The Guilty Secrets of the Rich Nations and the Threat to Global Prosperity.* London: Random House, 2007.

———. *Economics: The User's Guide.* London: Pelican, 2014.

———. *23 Things They Don't Tell You About Capitalism.* Harmondsworth: Penguin, 2012.

Chibber, Vivek. *Postcolonial Theory and the Specter of Capital.* London and New York: Verso, 2013.

Das, Satyajit. *Extreme Money: Masters of the Universe and the Cult of Risk.* New Jersey: Financial Times Press, 2011.

Deckard, Sharae, James Graham, and Michael Niblett, eds. 'Postcolonial Studies and World Literature' Special Issue of The *Journal of Postcolonial Studies,*48.5, 2012.

Derrida, Jacques. *Specters of Marx: The State of the Debt, the Work of Mourning and the New International.* Trans. Peggy Kamuf. New York and London: Routledge, 1994 [Galilée, 1993].

Dickens, Charles. *Oliver Twist.* London: Penguin Classics, 2003. [1837-8]

———. *Great Expectations.* London: Penguin Classics, 2002. [1860-1]

Dodd, Nigel. *The Social Life of Money.* Princeton, NJ: Princeton University Press, 2014.

Dorling, Danny. *Injustice: Why Social Inequality Persists.* Bristol: Polity, 2011.

Eagleton, Terry. *The Ideology of the Aesthetic.* Oxford and Malden, MA: Blackwell, 1990.

———. *Why Marx was Right.* New Haven and London: Yale University Press, 2011, Kindle Edition.

Engels, Friedrich. *The Housing Question.* New York: International, 1935 [1872].

Felski, Rita. *Uses of Literature.* Malden, MA and Oxford: Blackwell, 2008.

Fox, Justin. *The Myth of the Rational Market: A History of Risk, Reward and Delusion on Wall Street,* New York: HarperCollins, 2011.

Graeber, David. *Debt: The First 5000 Years*. New York: Melville, 2011.
Hargreaves, Deborah, et al. 'Cheques With Balances: Why Tackling High Pay is in the National Interest,' *The High Pay Commission*, 2012, http://highpaycentre.org/files/Cheques_with_Balances.pdf. 3 January, 2017.
Harootunian, Harry. 'Who Needs Postcoloniality?' *Radical Philosophy* 164 (2010), 38–44.
Harvey, David. *Seventeen Contradictions and the End of Capitalism*. Oxford: Oxford University Press, 2014.
Hodgson Brown, Ellen. *Web of Debt: The Shocking Truth About Our Money System and How We Can Break Free*. Baton Rouge: Third Millennium, 2007.
Hunt, Tristram. 'Urban Britain is Heading for Victorian Levels of Inequality,' *The Guardian*, 18 July, 2007, http://www.theguardian.com/commentisfree/2007/jul/18/comment.money. 3 January, 2017.
Jameson, Fredric. *The Political Unconscious: Narrative as a Socially Symbolic Act*. New York: Cornell University Press, 1981.
Jones, Gavin. *American Hungers: The Problem of Poverty in U.S. Literature 1840–1945*. Princeton and Oxford: Princeton University Press, 2008.
Judd, Denis. *Empire: The British Imperial Experience from 1765 to the Present*. New York: HarperCollins, 1996.
Kachka, Boris. 'On Tour With Rock-Star Economist Thomas Piketty,' *New York Magazine*, 21 April, 2014, http://nymag.com/daily/intelligencer/2014/04/on-tour-with-rock-star-economist-thomas-piketty.html. 2 January, 2017.
Kirby, Emma Jane. 'On the Trail of George Orwell's Outcasts,' *BBC News*, 6 August, 2011, http://www.bbc.com/news/world-europe-14372195. 3 January, 2017.
Lazarus, Neil. *The Postcolonial Unconscious*. Cambridge: Cambridge University Press, 2011.
Marx, Karl. *Capital Volume 1: A Critique of Political Economy*, trans. Samuel Moore and Edward Averling. Mineola, NY: Dover, 2011 [1867].
McKusick, James C. '"Wisely Forgetful": Coleridge and the Politics of Pantisocracy,' in *Romanticism and Colonialism: Writing and Empire, 1780–1830*. Eds. Tim Fulford and Peter J. Kitson. Cambridge: Cambridge University Press, 1998, 107–128.
Mertens, Maggie. 'The Great Gatsby is Really About the Housing Crisis,' *The Billfold*, 22 May, 2012, http://thebillfold.com/2013/05/the-great-gatsby-is-really-about-the-housing-crisis/. 3 January, 2017.
Moore, Heidi. 'Thomas Piketty is a Rock-Star Economist—Can he Re-write the American dream?' *The Guardian*, 27 April, 2014, http://www.theguardian.com/commentisfree/2014/apr/27/thomas-piketty-economist-american-dream. 3 January, 2017.
Nealon, Christopher. *The Matter of Capital: Poetry and Crisis in the American Century*. Cambridge, MA: Harvard University Press, 2011.
Ngũgĩ wa Thiong'o. *Globalectics: Theory and the Politics of Knowing*. New York: Columbia University Press, 2012.

Niblett, Michael. 'World-Economy, World-Ecology, World Literature,' *GreenLetters: Studies in Ecocriticism*, 16.1, 2012, 15–30.

Nixon, Rob. *Slow Violence and the Environmentalism of the Poor*. Cambridge, MA and London: Harvard University Press, 2011.

Ohneswere, Shahendra. 'Baz Luhrmann Speaks on Directing *The Great Gatsby*,' *Life and Times*, 4 April, 2013, http://lifeandtimes.com/director-baz-lurhmann-speaks-on-directing-the-great-gatsby. 3 January, 2017.

Piketty, Thomas. *Capital in the Twenty-first Century*. Trans. Arthur Goldhammer. Cambridge, MA and London: Belknap, 2014 [Seuil 2013].

Porter, Bernard. *The Lion's Share: A Short History of British Imperialism, 1850 to the Present*. Fifth Edition. London and New York: Routledge, 2005 [1975].

Quiggin, John. *Zombie Economics: How Dead Ideas Still Walk Among Us*. Princeton and Oxford: Princeton University Press, 2012.

Quirk, William J. 'Too Big to Fail and Too Risky to Exist,' *The American Scholar*, 4 September, 2012, http://theamericanscholar.org/too-big-to-fail-and-too-risky-to-exist/#.VCUacfmSyOM. 3 January, 2017.

Said, Edward. *Culture and Imperialism*. New York: Vintage, 1993.

Said, Edward. 'Orientalism,' in *Counterpunch*, 5 August, 2003, http://www.counterpunch.org/2003/08/05/orientalism/. 3 January, 2017.

Sedláček, Tomáš. *Economics of Good and Evil: The Quest for Economic Meaning from Gilgamesh to Wall Street*. Oxford and New York: Oxford University Press, 2011.

Sen, Amartya. *The Argumentative Indian: Writings on Indian History, Culture, and Identity*. New York: Farrar, Straus and Giroux, 2005.

Shapiro, Stephen. 'Marxism and Cultural Materialism'. *The Year's Work in Critical and Cultural Theory*, 20, 2012, 82–98.

Sherman, Sandra. *Finance and Fictionality in the Early Eighteenth Century: Accounting for Defoe*. Cambridge and New York: Cambridge University Press, 1996.

Wallerstein, Immanuel. *Historical Capitalism*. London and New York: Verso 2011 [1983].

Warwick Research Collective. *Combined and Uneven Development: Towards a New Theory of World-Literature*. Liverpool: Liverpool University Press, 2015.

Wilson, Janet, Cristina Sandru, and Sarah Lawson Welsh, eds. *Rerouting thePostcolonial: New Directions for the New Millennium*. London: Routledge, 2010.

Wood, Ellen Meiksins. *Empire of Capital*. London and New York, Verso, 2003.

Zahedieh, Nuala. *The Capital and the Colonies: London and the Atlantic Economy 1660–1700*. Cambridge: Cambridge University Press, 2010.

———. 'Overseas Trade and Empire,' in *The Cambridge Economic History of Modern Britain. Volume I: 1700–1870*. Eds. Roderick Floud, Jane Humphries, and Paul Johnson. Cambridge: Cambridge University Press, 2014, 392–420.

Žižek, Slavoj. 'The Need to Censor Our Dreams,' *Lecture at the London School of Economics*, 11 November, 2014, http://www.lse.ac.uk/newsAndMedia/videoAndAudio/channels/publicLecturesAndEvents/player.aspx?id=2698. 3 January, 2017

CHAPTER 2

Colonial Capitalism

THE IRRUPTION OF CAPITALISM

In November 2010 Prime Minister David Cameron and cabinet ministers on a trip to China caused a diplomatic stir when they refused the Chinese request to remove the red poppies they wore on their lapels. While the British regretted that the Chinese could not understand the cultural significance of the World War One remembrance symbols, the Chinese were offended by this reminder of a different variety of poppy—that which culminated in the Opium Wars of the mid-1800s, of which 2010 marked the 150th anniversary of China's defeat (Chapman 2010). The incident is a reminder of the extent to which Britain has forgotten its capitalist-imperialist involvement in China based on trade in a long history of tumultuous and imbalanced relations. The contemporary British eagerness to gain a bigger part of the export market share to China recalls the earlier attempt, with a similar uneasy apposition of being at once the weaker trading partner, in financial terms, yet imagining itself the stronger in terms of global geopolitical power. Today, the UK imports around £36 billion per annum from China, its second-largest trading partner. By contrast, China is only Britain's sixth most important export market, sending only around £14 billion, thus creating a significant trade deficit.[1] In the mid-eighteenth century, the imbalance was even starker, with British exports amounting to only 10% of its imports from China, predominantly tea and silk (Schirokauer and Brown 2013, 240). One response to this trade deficit, which depleted Britain's wealth and haemorrhaged the national cash reserves, was to establish tea plantations in India, where British rule controlled the market from the plantations and processing to export, and thus ensured greater profit margins (Schirokauer and Brown 2013, 248). The other response was to become the suppliers of China's opium habit, securing a lucrative niche market for a product which they could grow in their own colony in India. The resulting trade surplus with China was won through Britain's monopoly on the industry, controlling all steps from the production to shipping and sale, the latter of which was reinforced following the First Opium War and the requisition of Hong Kong as a colonial possession for the explicit purpose of facilitating the drug trade, construed as upholding the tenets of the global 'free' market. Britain's handing back of the trading hub to the People's Republic of China in 1997 makes Hong Kong the most recent secession of Britain's colonial possessions.

Along with his poppy-wearing diplomatic faux pas, Cameron's speech at Peking University was also highly ironic, even hypocritical in the light of the historical opium trade. Cameron boasted of Europe's human rights tradition and urged China to embrace the Western free-trade economic model. He claims, 'China has attempted to avoid entanglement in global affairs in the past. But China's size and global reach means that this is no longer a realistic choice' (Cameron 2010, n.p.). The speech, which assumes Britain's upper hand in the geopolitical domain, wilfully forgets the long history of British gunboat diplomacy, open warfare, and the harm of opium in China, all enforced in the name of global free trade.[2] Postcolonial studies also suffers a similar amnesia, with considerable work on Sub-Saharan Africa, the Indian subcontinent, and indigenous peoples of white-settler colonies detracting attention from other zones of European colonial aggression, such as China and South-East Asia. This chapter looks at a considerable body of historical fiction that brings back into the picture overlooked global spaces, in the Canton opium trade in Amitav Ghosh's Ibis trilogy, in the American form of imperialism in Hawai'i, in Kiana Davenport's *Shark Dialogues*, and in the Dutch, French, and British wrangling over the Dutch East Indies in Pramoedya Ananta Toer's work. The significant output of fiction written in the postcolonial era yet set in the colonial period indicates authors' motivations to join the dots between past and present eras of globalisation. Reading postcolonial historical fiction as reminders of forgotten pasts challenges the kind of short-sightedness that led Cameron to woo modern Chinese capitalism without regard to the historical relations between the two countries.

To focus on the early days of capitalism also exposes the range of responses colonised peoples took toward the new set of social relations, which in each unique colonial setting included members of a society who embraced nascent capitalism as well as those who resisted. The epic scope of much historical fiction, with large casts of characters and early examples of cross-cultural movement and contact, reveals how capitalism's irruption in the colonies differently affected members within colonised cultures, with pre-contact hierarchies and traditional cultural conventions of inequality reshaped into the capitalist model of wealth and income familiar today.

Finally, to write and read historical fiction of early capitalism in the colonies from today's framing position of neoliberal free-market globalisation is to highlight the similarities between these two periods. Far from imagining and portraying the past as a foreign country, these writers highlight the historical imposition of economic tenets central to the neoliberal time in which they write. The fiction dramatises the introduction of concepts such as the free market, user pays, and the uneven sharing of financial rewards based on meritocratic individual capability, as well as the privatisation of land and the conscription of the human body to labour that are capitalism's necessary foundations. Such beliefs and constructions, which are new, strange, and illogical for the historical characters, are familiar to the contemporary reader, who is placed in the uncomfortable position of witnessing the contested and forced birth of what has become, by our times, economic 'common sense.'

Just as Cameron's speech is representative of Britain's historical amnesia in regard to the opium trade, India's importance to British imperialism in China is a neglected aspect of Indian national history as well. India's role in the opium trade—such as the drug's production in Bengal, the key role of Indian ports in merchant shipping, Britain's financing of its Opium Wars with profits from India, and the significant role of a conscripted Indian army in the battle of Canton—all illustrate the global interconnectedness of the capitalist world-system in the colonial era. Indian historian and novelist Amitav Ghosh, in an interview about his research for his Ibis trilogy of novels about historical ties between India and China, comments thus:

> Like most Indians, I had very little idea about opium. I had no idea that India was the largest opium exporter for centuries. I had no idea that opium was essentially the commodity which financed the British Raj in India. It is not a coincidence that 20 years after the opium trade stopped,

the Raj more or less packed up its bags and left. India was not a paying proposition any longer. ... Opium was the fundamental undergirding of our economy for centuries. It is strange that [even] for someone like me who studied history and knew a fair amount about Indian history, I was completely unaware of it. (2008b, n.p.)

Ghosh offers a fictional redress of the historical amnesia he outlines in his 2008 novel *Sea of Poppies*, the first of a trilogy that maps the opium trade from its roots in rural Bengal to the British invasion of Beijing in the Opium Wars.

Throughout this novel and its sequels, *River of Smoke* (2011) and *Flood of Fire* (2015), Ghosh foregrounds the economic imperatives that motivate colonial-era capitalism. At its peak in the early-to-mid-1800s, opium accounted for up to 20% of all Britain's revenues from India, earning even more than the importation of Indian cotton for manufacture in England. If the cloth industry is the much-heralded backbone of the British Industrial Revolution, then opium is the product that funded it: the two are interdependent, both managed by the East India Company monopoly. It is this economic history that Ghosh's novel encompasses, locating a postcolonial epic in the Chinese port of Canton in order to pull together the three edges of the trade triangle—India, China, Britain—so usually held apart. Indeed, before the company was liquidated in favour of the state-run colonial management of British imperial rule, this private consortium generated revenue greater than that of the whole of Britain (Robins 2003). Throughout the 1800s India financed 40% of Britain's total trade deficit (Chomsky 1999, 26). By 1900, the colonies as a whole accounted for one-quarter of Britain's capital—on par with national agriculture and housing combined (Piketty, 116–121).[3]

Analysis of China, which is usually disregarded by postcolonial studies, illustrates the close imbrication of capitalism and colonialism, and further foregrounds the violence used to capture the market and enforce its conversion to capitalism. The interdependence of India and China that Ghosh explores at length in his trilogy stresses the global movement of capital and produce that was enabled by mobile and co-optable labour and military, as well as by new financial concepts invented for colonial trade, particularly the public limited company, of which the Dutch and British East India Companies were the first, and insurance, such as Lloyd's of London, founded to insure slave ships. *Sea of Poppies* describes the workings of the opium industry from a number of narrative perspectives, including farmer, factory worker, transporter, merchant, broker, purveyor, investor, and opium user. These multiple subjectivities each illustrate a facet of Britain's selective use of free-market principles to protect its own interests in the quest for profit and expanding market share, not only at the expense of the Indian subjects, whose land and labour made the industry possible, but also against other competitors aiming to wrest a share in this lucrative market. In calling on an enormous cast of characters from all social strata and cultural milieus, Ghosh narrates innumerable forms of violence done to characters lower down the economic pecking order, from domestic violence among poor opium farmers to hostile business takeovers among the international merchants. Ranging across caste, class, and culture, the novel acts out capitalist relations embedded into social interaction from the most intimate family relationship to the public spheres of East India Company directors and British parliament.

The novel's interwoven narrative, which eventually brings all the characters together on the *Ibis*, a boat bound for Mauritius, follows each character as they respond to narrowing sets of choices that led them to the *Ibis*, each pressured by the limitations of their respective social statuses. The lascar sailor Serang Ali and quadroon Zachary Reid are each condemned by their race to limited possibilities for promotion. Ah Fatt is crippled by his opium addiction; Paulette is circumscribed by the limitations European middle-class culture imposes on her gender; and Kalua acts within the bounds permitted by his status as an untouchable, the meagre rights to which he signs away in an indentured labour contract. Each storyline herein offers a version of the classic postcolonial trope of colonial abuse of the colonised. Even though the majority of characters have no direct contact with the white oppressor, internal social hierarchies such as class, caste, age, and gender produce and maintain inequalities that the British use and exploit.

In the various plot strands that bring the characters together on the *Ibis*, Ghosh demonstrates how economic inequality percolates through the entire fabric of the Indian social structure, with all sectors of society ensnared in the colonial economics of Britain's mercantile superiority. Indeed, the *Ibis* is the floating microcosm of the colonial economy, afloat in the very medium that enables it, the shipping trade routes and ports of the first era of globalisation. The ship physically embodies the combined and uneven composition of global capital of its time, in its history (slave transporter refitted for shipping opium) and trajectory (Baltimore, Patagonia, Calcutta, Mauritius, Java, Canton), as well as in the international composition of its provisions and its crew. In particular, two main characters representing opposite ends of the Indian social spectrum—Deeti, an impoverished land tenant, and Raja Neel, a wealthy zamindar—illustrate the impact of Western capitalist land relations on Bengali society. Deeti describes the shift from the mixed crops of subsistence farming to poppy monoculture, forced by local agents of the British sahibs who now own the land (31). Following a poor harvest and the cost of caring for her dying husband, Deeti becomes indebted to a moneylender (163). As a poor widow, she lacks both economic and social capital, and is thus rendered literally useless to her family and to capitalism. Her options are limited either to being bodily discarded through forced sati on her husband's funeral pyre, or to existing as an appendage through a coerced marriage to her brother-in-law. She chooses instead another form of co-opted labour, fleeing her family to join the *girmitiyas*, indentured labourers. At the other end of the socio-economic scale, Raja Neel, a highly educated Bengali zamindar, loses his fortune and estate, and ends up a convict deported to Mauritius following a devious about-face by his erstwhile business partner Benjamin Burnham, head of a powerful British opium-trading merchant firm. The zamindar lends his wealth of land, assets, and contacts among the Hindu elite as investment capital to the entrepreneurial Burnham. After enjoying twenty years of high returns from the expanding opium trade, the zamindar borrows capital from Burnham to invest in high-risk, high-return stock. In a classic speculative market bubble familiar also in today's neoliberal economy, the bubble bursts in 1837 and Burnham calls in the loan and repossesses the zamindary land and properties on trumped-up criminal charges that dispossess Neel and his extended family from their ancestral lands (87–93).

The long backstory that Ghosh attributes these characters brings back into contemporary memory the importance of forced agricultural monoculture and dispossession of local zamindar elites as key strategies in Britain's colonial policy in India. In the 1793 Bengal Permanent Settlement Act, the British government supported the East India Company's imposition of British land tenure laws on the area in order to guarantee 90% of income from the land, extracted from the tenants by the zamindar landowners, who received a 10% cut. The Act caused a series of famines, dispossessed twenty million smallholder tenants, and with the zamindars defaulting on their tax quotas created a commercial property market boom, in which properties were bought by other zamindars, by British investors as absentee landlords, or sub-divided into unprofitable microtenures among lower-caste Indians. Ghosh inscribes

Burnham's repossession of Neel's zamindary within this particular opportunity: 'merchants who controlled their own production [of poppies], rather than depending on small farmers, would stand to multiply their already astronomical profits' (226).

Far from heralding the transition to a modernity characterised by development and progress, Ghosh portrays capitalism as resoundingly negative even for many traditional elites. As Mike Davis succinctly summarises in *Late Victorian Holocausts*, his analysis of market-induced famines that killed millions in Bengal:

> Millions died, not outside the 'modern world system,' but in the very process of being forcibly incorporated into its economic and political structures. They died in the golden age of Liberal Capitalism; ... by the theological application of the sacred principles of Smith, Bentham and Mill. (2002, 9)[4]

The theorisation of the modern political economy, which emerged in the nineteenth century, conceives of development as the incrustation of capitalism everywhere, and of progress as a synonym for increasing profit. This commonplace emphasis on success, however, fails to register its hidden costs, often termed 'externalities'—the very word expresses the refusal of economic theory to see the myriad of indirect impacts as intrinsic to its practices. Davis's focus on the human toll of applying capitalist market principles to food as the basic necessity of human life, and the postcolonial insider views of Ghosh's *Sea of Poppies*, reveal the fundamental flaw or contradiction of classical economic theory that claims the superiority of the free market while causing death, dispossession, and devastation for a large number of people co-opted into its circle.

Ghosh is not alone in giving considerable narrative weight in fiction to this particular change of land ownership in redefining power relations in colonial Indian society. Sanjay Bahadur in *Hul: Cry Rebel* (2013) revisits a little-known historical moment in the dispossession of the Santal tribe by the East India Company and the resulting 1855 Santal rebellion. Similar to Ghosh's descriptions of Neel's dispossession from his zamindary, Bahadur, who trained as an economist, describes in considerable detail his characters' multiple financial motivations and accompanying strategies. The character of Bipin Roy becomes a rich zamindar by buying the land from a maharaja indebted to the East India Company. Demonstrating the capitalist accumulation and reinvestment of profit on land that has been divorced from the local inhabitants, Bahadur describes how traders dupe cash-poor but asset-rich maharajas into giving them the rights to collect land revenue (Section 'July 1830,' para 5). Maharajas who buy land in other regions simulate colonial relations by themselves becoming outside investors, who 'looked upon land as merely an asset and a means of generating more profit. They neither had nor desired any understanding of the people who survived on those lands' (Section 'July 1830,' para 10). While Ghosh follows the money of the poppy crop to take his story from Bengal's fields to Canton's opium trade, Bahadur's narrative focus remains with the wealth of the land itself. His novel is thus national in scope and local in focus, delineating how the Santal tribal peoples' traditional territories were increasingly restricted by encroaching crop monoculture, and their traditional relations with the maharajas changed by the latter's adoption of capitalist land relations. In portraying nineteenth-century Santal resistance, Bahadur offers a historical context to the ongoing discrimination and immiseration of twenty-first-century tribal groups. By centralising Santal characters and their culture, he inscribes the modern-day relationship between the indigenous group and the Indian state within a postcolonial dynamic, calling for recognition, respect, and redress for historical wrongs from this form of internal colonialism.

The fact that both writers draw for different narrative purposes from the same historical information about the precise ways in which land was wrested from local to foreign ownership attests to the pervasive impact of emergent capitalism on India and on world trade. While the Santal rebellion and the Cantonese Opium Wars are on the surface unrelated events, they may both be seen as separate violent responses to the same pressures of changing land relations in the violent co-option of colonised spaces into capitalist structures. The global geopolitics of early British empire-forming, which links India to China and the founding of Hong Kong, and the long history of indigenous immiseration which continues to occupy a marginalised place within Indian politics today, are both manifestations of local and global impacts of capitalist formation. Updated to a contemporary context, Gayatri Chakravorty Spivak, in her analysis of Mahasweta Devi's stories in *Imaginary Maps* (1995), names local complicity in the devastation of the environment in the name of free-flowing global capital, to the point where the map of the world is based on 'economic rather than national boundaries' (198). As literary explorations of a historically new financial map, both Ghosh's maritime journey and Bahadur's walking the tribal boundary structure their narratives by following the money.

The truth of Ghosh's and Bahadur's fictional renditions of the colonial-era foundations of land privatisation and dispossession, and resultant criminalisation of the poor and exploitation of a newly landless labour force, is supported in historical evidence of such facts and figures. Unlike a historical document, however, the novel does not present one coherent argument. Rather, the polyphonic form of the novel allows multiple voices to express a range of often vacillating attitudes to the colonial enterprise, including collusion from the locals and reluctance from sympathetic colonials. Ghosh's and Bahadur's claims to the longevity of practices of dispossession and resistance to it are also the subject of Noam Chomsky's history of the long-term inequality of capitalist globalisation, *Profit over People: Neoliberalism and Global Order* (1999). Chomsky shows how colonial-era British politicians and historians were keenly aware of the negative social impacts of inserting capitalist land practices into Indian colonial administration. He cites the Bengal governor general William Bentinck's 1835 report on the repercussions of the abrupt arrival of Western capitalist land ownership:

> '[T]he settlement fashioned with great care and deliberation has unfortunately subjected the lower classes to most grievous oppression,' leaving misery that 'hardly finds a parallel in the history of commerce,' as 'the bones of the cotton-weavers are bleaching the plains of India.'... The British governor-general observed that 'the "Permanent Settlement," though a failure in many other respects and in most important essentials, has this great advantage, at least, of having created a vast body of rich landed proprietors deeply interested in the continuance of the British Dominion and having complete command over the mass of the people.' (26)

The report from the Bengal governor general shows early British criticism of the rapacious origins and unfair distribution of colonial wealth. In their different prose mediums, Chomsky, Ghosh, and Bahadur bring back into contemporary consciousness historical voices of protest, which they apply to their contemporary political purpose of critiquing global inequality. In particular, both Chomsky and Ghosh quote from historical archives, either in direct citation or paraphrased through historical characters, to remind readers that there were vocal opponents to the unethical corporate practices of colonial times just as there are whistle-blowers and critics of neoliberalism today—alongside whom they position themselves.

The significant amount of recent postcolonial fiction that looks back to the historical moments of colonialism's implantation, such as Ghosh's and Bahadur's novels, invites readers to consider the contemporary relevance of long-forgotten events. In particular, these writers' emphases of economic history mesh with similar theories of long-range globalisation, such as the world-systems approach and longitudinal macro-economics. Certainly, the shift in moral norms that today condemns drug trafficking (while by no means managing to stamp out the practice or reduce its considerable part of world trade) allows a contemporary view of Britain's opium trade as a condemnable example of a now-outmoded imperialism. This change in attitude toward narcotics masks significant areas of continuity from past to present, in which the same principles of political economy pioneered by the East India Company, in particular, and British imperialism, in general, remain buried in global practices of privatisation and state military intervention normalised today.

Both Chomsky's non-fiction and Ghosh's fiction use their different mediums to expose the turbulent and violent historical birth of economic principles that are today seen as frictionless and imagined as timeless. In tracing the trajectory from colonial to neoliberal capitalism, they reveal the hidden traumas and structural inequalities on which the present system continues to be based. In his two histories of capitalism, *Kicking Away the Ladder* (2002) and *Bad Samaritans* (2007), economic historian Ha-Joon Chang exposes developed nations' 'bad Samaritan' attitudes to the developing world with strategies that preach the superiority of free-market liberal capitalism while 'kicking away the ladder' to growth, development, and wealth. Correcting the historical forgetting of the importance of the opium trade in the expansion of British capitalist political economy, Chang claims the 'real history of globalization' begins with Britain's colonial annexing of Hong Kong (2007, 24). Chang's economic histories have been popular with a general reading public interested in turning to the past to identify the roots of present economic problems. While Chang's economic histories have certainly sold particularly well, they are nowhere near as popular as Ghosh's fiction, or as blockbuster historical novels by other popular writers such as James Clavell, Bryce Courtney, and Wilbur Smith. While commonly snubbed by literary scholars, their bestsellers provide some of fiction's most vivid examples of the historical irruption of capitalism in their various geographical locations.

Ghosh's postcolonial history of early capitalism, Chomsky's recourse to history in his critique of neoliberalism *Profit over People*, and Chang's attention to a long tradition of unequal trade relations imposed by powerful economies over weaker nations, actively contradict contemporary economic dogma of the objective and rational 'free' market. Conveniently forgetting historical British–Chinese trade relations, in his 2010 visit to China Cameron called for '[p]artnership not protectionism': 'Britain is the country that argues most passionately for globalisation and free trade. Free trade is in our DNA. And we want trade with China. As much of it as we can get' (Cameron, n.p.). However, the history of Britain's changing policy on tariffs belies Cameron's neoliberal-era claim that free trade equates with freedom from tariffs. After embracing zero tariffs from the 1880s after fierce debate, Britain reintroduced trade tariffs after the shock of the Great Depression in the 1930s, repealed only in the early 1970s (Chang 2005, 52–56). In his 2005 address to the UN, President George W. Bush similarly forgot where isolationist policies historically came from—including 40% tariffs until 1945—when he blurred together the liberal philosophy of individual freedom with the liberal economics of free trade to claim:

> We need to give the citizens of the poorest nations the same ability to access the world economy that the people of wealthy nations have, ... to ensure that they have the same opportunities to pursue their dreams, provide for their families, and live lives of dignity and self-reliance. And the greatest obstacles to achieving these goals are the tariffs and subsidies and barriers that isolate people of developing nations from the great opportunities of the 21st century. (Bush 2005, n.p.)

Both Cameron and Bush promote laissez-faire capitalism in the present as if their relationship with China and other developing countries is based on an equal footing, a premise that their long histories of trade protectionism belie.

Both Cameron's and Bush's discourses further align with the World Bank, the International Monetary Fund (IMF), and core capitalist countries' pressure on undeveloped nations *not* to invest in state-supported development of industry and technology. Rather, economic theory argues they should allow the market to decide their areas of competitive advantage, which consist of cheap manufactured goods in China and raw materials from most developing nations. The significance of state-owned businesses in growing China, however, challenges this assumption.[5] Furthermore, as a concise example of Chang's argument that many of today's famous companies required years of state support and market protection before they could stand alone on the world market,[6] the former colonial Ghazipur Opium and Alkaloid Works featured in *Sea of Poppies*, now nationalised, is today the world's largest provider of pharmaceutical opium derivatives, specialising in high-tech production of opium alkaloids. The factory, founded by the East India Company and later run by the British colonial government, has always been a state-run monopoly that has never been subject to competitive free trade.

In *World Orders Old and New* (1994), Chomsky gives an example from colonial Bengal of the hidden coercion and manipulation behind the tenet of the free market that Chang's history and Ghosh's novel identify. Chomsky cites eighteenth- and nineteenth-century sources who describe imperial Britain's forced deindustrialisation of India and subsequent turn to cash-crop monocultures, particularly of poppies and cotton. In a historical example of a hostile takeover followed by asset stripping explicitly intended to quash competition, the East India Company invaded Bengal for its flourishing textile industry, which it promptly destroyed, leaving only the raw material of cotton farming, much of which was further converted to poppies. Dhaka, dubbed by the East India Company in 1757 'the Manchester of India'—'extensive, populous, and rich as the city of London'—was by 1840 reduced to an impoverished, backwards small town (Chomsky 1994, 115). Sven Beckert labels such strategies against competition as testifying to capitalism's 'illiberal origins' (2014, 37). Certainly, aspects of this historical transaction are familiar in corporate strategies today, including buying up the competition, corporate raids, and asset stripping.

As with the Bengal Permanent Settlement, described above, British analysts of the time were aware of the economic repercussions of their actions. One 1820s historian explains the benefit for Britain of this unfair market competition: 'the mills of Paisley and Manchester would have been stopped in their outset, and could scarcely have been again set in motion, even by the power of steam. They were created by the sacrifice of Indian manufacturers' (Horace Wilson [1826] qtd in Chomsky 1994, 115). Karl Marx gives a similar example of England's dismantling of Irish wool manufacture, a form of oppression by enforced backwardness that he claims to have been a common technique across European empires, which 'forcibly rooted out, in their dependent countries, all industry' ('Genesis of the Industrial Capitalist,' 830). It is this predatory strategy of reducing competition that leads Ghosh to claim in his interview about his Ibis trilogy that '[a]ll the empirical facts show you that British rule was a disaster for India. Before the British came 25% of the world trade originated in India. By the time they left it was less than 1%' (Ghosh 2008b, n.p.). Historical examples of such aggressive protectionist strategies contradict today's common understanding of market triumph as closely linked to superior technology: even the innovation of steam power would not have given enough competitive advantage to Britain's fledgling textile industry without the active suppression of overseas competitors. Chang, for example, describes several strategies of historical British and American protectionism, such as trade embargoes, unequal treaties, and high import tariffs, which only opened to the free international market in the late 1800s, once the protected industries were developed enough to dominate (2007, 25; 40–46).[7]

The misunderstood and misapplied concept of the free market of low tariffs and no state support or intervention exemplifies hidden inequalities within capitalism's mechanisms that are popularly construed as open and fair. Ghosh's Ibis trilogy brings back into view the highly contested, turbulent history of modern economics by revealing the unlevel playing field and 'bad Samaritan' behaviour most evident at the moment of capitalism's imposition in the colonies. In particular, the second novel, *River of Smoke*, dramatises the substantial tension and conflict in early colonial negotiation between private enterprise and state support. Whereas the first novel traces the product from Deeti's field, the Ghazipur factory, and river transport to the Kolkata trading docks, the second volume relates the merchant middlemen, international shipping, and the opium's sale at the port of Canton. Ghosh's focus on characters involved in the East India Company is a reminder of the importance of private investment in the development of modern capitalism that emerged out of the Industrial Revolution at home and colonisation abroad. The instantiation of British involvement in India through a private speculative business consortium is often overlooked in popular understandings of colonialism as primarily a state-led, political, and ideological endeavour of national desires for expansion of its purportedly superior civilisation.[8] Contradicting this misconception, economic historian Nuala Zahedieh[9] argues that '[p]olicy was not driven by a body of theory underpinning systematic rules' (2014, 392). Rather, she argues:

> Expansion was largely financed and organised by private individuals. ... The state did not direct the policy but it did provide support, both because the commercial classes were active stakeholders in government, especially

after the Glorious Revolution, and because the policy promised economic
growth and easily taxable revenue streams. (393)

This economic rather than cultural focus construes imperialism as quintessentially private rather than state led. Rather than being motivated by a national desire to spread its civilisation, expansion was primarily driven by the emerging theories of modern economics, and pioneered by self-interested, individual entrepreneurs free to circulate and to trade around the globe.

Supporting Zahedieh's argument for the avant-garde position of private investors ahead of the state, in *River of Smoke* Ghosh portrays the European merchants of the Canton Chamber of Commerce as a law unto themselves. They make illegal forays into northern Chinese ports looking for new markets by bribery or force (307), and take into their own hands decisions of local justice and its enforcement, yet claim impunity for their own illegal actions through protection as British citizens (368). The novel's climax portrays the standoff between European traders and Chinese compradors over the opium trade in Canton immediately preceding the First Opium War of 1839. The entrepreneurs defend their actions through recourse to economic 'common sense,' a belief in the scientific and objective nature of the market, which they tout as fact, thereby drawing the nascent discipline of economics into the Enlightenment principles of rationality.[10] With their insight into political economy, the East India Company and other British trading barons proclaim that the government representative in Canton 'understands nothing of financial matters' (251) and that 'he should trust our leading merchants to represent our own best interests' (252). In the words of Burnham, regarding the merchants' power to declare war on the Chinese Emperor for his threatened opium embargo without consent from the British government, 'if such matters were left to Parliament there would *be* no Empire' (Ghosh 2008a, 123, italics in original). The traders' confidence that Britain will not pass unfavourable laws against the lucrative trade is furthered by their knowledge that a number of members of parliament have vested interests in the trade, as investors in the East India Company, shipping, banking, or colonial possessions (425).

In these plot developments, Ghosh's background as a historian is in strong evidence, with his fictional narrative closely following historical fact and argument. Writing about the close relationship between politics and business under early empire, Amartya Sen claims 'nearly a quarter of the members of Parliament in London owned stock in the East India Company in the 1760s. ... The commercial interests at the beginning of the empire in India reached far into the British establishment' (2007, n.p.). Explaining eighteenth- and nineteenth-century patronage and corruption, R.R. Neild states, '[p]ublic offices were private property to be bought and sold' (62). The influential economist John Stuart Mill, for example, was an executive of the East India Company as well as a member of parliament. Overt in his dependence on historical research, or perhaps positioning his novel as biographical fiction, Ghosh retains in his novel the names of real-life British opium traders and members of parliament William Jardine and James Matheson, and John Dent, a trader who went on to become a leading official in Hong Kong after its annexation following the First Opium War.

Ghosh's merchants' claims that the function of government is to support and not to meddle in the market is a founding tenet of economic liberalism, upheld today even following economists' and financial analysts' catastrophic miscalculations that led to the 2008 global financial crisis. In concordance with capitalism's dependence on state support structures of policy, law, and the military, identified in neoliberal critique, Ghosh demonstrates the opium traders' reliance on British support for their illegal activities in China. The premonition that Great Britain would rather wage war against China than accept the Emperor's opium ban—and thus lose the British Empire's most lucrative industry—is foreshadowed in the earlier *Sea of Poppies*. From the privileged position of historical hindsight, in which the reader knows the outcome of China's attempt to reject the West's imposition of global free trade, Ghosh spells out the economic grounds for a war that has been largely forgotten today. Using the narrative opportunity of the unworldly aesthete Raja Neel asking Burnham the reasons for the downturn in the opium trade, Ghosh explains the threat to Britain's economy of a potential end to the opium trade to the equally uninformed reader:

> But Mr Burnham! Are you saying that the British Empire will go to war to force opium on China?
>
> ... The war, when it comes, will not be for opium. It will be for a principle: for freedom – for the freedom of trade and for the freedom of the Chinese people. Free Trade is a right conferred on Man by God, and its principles apply as much to opium as to any other article of trade. More so perhaps, since in its absence many millions of natives would be denied the

lasting advantages of British influence. ... Do you imagine that British rule would be possible in this impoverished land if it were not for this source of wealth? (120)

Burnham's didactic language, ostensibly simplified for Neel and thus also the reader, offers a simplistic explanation of free-market liberalism and its hidden ideological foundations. Burnham's patronising tone conveys the alleged superiority of this economic system, and thus also the superiority of the British trader over the local Indian zamindar and the Chinese opium user. He further makes clear the drive for wealth as being behind Britain's God-given mission of expanding its sphere of 'influence,' thereby unmasking the economic over the civilising motivation of empire. In his emphatic proclamation, the primacy of the market renders Neel's humanist concerns secondary, as Burnham, in Chomsky's terms, privileges 'profit over people.'

Like the character of Neel in *Sea of Poppies*, whose high status in Indian society brings him in direct contact with the colonial administration, *River of Smoke* also features a narrator ambivalently positioned between the dominant foreigners and subjugated natives. Bahram Modi, a Parsi Indian merchant, is a private individual who acts out of his own entrepreneurial interests to gain respect from his wealthier in-laws in Bombay, boat builders contracted to the East India Company (47–60). As an Indian tai-pan in Canton, he is a cultural outsider, and although he is primarily in collusion with the British, he is emotionally aligned with the victims of colonisation, a useful position with which to expose the impact of merchant imperialism on both Indians and Chinese. Modi, to whom all European ideas and manners are foreign, narrates from his ideological remove the actions and claims made by Canton's British traders and merchants. His gaze exposes as strange the British beliefs and motivations that the modern-day Western reader may find unremarkable or even normal, and thus not notice. Modi's narrative control prepares the reader for speeches by British and American opium traders defending their trade that are shocking to the point of ludicrous, reinforcing through repetition Burnham's speech on free trade from the previous novel, quoted above:

> I am quite confident that the attempts to ban opium will wither in the face of growing demand, it is not within the mandarins' power to withstand the elemental forces of Free Trade. (425)

> Free Trade, Universal Free Trade, the extinction of all monopolies, and especially the most odious one, the Hong monopoly! ... 'To Free Trade,

gentlemen! ... It is the cleansing stream that will sweep away all tyrants, great and small!' (428)

[I]t is not my hand that passes sentence upon those who choose the indulgence of opium. It is the work of another, invisible, omnipotent: it is the hand of freedom, of the market, of the spirit of liberty itself, which is none other than the breath of God. (486–487)

Is freedom not a principle as well as a right? Is there no principle at stake when free men claim the liberty to conduct their affairs without fear of tyrants and despots? (488)

Coming at the end of the second novel, after several hundred pages outlining the mechanisms through which opium is extracted, transported, and traded, the reader knows that the 'freedom' expressed in these quotes is heavily compromised. The pompous and earnest sincerity of these utterances ought to render them highly parodic to the contemporary reader. Yet, any sense of farce is undercut by the very real power wielded by these merchants, on behalf of the British Empire, which waits in the wings with a naval fleet, ready to invade the bellicose, protectionist China. Although these phrases sound absurd, the pantomimesque narrative takes a turn to realism when the reader learns from the Author's Note that in many instances Ghosh is quoting verbatim from archival newspapers and letters (582). Indeed, the majority of the Western characters are based on famous historical figures, including Benjamin Burnham, Lancelot and John Dent, William Jardine, James Matheson, Charles King, Charles Elliot, and John Slade. In citing passages from, for example, Slade's (2007) journalism from *The Canton Register* and King's 1839 appeal to the colonial administrator to end the opium trade, Ghosh suggests that the location of fiction is not the novel but rather the tenets of free-market capitalism itself. In the absurdity of the above phrases about free trade, the reader sees the illusionary nature of key principles of the modern political economy.

If the language of such quotes rings anachronistic, the ideas they propound are not out of date. The liberal theories of freedom proclaimed by the tai-pans, both of the market and of the individual's choice to consume, are indebted to Adam Smith's concept of the free hand of the market and John Stuart Mill's philosophy of individual freedom. The neoliberal interpretations of these classical economists' theories, which are today taken for granted as common sense, are uncomfortably jarring to the modern reader familiar with many of the principles espoused by the traders. The above medley of citations voices key concepts of the power of the individual as consumer, trade freedom as a principle, the invisible hand of the market, consumer-driven supply and demand, and anti-monopolies. Rather than the obscuring economic jargon and matter-of-fact tone of today's descriptions of the free market, Ghosh's bombastic, quasi-religious nineteenth-century idiom foregrounds the ideology of capitalism that is today usually hidden behind mathematical formulae and data. Ghosh thus provides a powerful critique of capitalist political economy by conveying familiar principles rendered suspicious and unethical by the unfamiliar language and unfamiliar setting of now-forgotten British imperialism in China. Known as a postcolonial writer, Ghosh's rewriting of the economic history of the opium trade asks for postcolonial studies to incorporate into its remit the injustice of British imperialism in China and the injustice of capitalism.

Britain comes out looking the villain on both economic and imperial fronts, as the contemporary reader takes a moral position against the blatant British greed to profit from now-illegal international drug trafficking. The trader's invocation of a God-given right to trade also sits uncomfortably with modern secular society's expectations of clear separation between church and state, and the shift of religious practice to the private sphere. At the same time, the elevation of money-making to such an exulted level of mystification, here rendered in ecclesiastical tones, is unnervingly close to contemporary society's thrall to Mammon. While the contemporary (white Western) reader might emotionally reject the opium traders' beliefs, he or she is cognitively aligned with the tenets of free-market liberalism that dominate today in a political economy directly descended from such historical figures, corporate strategies, and moments of state intervention.[11] It is exactly in such dissonant moments of recognition that Rita Felski locates the power of literature's epistemic and ethical insights (29–30). To recognise one's complicity in a system that has subjugated and marginalised the colonised Other is, of course, intrinsic to the white Western reader's experience of postcolonial literature. Ghosh's novel expands this complicity to include the reader's collusion in capitalism.

Ghosh's Ibis trilogy exposes the illegal and underhand dealings of both private interests and the state in a distant historical and cultural setting; however, his novels have particular resonance in regard to the 2008 financial crisis and its aftermath. For Felski, the flash of recognition experienced while reading, of seeing a part of one's own world exposed on the page, confounds the reader's 'sense of who and what they are' (23). Reading *River of Smoke* at the time of its publication in 2011, when debate over state bailouts of banks and companies deemed 'too big to fail' was still prominent in the media, the reader recognised in a little-heard-of historical context similar dynamics of the neoliberal political platitudes that smoothed over the bullying of powerful private investors pushing the state into backing them up. Corroborating the truth of fiction and the fiction of economics, post-crisis pop-economics texts such as *Too Big to Fail* and *The Big Short*, which explicitly blame individuals and institutions for the 2008 crisis, offer contemporary versions of the crookedness of antipathetic characters in the opium trade. Indeed, if we shed the nineteenth-century idiom of Ghosh's narrative, the ideas expounded by the opium traders are familiar to key twenty-first century neoliberal arguments. These include George W. Bush on American oil deals in post-invasion Iraq—'[b]y expanding trade, we spread hope and opportunity to the corners of the world, and we strike a blow against the terrorists' (2005, n.p.)—and Ben Bernanke, chairman of the US Federal Reserve, who supported Smith's concept of the invisible hand in relation to trusting commercial banks and hedge funds just months before the collapse of sub-prime mortgages in late 2007 (Bernanke 2007, n.p.). Common across the pronouncements made by each of these advocates of free trade, from nineteenth-century opium traders to modern-day leaders such as Cameron, Bush, and Bernanke, is their great confidence in the political apparatus that supports them, even when their economic models are proven to be wrong.

In accounting for the extraordinary lengths to which the rich cling to disproven or controversial economic concepts, Thomas Piketty brings together examples from France's *Belle Époque* and the contemporary USA to claim: 'no hypocrisy is too great when economic and financial elites are obliged to defend their interests—and that includes economists who currently occupy an enviable place in the US income hierarchy' (514). Piketty's example of the tendency for the elite to package their self-interest as general norms chimes with the indignation with which Ghosh's opium traders berate the appointed British governor to Canton's attempts to curb the opium trade in the name of law rather than the free market: '[i]t is appalling that a man whose salary we pay should take it upon himself to impose Celestial misrule upon free man' (382). Paul Krugman, in his review of Piketty's *Capital*, refers to a similar Upton Sinclair quote on the US Gilded Age of the 1920s: 'it is difficult to get a man to understand something when his salary depends on his not understanding it' (2014, n.p.). Krugman, who argues that the 2010s represent a contemporary gilded age, claims the phenomenon is today repeated in the deluded businessman's notion that his great wealth benefits the public good, as a contribution to the economy. Andrew Sorkin is more direct about the self-serving response of the public and private engineers of the crisis. He briefs his early post-crisis pop-economics book *Too Big to Fail* as 'the inside story of how Wall Street and Washington fought to save the financial system—and themselves' (Sorkin 2009, front cover). Nick Robins extends the logic of private–public collusion back to the East India Company, which he calls the forerunner of the modern multinational and the original 'too big to fail' corporation (2013, n.p.). Certainly, state intervention to rescue or regulate private corporations in the wake of the 2008 crisis, and the vigorous growth of some state companies in recent years, particularly in Brazil, Russia, India, China and developing countries, has renewed interest in such 'public-private hybrids,' of which the East India Company is a model (Robins 2013, n.p.). Just as the US government felt compelled to support the failing banking industry and key companies such as General Motors for the national good, in the nineteenth century the British government effectively nationalised the East India Company rather than lose its significant contribution to national wealth. Company shares were converted to government bonds, of which its parliamentarian shareholders held a significant stake, and its infrastructures of land tenure, trading, and military support continued under the British Raj from 1858, as capitalism continued under formal colonialism (Robins 2006, 6).

Ghosh's Ibis trilogy makes an important link between colonial India, which is the nation and literature most privileged in postcolonial studies, and China, which does not feature in the discipline at all. Ghosh's *oeuvre* is a reminder of the forgotten areas of British imperialism, set in such locations as China in the Ibis trilogy; Burma, Malaya, and Thailand in *The Glass Palace*; and Egypt in *In an Antique Land*. The ongoing interest for postcolonial writers of revisiting the colonial contact period in lengthy historical novels stakes a claim for the continual significance in the present of the historical introduction of capitalism to the colonies. As all history reveals as much about the concerns of its time of writing as it does of the past it records, confluences and parallels between past and present political economies in historical fiction, particularly epics, are integral to the social realm and cultural imaginary these writers wish to convey. The broad panorama and multigenerational epic timeline of Ghosh's novels offer valuable longitudinal studies of the impact of the irruption of the capitalist world-system in colonial times and its continuation in its present neoliberal manifestation. This *longue durée* approach reveals recurring structures of political economy and patterns of inequality both within a country and across colonial spaces, offering, in effect, an overview of the spread of globalisation through important routes and nodes in its web, mapping the international movement of capital—monetary, human, and ideological—in the first era of globalisation.

Ghosh's exploration of the British Empire in East and South-East Asia significantly broadens the postcolonial outlook to encompass the opium and spice trades; however, Britain's colonial endeavours must also be situated in the larger geopolitics of pan-European international relations of the colonial period. While most postcolonial analysis pays heed to the relationship between the coloniser and the colonised, scholarship has altogether less to say about the allegiances and tensions between the colonisers, whose political wrangling at home was often enacted as dramas played out in the colonies. This academic bias is perhaps understandable when the subject of analysis is social and cultural influence, such as British education, religion, and cultural values imposed on and translated in British colonies, but it becomes untenable when applied to geopolitical factors such as strategic territories, extraction of resources, and investment and debt structures.

Positioned outside of the Anglocentric domination of histories of Western capitalism and of the British Empire, as well as the English-language dominance in postcolonial studies, the Dutch East Indies, viewed through the work of Indonesian writer Pramoedya Ananta Toer, focuses attention on the wider geopolitical environment of the first age of globalisation. Pramoedya's Buru Quartet novels,[12] *This Earth of Mankind* (1982), *Child of All Nations* (1984), *Footsteps* (1990), and *House of Glass* (1996), map the history of Dutch colonialism in the East Indies from the Dutch East India Company's trading monopoly to Indonesian independence. Based on extensive archival research, Pramoedya's relentless advocacy of the power of the written word for nation-building is tempered by his imprisonment under both the colonial regime before independence and the second national government under Suharto throughout the 1970s, and his subsequent house arrest until 1992. Although he wrote in Bahasa Indonesia, Pramoedya's works were banned in Indonesia from their time of publication until 2005; he is most widely read outside of his country and in translation, of which Australian diplomat Max Lane's English translations were among the first.

The four-part historical epic traces the tumultuous rise of Indonesian nationalism amid and against Dutch colonialism, which Pramoedya situates within a global context of power relations and political posturing among the colonial players in South-East Asia, which include Britain, France, Spain, Germany, and the USA, with Japan further waiting in the wings. Pramoedya's novels resonate particularly with Ghosh's Ibis trilogy because of the similar motivations and strategies used by the Dutch East India Company (VOC) and the British East India Company in Bengal and Canton. Both India and the Indonesian archipelago were ruled for over 200 years as royally sanctioned monopolies before being taken over by the state as administrative colonies. The British and Dutch charter companies, formed barely a year apart, were closely modelled on, influenced by, and competed with each other. Pramoedya's fictional portrayals of the violent insertion of Dutch colonial forced cultivation methods onto the land and into the cultures of the Indonesian isles echo Ghosh's representation of Bengali cash-crop monocultures. Like Ghosh, Pramoedya renders as fiction speeches and popular economic arguments of the colonial period, in which the historical language rings anachronistic although the arguments sound familiar to the modern reader. In their ability to make the past resonate in the present, such epics bridge the gap between different yet simultaneous forms of colonial capitalism, and between early and present forms of capitalism.

Pramoedya spells out the connecting threads of economic dependency that tie the Netherlands to their resource-rich colony and to the other European empires. For example, a fictional version of Dutch parliamentarian and radical liberal H. van Kollewijn makes a cameo appearance to explain 'that the first decades of the *Culture System*, also called Forced Cultivation, had saved Holland from the bankruptcy it faced due to the huge debts that were incurred through the wars in Europe in which Holland too was involved' (1990, 38, italics in original). In such passages, Pramoedya emphasises the Dutch East Indies' role in the global flows of colonial-era commerce, which extend far further than a simple relationship between the Netherlands and the East Indies. In other examples of international connectivity, the Indies are involved in the opium trade through Chinese guilds circumventing the British monopoly by smuggling Burmese opium overland through networks of ethnic Chinese Indonesians (1996, 2). The islands are constantly on their guard against American ships working out of the Philippines kidnapping Javanese to supply the South American mining industry (1996, 59). They are alert to the implication of Japan's 1904 colonial ambitions in Manchuria, Russia, and Korea, as Meiji-era Japan joined the European imperial drive to claim foreign territories so that '[t]he non-European world, even to the smallest island in the ocean, had been swept up' (1990, 136). Made anxious by the Philippine–American War (1899–1902), the narrator of the final tome is aware of the precarity of colonial rule, and likens the insecurity in the early 1900s with earlier changes of colonial masters a century earlier[13]:

> You must all pay more attention, gentlemen. If not ... we could have a second Philippines here in this pearl of a colony of ours. We could be kicked out. Another one of the Western countries will come in, perhaps America, perhaps Germany, or perhaps even England. ... It seems that none of you pays attention to colonial developments outside the Indies. That is very bad, gentlemen. Colonial affairs in Asia are all interconnected, like links in a chain. (1996, 48–49)

The speaker's admonishment of his audience of Dutch colonial administrators and nascent Indonesian nationalists might equally apply to the contemporary reader. The reminder to always consider the global politics of colonialism as well as its local manifestations unique to each site is a refrain throughout the novels. For Pramoedya, ending the final novel of his quartet before Indonesia's independence allows him to keep to the fore the uncertainty of the next stage of colonialism. Thus, his text brings back into focus the moments before this bifurcation, reminding readers of continuities and confluences later forgotten. Pramoedya's work may be considered postcolonial for its recuperative act of centring the colonial experience and indicting colonial abuse and injustice, yet his work is innovative for the way he does not lose sight of the very real Eurocentrism at the heart of empire, a mistake postcolonial analysis often makes in its haste to recuperate and validate heretofore silenced voices.

As Pramoedya understands, colonies are possessions to be fought over, delegated, and even swapped among the European powers according to geopolitics in faraway Europe: 'colonialism was not simply a local problem but an international one' (1996, 228); '[e]verything that is born here on Java is nothing but the echo of what happens on mainland Asia, and now Europe too' (1996, 264). Far from a one-way flow of influence, however, European geopolitics is also a source of inspiration for growing nationalism in the Asian sub-continent. Pramoedya outlines East Indian workers' movements organising around the Irish concept of boycott (1990, 261) and close interest in the Chinese nationalist movement, which resulted in the overthrow of the Manchu dynasty and the founding of a republic in 1912, tracked throughout the quartet of novels. Similarly, Ghosh, in his earlier novel *The Glass Palace*, points to colonial interest in the conflict between European Russia and Asian Japan in the 1904–1905 Russo–Japanese War as fuelling Indian and Burmese nationalist movements, twinning support for Japan's imperial victory with the early Swadeshi movement, boycotting British-made goods, and burning imported Lancashire cloth (105).

As pawns in a larger game, analysis of the colonies is incomplete without concomitant analysis of the dynamics in and between their imperial masters. This includes Japanese imperialism and its challenge to European empires, which culminated in the invasion of South-East Asia in the Pacific War, which Ghosh portrays in the Malayan section of his novel *The Glass Palace*.[14] Of more prominence is the power-brokering within Europe over the Ottoman Empire, which led to World War One and resulted in a shift in, rather than an end to, colonial management, particularly in the Middle East. Whereas the great majority of World War One histories centralise only European politics,[15] Pramoedya's frequent reminders of other colonial contestations happening simultaneously yet off the pages of his books helps recall the importance of imperialism within Europe's internal colonies of the Prussian, Austro-Hungarian, Russian, and Ottoman Empires. Both Ghosh (2001, 201) and Pramoedya (1996, 159) mention the Sarajevo assassination of Archduke Franz Ferdinand that sparked World War One for its impact on their respective colonial economies. Outside of the apparent colonial connection, however, the Balkan question represents Europe's own site of colonial contest between the competing empires, as well as an early example of a successful national independence movement. Similar to the external colonies, the Balkans were swapped between European powers, partitioned, remapped, and carved up with little regard to the area's own interests: 'a plaything of the great powers' (Romein and Wertheim 1956, 85). As one policy historian states, '[t]he failure of the powers to agree on Serbia's status—that is, whether she was "oriental" or "European"—was in a sense one of the major factors that led to the war' (Trachtenberg 1993, 25). Lenin, who wrote *Imperialism: The Highest Stage of Capitalism* during the war, labels it 'an annexationist, predatory, plunderous war ... for the division of the world, for the partition and repartition of the colonies, "spheres of influence" of financial capital, etc' (1999, 27). Rosa Luxemburg, in her excoriating, poetic *Junius Pamphlet* 1916, enumerates the multiple ways in which the German bourgeois profited from the industries and supply chains that provisioned the war, as '[b]usiness thrives in the ruins' (Chap. 1, n.p.), booming in an 'imperialist war [covered] with a lying mantle of national self-defence' (Chap. 7, n.p.). While the war certainly took a heavy toll on all participant nations, the post-war redistribution of colonial spaces concentrated colonial sources of wealth in favour of the Western allies. Germany's colonies were predominantly split between Britain and France,[16] while Russia and the extensive Ottoman Empire were carved up, with Britain and France taking over protectorates in Egypt, Palestine, Iran, Iraq, Syria, and Lebanon at the precise moment when the potentials of oil were discovered.

In order to fulfil its own remit as the discipline dedicated to historical empire and its contemporary repercussions, postcolonial studies has much work to do in tracing the continuities rather than the ruptures between past and present forms of colonialism and across all its many sites. Ghosh's and Pramoedya's historical fiction return to view the economic functions of the colonies within the global commodities market by foregrounding British and Dutch economic theories more familiar to readers today than to the Indian, Chinese, and Indonesian characters confronted with them for the first time. The fiction demonstrates great knowledge of the wider geopolitical plain on which colonial history played out, which includes the conditions underpinning World War One and the influence of nationalist movements such as in the Balkans, Ireland, and China. Drawing attention to the geopolitical economic history of the colonies for their role within the European-led world-system challenges the shape of postcolonial studies to think past centring the margins as its main objective. It is only by following the historical trajectory of capitalism's spread that Britain's past trading relationship with China and the prominence of Indian opium production becomes evident. Both Cameron's and Bush's ignorance of this economic history signals the extent to which the narrative of capitalism has been written out of popular history, an oversight that postcolonial historical fiction does much to rectify.

Capitalism in Settler Colonies

The above study of colonial history emphasises how the motivations of empire were informed and shaped by the concepts of classical economics that already dominated discourse at home in Britain and Europe. All forms of colonisation revolved around the expansion of British trade: exploring shipping passages, claiming and developing new land in farming, plantations, and mines, and new industries and forms of commodity production, as well as widening the base of the mercantile industry of finance, insurance, transport, and distribution (Zahedieh 2010, 392–393). These different expressions of imperialism cover all forms of colonisation, including white-settler nations, extractive and commodity colonies, and protectorates of strategic location. Although certainly colonisation was experienced differently in each unique space, they each shared a common quest for profit by instigating capitalist relations. All colonies are marked by negotiations for the commodification of land, natural resources, and human labour, as well as the financialisation of intangible concepts such as risk (insurance, speculation) and futures (credit, bonds, indentured labour). The capitalist underpinnings that drove the East India Company's rule in India to facilitate trade, and which motivated British naval warfare to annex the strategic-position colonies in Hong Kong (1841), Singapore (1867), Cyprus (1878), and Egypt (1882), are also evident in the white-settler colonies such as Australia and New Zealand.

Postcolonial study of the white-settler colonies has tended to centralise the relationship between settlers and indigenous peoples through which to analyse cross-cultural interaction and the building of national identity. Questions of class inequality within the settler group and social hierarchies within the indigenous society are, however, underanalysed. Today's spotlight on internal inequality within the nation makes it timely to investigate colonial-era access to capital and its present-day legacies. Structures and mechanisms of capitalist inequality instituted in early settlement have long-lasting repercussions, continuing today in the disproportionate poverty of indigenous peoples within developed nation-states. This section focuses firstly on internal relations within the settler society to tease out the new forms of capitalist-inflected social relations that stratified colonial society and continued British class relations in the new land. The second focus, on internal inequality within indigenous communities, challenges the tendency in postcolonial literary analysis to romanticise indigenous societies as egalitarian, equally victims of an imposed colonial system, and as always resistant to the capitalist processes that have all but destroyed their social and cultural practices. Identifying how, at the colonial moment, capitalism was integrated into pre-contact societies which already contained their own hierarchies is necessary for the explanation of how native comprador elites later propagated capitalist economic structures at the time of independence. Such focus on internal inequality, also known as internal colonialism, allows analysis of the structures and mechanisms by which economic inequality has been sustained from colonial to neocolonial to neoliberal times.

The importance of the colonies to the development of modern economics is evident in the frequency with which many of the classical economists write on the mechanics and ethics of imperialism, well before Lenin's *Imperialism, the Highest Stage of Capitalism*. Smith, in *The Wealth of Nations* (1776), writes dedicated chapters on the British colonies, in which he resoundingly condemns the East India Company's unethical business practices, its colonial brutality, and its unbridled power as a monopoly. His voice was only one of the many critics of the well-known rapacity of the East India Company's rule in India, which not only concerned early socialists such as Marx and Luxemburg but also featured in the work of much earlier economists of the seventeenth and eighteenth centuries, notably John Locke, David Hume, Daniel Defoe, Malthus, Jeremy Bentham, and John Stuart Mill. Both Malthus and Mill were directly involved in the East India Company.

Colonial companies in the settler colonies were not necessarily based on a more equitable business model. Marx critiques Edward Gibbon Wakefield, British speculative investor in Canada, Australia, and New Zealand settlement companies, thus: '[i]t is the great merit of E.G. Wakefield to have discovered, not anything new about the Colonies, but to have discovered in the Colonies the truth as to the conditions of capitalist production in the mother country' ('The Modern Theory of Colonisation,' 839). The quote illustrates the understanding of colonialism as the continuity of capitalist relations already at work in the imperial centre; it further recognises the key role of the private company in expanding investment opportunities by moving capital abroad. In the case of settler colonies, this expansion includes human movement as another form of capital. As Jean-Paul Sartre tersely summarises in his portrayal of French imperialism in Algeria, '[t]he colonist is above all an artificial consumer, created overseas from nothing by a capitalism which is seeking new markets' (2001, 34). While Marx's and Sartre's comments might be interpreted from a postcolonial or an anti-neoliberal perspective as a critique of the colonial speculator's imposition of capitalist social relations on unsuspecting civilisations, for Wakefield the charge is merely common business sense. He heads his theory of colonial settlement, *A View of the Art of Colonization* (1849), with an epigraph from Mill: '[t]here need be no hesitation in affirming, that Colonization, in the present state of the world, is the very best affair of business, in which the capital of an old and wealthy country can possibly engage' (2001, n.p.). There is no hint of imperialism's civilising mission underpinning this comment.

In fact, the human dimension is absent, as profit over people is the unashamedly stated governing logic of this expression of colonial mentality.

Marx's reproach of Wakefield usefully identifies the way in which the capitalist means of production are clearer to see in the colonies because of the suddenness of their adaptation to capitalism, a point also made by Wakefield in his didactic accounts of the emerging colonial political economy that was already entrenched in Britain. The ideological motivations and mechanics of the insertion of capitalist social relations in the colonies are evident, whereas in Britain they had become so ingrained by the early 1800s as to appear normal and thus invisible. In the rapid and often-violent expropriation of indigenous peoples from their land, and their subsequent conversion to wage labourers or their isolation on reserved land, Marx's principles of primitive accumulation are seen in action, with British and colonial government policies and private investment strategies colluding in what Marx calls 'artificial means to ensure the poverty of the people' in the colonies in order to extract the maximum profit destined for Britain, 'in the interest of the so-called national wealth' ('The Modern Theory of Colonisation,' 839).

The irruption of colonial capitalism is perhaps most evident in the settlement of Australia. According to Marxist historians Ken Buckley and Ted Wheelwright, the prison colony, 'which initially contained no capitalists, no free labourers, and no peasants' (1988, 1) established a working capitalist structure within one generation. There was in effect no capitalism from the First Fleet arrival of convicts and salaried army officers at Sydney in 1788 until the arrival of free-settler immigrants with start-up capital around 1820; until then the penal colony was financed and provisioned by the British government. Yet by 1800, 30 officers and officials were the dominant landowners (35); by the mid-1800s, 42 squatters owned a further 13.6 million acres (3); and by the 1880s, 500 large land holdings accounted for half the land of New South Wales (9).[17] While some ex-convicts were awarded small land allotments in the early years, this practice was soon stopped following parliamentary petitioners in London, including Wakefield, who argued for the need to keep land prices high in order to deter uneconomical subsistence farming. Instead, he encouraged a model of large-scale farming worked by a surplus labour force (Buckley and Wheelwright, 68–72; Wakefield, 52–55).

From early in its settlement history, the emerging Australian society was split between the officers and colonial administrators who granted land to themselves and a select group of moneyed immigrants, and a large landless peasantry of convict labourers, ex-convicts, and displaced Aborigines (Buckley and Wheelwright, 34–42). This same government-employed elite monopolised the arriving cargoes of supplies from Britain in a method that Buckley and Wheelwright call Australia's 'first import cartel' (4). Both for land and resources, then, public (state) goods and money shared among a small elite at the expense of an impoverished majority established in the colony a capitalist political economy based on stark economic inequality. The soldiers initially brought to Australia to run the convict colonies were integral support for this emerging capitalism, quelling Aboriginal protest against land dispossession. Similarly, in New Zealand, permanent British troops subdued Maori unrest at having their land stolen or swindled by settler land companies such as Wakefield's. The clash culminated in the New Zealand Wars from the 1840s to the early 1870s, which resulted in confiscation of the land, which was redistributed among white settlers.

The speed at which capitalism was established in the settler colonies speaks to the importance of economic concerns inherent to colonisation, with Britain's eagerness to minimise costs resulting in significant power residing in the colonial elite as well as in the selective, expedient, and unequal application of British law. In his overview of the British Empire, historian Bernard Porter argues that the laissez-faire, minimalist intervention of British colonial law was in line with the newly popular economic liberalism at home, which rewarded entrepreneurial enterprise:

> The colonists ... were British subjects, in nominally British territories, and under the ultimate protection of British arms; which made them the British government's responsibility. The latter should have kept them on a tighter rein. That it did not do so was a matter of choice, not necessity. The motive was to save the cost, both human and financial, of policing them properly. Behind *that* was the growing spirit of early nineteenth century Britain that all government, including policing, should be kept to a minimum, in order to allow enterprise to thrive – the sort of enterprise that had created the colonies in the first place. (2005, 7, italics in original)

Ghosh's portrayal of the British Canton opium traders' open disregard of their administrator's decrees offers a fictional corollary of Porter's argument. In Cecil Rhodes's settlement of Rhodesia, historian Muriel Chamberlain offers another example of Britain's hands-off approach, motivated by an 'almost obsessed' desire to keep costs low (1999, 52). She writes: '[i]n theory, the British government retained some control over Rhodesian legislation and could veto any which was racially discriminatory. In fact, however, it did not exercise this right. The prejudice in favour of "the local man knowing best" was very strong at this time' (53). Rhodes's company ran Rhodesia until 1923.

Writing from the late 1980s of the new neoliberalism in Australia, Buckley and Wheelwright's study of the emergence of capitalism in New South Wales directly contradicts the nationalist myths of meritocratic competition that underpin neoliberalism's proclaimed freedom and equal opportunities for the individual to thrive. Instead, the historians insist on an altogether different set of skills and attributes that dictated economic success in the new colony:

> Thrift and abstinence, the economists' traditional explanation, had nothing to do with it [success]. The essentials were social status and patronage, which entailed access to modest amounts of initial capital, plus a certain degree of intelligence or low cunning. Luck played a part and ruthlessness was another useful attribute, especially in the case of ex-convicts who started with nothing but were able to make their first gains through petty trading which was beneath the dignity of their social superiors. (34)

For both Porter and Buckley and Wheelwright, injustice and inequality go hand in hand, a stance that in their era labelled them Marxists but today reads equally well as neoliberal critique.

The injustice and illegality of many of the structures and processes that typify settlement colonisation and subsequent colonial-era administration is the mainstay of postcolonial studies and its literary analysis. Nowhere is this injustice more blatant than in the colonisers' treatment of indigenous peoples. And yet, in a number of postcolonial novels that revisit the early contact years, the pervasive violence that marks dispossession, marginalisation, and degradation into emotional and material poverty is portrayed as not only of whites to autochthones but more generally of rich to poor everywhere. Analysis of the generation and distribution of material wealth in the settler colonies makes evident the poverty in which a vast number of people—both native and lower-class settler—lived throughout the nineteenth century and up until the Great Depression of the 1930s, when inequality peaked. Many years before Piketty's percentile breakdown of capital inequality revealed the high concentration of wealth and the absence of a middle class until the mid-twentieth century, Buckley and Wheelwright cited the findings of

Australia's 1915 census, which showed that the top 10% of income earners received 40% of all national income, and the top 5% owned 66% of national wealth, with the vast majority of people owning nothing at all (15).[18] Focusing on this historical economic inequality debunks the tenacious myth that the settler colonies were—and are—classless and egalitarian within the white majority.[19] Structures of historical capitalism are the precursors of contemporary inequality, which follows the same patterns in the neoliberal era.

In *That Deadman Dance*, Aboriginal Australian writer Kim Scott portrays the contact between Aborigines and the first generations of settlers in Western Australia. A bestselling, prize-winning novel that is recommended high-school English reading on the national curriculum, Scott's fictional narrative paints a vivid picture of the emergent economic and social structure historicised by Buckley and Wheelwright, with his characters filling the Marxist critics' class schema uncannily closely. The first part of the novel, set 1833–1835, portrays the shift from military outpost to colony. Dr Cross, a retiring military surgeon who uses his wife's inheritance, his rank, and his connection with the colonial governor to purchase land for himself[20] advises the new governor on how to develop the harbour town by attracting settlers with capital and by encouraging trade with the itinerant sealing and whaling ships. Wealthy settlers, he continues, will 'create a mutual demand and supply,' 'secur[e] against want,' palliate inflation of the 'extravagant prices of the necessities of life,' and 'attract the labourer, who is of paramount importance' (37). The type of capitalist immigrant Cross intends is represented in the novel by new arrival Geordie Chaine, who arrives on the boat with 'two prefabricated houses. He had money and stock, tools and enterprise, which he'd been promised was enough for him to be granted land' (18). With the right permits and official recognition, Chaine quickly sets up business and his entrepreneurship expands constantly throughout the novel, hiring more and more people to work for him in his various businesses, which include a bar, a farm, whaleboat crews, and merchandise.

The need for labourers to work for settlers such as Chaine, identified in Cross's recommendation and also considered at length in Wakefield's theory of colonisation, is exemplified in the novel by Killam, the only working-class white character given an inside narrative perspective. A low-rank soldier who struggles to get a foothold in the capitalist economy, Killam supplements his meagre government income with the most basic forms of profit-skimming from privileges he accesses through his army duties: petty stealing, bartering, and smuggling. Thus, while working on the state vegetable garden, he holds back a little 'surplus' (185) to trade for himself (121). From his customs-officer duty to row out to the whaling boats, he smuggles grog which he resells in his shebeen. Yet such informal economy is quickly taken over by those with permits and official recognition. Thus, the new governor takes over the garrison garden for his private use (185), and Chaine buys the first official town liquor licence and employs Killam to work in it for a low wage. Killam's entrepreneurship is thwarted, a phenomenon identified by Buckley and Wheelwright as typical: '[o]nce rigidities of structure set in, there was very little opportunity' (41). Describing himself as '[j]ust a man trying to make his own way. Trying to advance his-self' (186), Killam recognises that his own brain and brawn are not enough, and in order to make a profit rather than merely scraping by, he needs luck, capital, patronage, and labourers to work for him (187).

The social structure of first-generation settlement that Scott portrays reads as a textbook illustration of Wakefield's theories of emergent capitalism. Structuring the novel through the various narrative viewpoints of characters representative of each social class allows readers a window into the motivations underpinning colonial relations. The social-realist voice used for white-settler perspectives conveys several aspects of capitalist logic: forward-thinking scheming for social advancement; calculations of labour and capital in terms of expenditure and rewards; and the matter-of-fact rationale that excuses morally dubious behaviour as necessary and logical to meet these ends. These patterns are seen to repeat on each level of the class hierarchy: Chaine exploits Killam, and the latter, aping Chaine's business strategies in his efforts for upward mobility, reproduces the same social relations to those lower down on the social scale.

In the use of unfree convict labour, colonial Australia practiced a form of internal colonialism by submitting people of their own ethnicity and nationality to the exploitation and subjugation more commonly understood in the unequal power relations between the coloniser and the colonised. Importing capital class relations entailed, to a certain extent, importing a form of British class relations into settler colonies. Ellen Meiksins Wood argues that 'traditional imperialism had much in common with certain domestic class relations' (2). Both class and colonialism create and maintain hierarchical relations based on economic forms of coercion that are backed up by political, military, and judicial forms of control (4). The term 'internal colonialism' is useful for the way in which it registers structures of economic inequality within a nation, ethnic group, or community, while retaining in focus the colonial roots of these iniquities—which are also concomitantly capitalist roots.[21] In their unpaid work and restricted movement, convicts were subject to the discriminatory practices and attitudes of British colonists, who imported British relationships and hierarchies of class, gender, and region, with particular marginalisation of the Irish, as well as the significant yet undervalued non-paid labour of women.

In one well-known example of internal colonialism in Australian historical fiction, Kate Grenville's *The Secret River* (2005), the freed convict and new landowner Thornhill replicates the harsh treatment he was subjected to as a convict labourer, to lord it over his former friend and fellow convict assigned to him as indentured prisoner (175). Contradicting Grenville's tale of Thornhill's upward mobility, however, the historical record suggests that most unskilled ex-convicts did not have access to land ownership. Constrained by the social stigma of their criminal background to a life of low wages and itinerant and insecure work, discrimination from the moneyed settler community often resulted in precarity or poverty that lasted several years or even several generations. Peter Carey gives a poignant example in *True History of the Kelly Gang* (2000), a hard-hitting novel that portrays from the victims' perspective the relentless persecution of three generations of the Irish Kelly family by colonial administrators, police, social superiors, and members of their own Irish underclass. In each case of unjust or illegal maltreatment, which offer multiple instances of Buckley and Wheelwright's formula for upward mobility, the Kelly family loses out in order for others to profit. Throughout the novel, the Kellys' struggle for land tenure represents the broader class struggle of the emergent society. Inequality is inscribed in the quality and quantity of land, from the large stations occupied by wealthy squatters to the marginal land of small selection leases, bought by precariously employed labourers and ex-convicts such as Ned Kelly's father. This class struggle is played out, quite literally, on the land, which must be adequately cleared, fenced, and stocked, or else it will be confiscated. The Kelly family's failure to conform to genteel Anglo farming expectations is interpreted by the administrative powers that persecute them as reflecting a moral failure, and they are deemed unfit to represent the landed class on which Australia's nationhood is based.

Like Killam's efforts in *That Dead Man Dance*, each of the Kellys' efforts of entrepreneurship are thwarted by those who maintain their advantage through political connections, capital, and illegal means, which reveal the unlevel playing field of capitalist competition and lock them in the poverty trap. The fact of historical inequality and the ruthless means for gaining land are still acknowledged in Australia's contemporary narrative of national cultural identity. In Baz Luhrmann's movie epic Australia (2008), the station worker Fletcher kills his boss, takes over the role of cattle baron, and justifies his hostile takeover attempts of the neighbouring farm thus: 'Your land? My family worked this property for three generations. My father died making people like you rich. Faraway Downs belongs to me.' The construct of the 'great Aussie battler' comprises not only an embattled position against the hostile land but also a fight for upward mobility against imported British class structures. What both the novels and the film suggest, however, is that the poor can only win the battle if they are prepared to cheat, steal, or kill; in stark contrast to the sportsman-like notion of 'fair play,' the playing field of economic success is shown to be rigged. The sympathetic portrayal of such battling characters as Killam in *That Deadman Dance* and Ned Kelly in *True History of the Kelly Gang* exposes the foundations of the nation as neither wholly heroic nor utterly barbaric. Rather, the 'average' Everyman settler is a willing hard-worker turned into a petty criminal by the competitive scramble encouraged within the logic of possible upward mobility.

Analysis of the reproduction of British class structures in the newly settled Australia tends to be overlooked in postcolonial analysis in favour of sustained attention to socio-cultural relations between settlers and indigenous peoples. The benefit of the above economic analysis, however, is that it exposes the structures and mechanisms of capitalism's tendency to inequality even within the largely culturally homogenous British settler society. This optic allows analysis of settler relations with Aborigines to be inscribed within the same logic of accumulation, dispossession, and hierarchical labour relations, seeing herein how the indigenous were co-opted into a place on the bottom rung of the capitalist ladder. On the sliding scale of inequality, multiple instances of oppression compound from the top to the bottom of the socio-economic scale. Thus, Chaine exploits Killam, who in turn exploits his two unpaid labourers—Aboriginal youths taken from their homes to be raised as domestic labourers for settlers, literary examples of what became later known as the stolen generations. Far from opting out of the capitalist social relations in which they struggle to get ahead, the poor white settlers in turn discriminate against Aborigines, transferring British domestic class relations to the newly colonised, a step made easier by the legal dispossession of Aborigines who were denied not only land ownership rights but also voting rights (no universal suffrage until 1962) and access to the formal labour market (no minimum wage until 1968).

Scott's careful delineation of the economic pressures of the new colony in South Australia, from the richest settlers to the poorest convicts, enables him to trace in close detail the incremental degradation of settler–native relations that lead to their violent dispossession at the novel's end. Whereas the novel starts out by portraying close, mutually satisfying relationships between whites and Noongar, this changes as the balance of power tips from the first settlers relying on Aborigine hospitality for land and food to the increasing persecution of Aborigines as the white population grows to overtake the indigenous numbers. As the novel progresses, the original inhabitants are increasingly shut out of the sharing of resources, just as Killam and Ned Kelly are in the white community. As capitalism takes root as the dominant and exclusive system of social relations, all other options offered by the 'blank slate' of creating a new settlement, or by recourse to Aboriginal values, are foreclosed. A passage near the end of the novel—narrated by Chaine's daughter, who embodies the European conception of development as progress, inculcated by her successful entrepreneurial father—captures the shift:

> Laws were being enforced now, thankfully. Natives must be clothed and without spears if they were to enter town. ... Bobby had got into trouble because the policeman and his native constable had tried to prevent the old man with Bobby from entering town. The old man claimed it was his right, that it was his town! Papa laughed recounting it, said it was true in a way. And it was also true, as Bobby apparently claimed, ... that the old man had received a ration of flour from previous authorities, and had even been dressed, accommodated and fed at government expense. Why? Because he was the landlord. (376)

Explaining further that such measures 'may have been expedient at one time, but [are] no longer necessary' (376), the earlier right to take food from gardens, farms, and storehouses as an acknowledged return for use of tribal land is rescinded so that Bobby Wabalanginy and Menak are arrested for trespassing and stealing. Bobby is imprisoned and Menak is sent to a native camp (377), a systematised restriction on Aboriginal movement that Scott develops in his earlier novel *Benang*.

The privileged white child's condescending tone in the above passage mimics her father's attitude, which exemplifies the common racial stereotyping of the unintelligent native that pervades colonial discourse. Contrary to this aspersion, however, Menak has not misunderstood his entitlement to payment as acknowledged landlord; rather, the colonists have changed the rules to render null and void the exchange system previously agreed upon. Similarly, Bobby's extraordinary abilities as cross-cultural broker and interpreter between Noongar and settlers are not up for question when he is treated as a criminal at the end of the book: the settlers' trumped-up charges against their former helper are an expedient way to get rid of a no-longer-necessary go-between. One of the achievements of Scott's narrative is to capture empathy between Noongar and settlers—mutual curiosity and a great deal of learning from each other in the early days of settlement. Yet, as these fluid relations solidify into unequal capitalist relations based on rigid structures of owner–renter, employer–employee, and citizen–criminal, the novel can only end unhappily, with Bobby and Menak relegated to prisons or native reserves, forcibly excluded from the new society their cultural brokering helped establish.

The focus on the dynamics of economic transactions in colonial contact encounters demonstrates native understanding of and interest and involvement in colonial economies until they were forced out—not by fair competition or lack of merit, but by the same mechanics of capitalist inequality outlined by Marx, Wakefield, and historians Zahedieh and Porter, and also experienced by many working-class white settlers, as represented by Killam and the Kellys. In the similar settler context of New Zealand, Mark Williams summarises nineteenth-century Maori political leaders' attitudes to capitalism to claim that the Maori 'were eager to adapt the opportunities provided by technology and capital to their communal forms of life. It was settler protectionism that denied them access to loans for the development of tribal land, not the inherently "communistic" structure of their own society' (2006, 221). Instead, '[t]he economic benefits of globalisation in the late colonial period were reserved for Pakeha [white settlers]' (213). Historical novels by indigenous writers such as Scott provide valuable counter-narratives that combat the erroneous Western conception of the backwards indigene by portraying native adaptability, ingenuity, and constant negotiation between tradition and change. The complex and sophisticated indigenous life-worlds fruitfully counter Western conceptions of indigenous pre-modernity at the same time as the novels' pathos lies in representing the subjection of these socio-cultural structures to the dominant capitalist social relations.

Both fictional and non-fictional accounts of indigenous openness to modernity include active involvement in capitalist practices, beginning from early colonial contact. Scott's novel explores Aboriginal interest in the incoming technology and in adopting aspects of European culture, such as in trading, farming, and joining whaling crews. Similarly in New Zealand literature, Maori writer Witi Ihimaera—in *The Matriarch* (1986) and in *Whanau II* (2004), two of his several historical epics portraying a long history of Maori resistance—describes Maori entrepreneurship, including quoting a historical document by a British missionary that the Maori 'have attained a [business] intelligence beyond what might have been expected in so short a period. Their motto is now: "Ploughs, sheep and ships"' (1986, 50; 2004, 63). Hamish Clayton's historical novel *Wulf* (2011) details the flax-trading 'empire' of Ngati Toa chief Te Rauparaha, for whom Clayton uses the now-outdated nineteenth-century moniker 'the Southern Napoleon' (181–182). These novels corroborate cultural theory such as Stephen Muecke's work on Aboriginal 'indigenous modernity' (2004, 138), James Clifford's claim for the 'hybrid authenticity' of highland Papua New Guineans and North-West Coast Native Americans (1997, 185), and Anne Salmond's argument for Maori incorporation of Europeans into their own settlement, trading, and farming patterns. Such examples of indigenous adaptability might be construed as a form of colonial mimicry, however, not of identity and culture, to which the term is usually applied, but of capitalist practices. This trend in indigenous studies to record a long and active history of indigenous capitalist practices has recuperated native agency and attention to cultural adaptability from the earlier negative discourse of passive victimhood and an assumed reluctance to change that carried echoes of the now-debunked primitive–modernity dichotomy. However, to celebrate indigenous peoples as talented capitalists is in itself problematic, suggesting capitulation to the 'there is no alternative' mindset that normalises capitalism and thus construes indigenous winners and losers in capitalist terms of competition and individual merit, which is the topic of Chap. 4.

Kiana Davenport's historical epic *Shark Dialogues* outlines the steps by which indigenous Hawai'ians were brought into the capitalist world system, showing the dynamics between the encroaching Americans and Hawai'ians, as well as between Hawai'ians themselves and in their interactions with other immigrant groups.[22] Davenport details military and police intervention and government policy decisions that support the economic interests of the elite despite intensive protest. Thus, she offers a Hawai'ian example of the state, military, and legal support structures necessary for capitalism already seen in regard to the British invasion of Bengal, the Canton opium trade, and Australian settlement. Again, imperial aggression is couched in an ideology of progress, democracy, and equality, first broached in the Hawai'ian sovereigns' protest against US annexation. Hawai'ians lost exclusive land rights in 1848 when King Kamehameha III 'let himself be persuaded by white merchants and ex-missionaries to "abolish feudalism and make land-rights equal"' (Davenport 1995, 46). Once Americans owned land and thus voting rights, they increasingly lobbied for annexation with the USA to combat Hawai'ian sovereign power. When, in 1892, Queen Lili'uokalani attempted to make a constitutional change to allow all Hawai'ians to vote, not just landowners, she precipitated a military coup led by the 'white elite' (66)—notably sugar barons—which overthrew the monarchy and established a white-led republic that, despite being condemned by the US government, was not disbanded.[23] As with the First Opium War against Canton, the military operation against Hawai'i was not state led but engineered and executed by the private sector. This pattern by which private wealthy investors influence political, legal, and military action in their favour is familiar from the Bengal Permanent Settlement, the Canton opium trade, and in Australian requisitioning of Aboriginal land.

Davenport uses her epic schema, which spans from a Dutch orphan immigrant to New York in 1655 to sovereignty demonstrations in Honolulu in the 1990s, to show the replication and repetition of colonial-era control mechanisms throughout Hawai'i's history. Her application of contemporary business jargon to an epic sweep, from the 1790s gunboat diplomacy of the American military opening of Hawai'i for trade to the twentieth-century sugar cane and pineapple processing, bridges the assumed gap between historical and contemporary Hawai'ian agitation for plantation and factory workers' rights, ecological activism, and the 1990s Hawai'ian independence movement. Thus, the reader is told, 'in 1853 there was no middle class. White traders and merchants were becoming millionaires in Honolulu' (48–49). The trans-Pacific opium trade, illegal traffic in Chinese coolie labour, and the buying up of indigenous land are described as strategies of wealth accumulation (27, 45). Honolulu in 1834 was 'the business center of the islands' (45);

'white monopolies control every aspect of the sugar and pineapple business. Banking. Insurance. Utilities. Merchandising. Transportation. Shipping. Labor' (88). Labour inequality is described in a cluster of phrases that blur imperialist and capitalist motivations, applied to different labour groups and across the economic sectors. For example, 1892 indigenous Hawai'ians' and indentured Asians' '"slave work" on plantations' (66) becomes, in the 1970s, 'economic slavery of [Hawai'ian] people' (196) and '[h]undred-thousand-acre ranches owned by rich *haole* in Palm Springs,' men who 'owned you for three bucks an hour. ... indentured' (225, italics in original). Davenport's repetition of such language emphasises the continuity of economic practices throughout the historical time frame. Across time and space, she claims, '[t]he pattern kept repeating itself' (225).

The emphasis on indigenous economic agency negates the split between pre-modern and modern through indigenous peoples' active participation in capitalism, which includes efforts to align those imported Western values with aspects of their pre-existing traditional cultures. Indeed, all civilisations contain systems of valuing and distributing resources, such as in sharing and trading, of which capitalism is merely the most recent, notable for its incursion into all aspects of social life. Indigenous adoption of and adaptation to Western capitalism—and, to a lesser extent, capitalism's local shaping to indigenous practices—attests to the durability and mutability of this economic system. Indigenous modernity also muddies the question of indigenous victimhood by showing their own collusion with the new system: more or less reluctantly, under varying degrees of coercion, and unevenly experienced by different social groups within indigenous hierarchies. Just as pre-contact traditional societies contained structures of trade and value, so too did they contain structures of social inequality, with forms of exclusion and domination. In her discussion of the uneven repetition of capitalist logic across the world, Doreen Massey rejects the logic by which small nations or colonies are seen as belatedly inserted into globalisation as passive or unwilling victims (167). In every traditional society, there are agents who benefit from the new capitalist regime, or who embrace its logic as an extension of their own structures of trade and distribution.

Traditional hierarchies such as chieftainship, kin-based functions, roles of women and children, and slavery are thrown into sharp relief as they are adapted to fit the new political economy. In Clayton's novel, as in the historical record, Te Rauparaha is portrayed as a ruthless and cunning leader, usurping conventional Maori protocol and inherited hierarchy to claim land and domination over neighbouring tribes. His flax-trading empire built on the slave labour of conquered tribes buys him British muskets, and his bargaining power and negotiation skills are great enough to co-opt a British merchant brig to launch a guerrilla raid on a distant southern tribe. Te Rauparaha's mastery of capitalism's prerequisites—wealth, contacts, political influence, military support, underhand tactics, and luck—are acknowledged and respected by the British traders who narrate this early, little-known episode of New Zealand's history. As an experienced veteran of British mercantilism, Clayton's sea-faring narrator comprehends the Maori chief within the terms of trade familiar to him:

> [T]here was no such thing as innocent trade, for whenever a European ship sailed from these islands laden with flax it sailed with a hull bloated on native blood. And because of that we could admire Te Rop'raha for the way he'd controlled his dealings with Europeans, the way he'd used the great shifts and flow of people around him to fashion an empire. (182)

The admiration for Te Rauparaha in the narrator's voice suggests an altogether different basis for understanding the Maori–Pakeha relationship than that of cultural distinctness, positing trade as a lingua franca that binds rather than separates. While the novel artfully refrains from making moral judgements of Te Rauparaha's actions, the reported documentary of his Tuhoe massacre makes it difficult to condone his brutality. This puts the postcolonial reader in an unaccustomed position of siding with the white narrator and disliking the Maori chief, who is presented in national history as a warrior and a hero, embodied in popular culture as the author of the famed All Blacks' haka.

While New Zealand Maori writers have almost unanimously represented Maori society as a positive source of cultural inspiration, cohesive against an outside Pakeha Other, Tina Makereti's *Where the Rekohu Bone Sings* (2014) portrays unequal hierarchies within nineteenth-century Maori society. The novel traces a long history of Maori persecution of Chatham Island (Rekohu) Moriori, including a profound silence and lack of acknowledgement of the 1835 Ngati Tama and Ngati Mutunga raid of the Chatham Islands, massacre, and subsequent enslavement of Moriori survivors. Beginning in the 1880s, the novel outlines a rigid hierarchy in the Maori community. Mere's grandfather, a tribal chief, negotiates land from Wakefield's New Zealand Company purchase to ensure a livelihood of farming and trading with the Pakeha, while at the other end of the social spectrum, Iraia, a 'half-man-servant-slave' (Chap. 3, Sect. 2, para 2) is poorly treated by the family. The child of a Moriori slave, Iraia is malnourished, poorly clothed, and lives outside in a shed, an uncomfortable 'reminder of [the] dark times' (Chap. 3, Sect. 4, para 5). While the novel is sympathetic to the immense effort of the Maori to retain their land, culture, family cohesion, and personal dignity in the face of colonial pressure, Makereti does not shy away from addressing the injustice of social inequality and its contemporary repercussions, notably the effacing of Moriori ancestors from tribal genealogy and the denial of land rights and tribal support for their descendants to the present day.

Indigenous and postcolonial studies have thoroughly addressed the importance of land ownership in indigenous cultures as symbolic of continuity and life, and for its spiritual role, including in native cosmology. Much less analysed, however, is the connection between land and material wellbeing. The original source of primitive accumulation on which capitalism is based, in Marx's terms, and the primary form of wealth, in Piketty's schema, land ownership was the primary site of contestation between settlers and indigenous peoples during colonisation. Property remains today the dominant form of investment wealth in New Zealand, as elsewhere, and the ability to live rent-free, to produce, and to generate income from the land is a key source of savings and revenue, one embraced by Maori iwi. In the above example, Mere's family land ownership forms a base of emotional belonging and tribal togetherness, a concept known as *turangawaewae* that is instrumental to cultural identity but also ensures a level of economic comfort that stretches into the young generation of inherited landowners in the novel's twenty-first century present. By contrast, Iraia's material dispossession and ethnic marginalisation continues in the nineteenth-century storyline, when he moves to the colonial city of Wellington, where he is again relegated to living in a shed and working as a day labourer on the docks. Like their ancestor, his descendents in contemporary New Zealand have been emotionally and materially shunned by their Maori family, without an inheritance right to family tribal land, an exclusion corrected in the story's close as his descendents are 'gifted' their Maori family land on the Chathams, originally appropriated as spoils of war from their Moriori ancestors.

More explicitly than in Makereti's novel, in *Shark Dialogues*, internal inequalities within traditional Hawai'ian society are also converted into the capitalist structure of accumulation and dispossession. While Davenport clearly shows that all Hawai'ians have suffered loss of sovereign autonomy, some characters fare significantly better than others. That the novel's pivotal indigenous couple, Pono and Duke, own a coffee plantation is testimony to a nineteenth-century Hawai'ian character's summary: '[y]our husband is successful. Your children will be privileged' (48). Duke is descended from Hawai'ian royalty, his ancestor a doctor to King Kamehameha the Great (327), and thus privy to royal privileges and networking within the colonial and indigenous elites. Pono is a descendent of a Tahitian daughter of a high chief, whose dowry of black pearls provides the venture capital for her entrepreneurial Yankee husband to make his fortune in real estate, plantations, slavery, and the coolie trade (36, 40). Pono and Duke live in a coffee plantation manor house filled with oil paintings, globes and maps, East Asian furniture and silks, Persian rugs, and European books, while outside the plantation workers pause in their labour to bow to them, as descendants of royalty, perhaps, but more directly as their bosses (106–107).

In its tendency to emphasise the damage of colonialism on non-Western societies, postcolonial literary criticism often misses the complex, contradictory differences present within the local community, which include unpleasant aspects of pre-existing traditional culture. In the examples of colonial India and the Dutch East Indies, Ghosh and Pramoedya represent the friendly complicity of zamindars and *priyayis* with the colonial elite, and show how these indigenous plutocrats upheld the unequal and unfair colonial policies under which they retained a certain amount of prestige and power. Ghosh's *The Glass Palace* clearly registers the different layers of domination and subjugation of external and internal social hierarchies. At first glance, the following monologue by the Burmese queen deposed by the 1885 British invasion that seized control of the teak industry reads as a typical postcolonial positioning of the native as victim of colonisation:

> [W]e who ruled the richest land in Asia are now reduced to this. This is what they have done to us, this is what they will do to all of Burma. They took our kingdom, promising roads and railways and ports, but mark my words, this is how it will end. In a few decades the wealth will be gone – all the gems, the timber and the oil – and then they too will leave. In our

golden Burma where no one ever went hungry and no one was too poor to write and read, all that will remain is destitution and ignorance, famine and despair. (88)

In a few short sentences, Ghosh links colonial plunder of the material and cultural wealth of pre-colonised Burma to postcolonial material, intellectual, and spiritual impoverishment. Indeed, Myanmar (Burma) today occupies a very low position on the Human Development Index: underdeveloped, riven by ethnic strife, corrupt, its failed attempt at socialism through military dictatorship ridiculed by heavy economic sanctions. While the Queen's premonition might be said to have been realised, her sense of victimisation masks her role as royalty in upholding gross inequality within pre-colonial Burmese society itself, which includes a caste-like hierarchy of social position, including a trade in child servants (20), held in place by the Queen's reputation for cruelty, which includes executions, exile, and fratricide among the royal family (31, 38).

Whereas Davenport employs the language of neoliberalism to mark the similarity and continuity of political economy from past to present, Ghosh traces the same trajectory with the term 'imperialism,' which he applies in turn to the Burmese monarchy, British colonialism, the immigrant Indian elite of plantationers and industrialists, and the post-independence Burmese military junta. Thus, the monarchy hordes the riches of Burma's ruby mines as a sovereign right to the wealth of the land (43), and the Indian merchant minority in Burma is described as 'rich Indians liv[ing] like colonialists' (240), who believe in 'the pattern of imperial rule and its policy of ensuring its necessity through the division of its subjects' (243). The radical change announced by the 1962 military coup is derided: 'in fact, it is they who invoke the old imperial laws and statutes to keep themselves in power' (543), the regime's censorship 'growing out of the foundations of the system that that had been left behind by the old Imperial Government' (535). The epic novel documents dramatic inequality that continues despite radical changes to different political systems of monarchy, colonialism, and socialist military junta.

These historical novels describe in detail the complicity between some parts of indigenous society and colonial capitalism, and the merging of internal structures of social hierarchy with those of the new regime. Attributes such as greed, individualism, and blatant acts of injustice, usually ascribed to the rapacious colonisers, are also found within the local community: indeed, Buckley and Wheelwright's list of the keys to economic success in early Australia, namely status, patronage, intelligence, low cunning, ruthlessness, and luck, equally apply to the local rulers and wealthy in other colonies. In *Sea of Poppies*, Neel's wealth comes from opium profits and maintaining 'half-starved coolie farmers' on his land (123); Deeti's predicament comes from her brother-in-law's patriarchal legal rights that allow him to take over her land or marry her, on the death of her husband. In response to these blatant inequalities, both Neel's servants (110) and Deeti's hired hands (162) cheat their bosses and steal whatever they can to improve their own modest situations. In *The Glass Palace*, the deposed royal family can only stand aside as the townspeople enter the forbidden citadel to loot the riches cached there (30–34). In Pramoedya's *Footsteps*, the native elite *priyayis* and *bupatis* boast of their inherited rights to 'govern over thousands of people, to be honoured, to be bowed down to' (292), and the mixed-race Indos are the local middlemen, 'the trusted tools of the sugar companies who ensure that no Native can ever better his income even when he deserves it' (312). Davenport uses Hawai'ians' participation in the money economy to deflate the pro-sovereignty movement's separatist rhetoric of Americans versus Hawai'ians. Her characters' criticisms are harsh, and come from both cultural outsiders and insiders: '[y]our cause is lost. It was lost the day you started trading with the white man' (353); '[w]e were lost when we were born because we're Polynesians, intelligent, competitive, vain. We coveted things *haole* owned. They gave us progress, we gave them land' (385, italics in original); '[w]hen environmentalists go up against billion-dollar businesses, business ... always ... wins. ... But they didn't steal the land, Vanya, Someone—a farmer, or rancher, or Boards of Trusts—someone *sold* that land' (384, italics in original). In such passages, Davenport does not permit her Hawai'ian characters to sustain a comfortable narrative of victimhood which would allow them to hold the moral high ground in their sovereignty claims. In this novel, all characters are conflicted and troubled, which allows Davenport to subvert and twist stereotypical plotlines such as those of redemptive love, maternal instinct, attachment to land, and solidarity through hardship.

Each of these epic historical novels conveys a complex world in which unresolved tensions stand to break down assumptions of clear-cut behaviour patterns of colonisers and colonised. Implicating the main characters in capitalist processes of alienation and subjugation complicates the colonial–neocolonial–postcolonial divide, refusing to imagine a neat split between coloniser and colonised, oppressor and victim, modern and pre-modern. Rather, these binaries are broken down by the presence of capitalist practices—and desires—on both sides. These novels' portrayals of characters who occupy different ranks of their own social hierarchies, from local royalty and chiefs to workers and slaves, ask the reader to pay attention to the unevenness with which capitalism impacted on the colonised. The flows of finance, forms of land ownership, and control of production, extraction, and trade adumbrated in this chapter were pivotal to colonisation. These structures, which inserted colonial spaces into the global world economy, endure today in the modern age of globalisation. In linking the colonial past with the neoliberal present, these novels reveal historical variations on contemporary forms of global finance, the behaviour of big business, and economic geopolitics, as well as forms of injustice and inequality suffered by the poor, often at the hands of the rich in their own culture and community.

Racism as Capitalist Ideology

Postcolonial fiction is a valuable source of insider perspectives from under-represented cultures and communities, whose responses to capitalism are rarely registered in other social sciences based on written documentation, such as history, law, politics, and economics. In its large corpus of works, postcolonial literature offers a significant body of work that usefully reveals the patterns, structures, and mechanisms of capitalism and its tendencies toward exacerbating inequality, embedded in political economies of different periods and nations. The function of 'writing back' to the imagined centre, which has been largely accepted in literary studies as a corrective amendment to national literary canons, might also be read as such in other disciplines with a similar gap in their records. The historical novels discussed in this chapter narrativise the incremental steps by which European, predominantly British capitalist structures and ideology were imposed on colonised peoples, who variously resisted, adopted, and adapted a system that increasingly encroached on all aspects of society. Fiction does not merely document the impacts of free-market economic practices on indigenous peoples, however; its subjective, often-multiple narrative perspectives emphasise the violence of capitalism's impact, such as its fracturing impacts on social cohesion, changes to family and community culture, and psychological and physical rending of the body. Far from describing culture-centred reasons for indigenous economic underperformance, the novels locate inequality and its injustice as intrinsic to colonial capitalism itself. The colonised who accept the tenets of capitalist commodification, privatisation, labour relations, and competitive accumulation find that, despite their efforts, they struggle to succeed in capitalist terms due to overt and covert discriminatory practices. Those who resist face military, judicial, and political repercussions from the colonial state apparatuses, as well as pressure from social and cultural expectations and obligations from within their own societies. Drawing on colonial historical documents and local oral histories, these postcolonial historical novels portray the explicit marginalisation and forcible exclusion of the indigene and autochthone instigated by the British government, colonial administrations, and private settlers and traders.

As a form of cultural expression, fiction reminds readers that the economic is deeply embedded in the social and cultural. Indeed, the financially motivated injustices that create economic inequality can only be expressed through cultural values and practices. As capitalism is an all-encompassing social system, the shaping of appropriate cultural values is crucial to normalise and uphold the principles of the political economy. Of particular relevance to the colonial capitalism registered in these historical novels is the language of racism in the colonies and the concomitant emergence in nineteenth-century Britain of a new definition of poverty as a crime—the result of individual failure in a competitive meritocracy that celebrates opportunity for upward mobility. The classical economics-based attitudes toward poverty reverberate in the neoliberal present, in stereotypes that tie the poverty of ethnic groups that are economic underachievers to a language of backwardness and laziness.

In his critique of the Western bias of international aid and development discourse, Chang documents the attitudes of visitors from developed countries toward the less developed:

> My impression as to your cheap labour was soon disillusioned when I saw your people at work. No doubt they are lowly paid, but the return is equally so; to see your men at work made me feel that you are a very satisfied easy-going race who reckon time is no object. When I spoke to some managers they informed me that it was impossible to change the habits of national heritage. (*Bad Samaritans*, 182)

This is an Australian management consultant about the Japanese in 1915. About a century earlier, before German industrialisation, the British also considered the Germans a slow, dull-witted, dishonest people with abominable roads and a tendency to excessive emotion (184). As Japan's and Germany's post-World War Two industrial and technological boom resulted in a shift in global power in their favour (they are currently the third and fourth largest economies by Gross Domestic Product), today's characterisation of these nations is altogether more positive: the above-quoted historical stereotypes are ridiculous because we can today imagine their very opposite, with Japanese criticising Australians for their laid-back lifestyles and Germans complaining about poor transport in the UK. In these above examples, the positive factors are those conducive to extracting maximum profit margins, such as punctuality, seriousness, efficiency, discipline, and organisation.

The merging of negative judgements of race and work ethic is familiar in past and present stereotypes about indigenous and minority cultures, from colonial-era missionary prospectuses calling to civilise pagans in Africa to contemporary media reports and political campaigns in rich countries decrying benefit-draining immigrants, enacted in 2016 in the UK's Brexit 'Leave' campaign and in Trump's successful election bid for the US presidency. Chang uses the above historical examples to argue that culture is deployed to excuse the failure of neoliberal policies, such as the 1980s Structural Adjustment Programmes throughout Sub-Saharan Africa, and current austerity measures in Spain, Portugal, and Greece. The cultural argument claims that the fault lies not with inherent problems of capitalism's tendency to inequality but with the individual's character, extrapolated to overarching faults in national organisation that hinder productive efficiency (Chang 2007, 186). Unable to imagine that the neoliberal system is at fault, it is easier to believe the people are to blame.

The idea that economic success or failure is related to personal or cultural traits is a particular characteristic of the modern political economy. Already by the mid-1800s, Marx was able to mock the value-laden assumptions that align wealth with merit, and poverty with laziness. He attacks classical economics' analyses of inequality by demoting their argument to a fairy tale narrative, as if it were myth or fiction:

> In times long gone by there were two sorts of people; one, the diligent, intelligent, and, above all, frugal elite; the other, lazy rascals, spending their

substance, and more, in riotous living. ... Thus it came to pass that the former sort accumulated wealth, and the latter sort had at last nothing to sell except their own skins. And from this original sin dates the poverty of the great majority that, despite all its labour, has up to now nothing to sell but itself, and the wealth of the few that increases constantly although they have long ceased to work. ('The Secret of Primitive Accumulation,' 784)

Marx's satirical tone ridicules the underlying yet unvoiced assumptions of the market as a level playing field, a fair but competitive system in which individuals are judged by their ability to succeed. Instantly recognisable to the contemporary reader is the cluster of judgements around the laziness of the poor and intelligence of the rich, which Marx identifies and satirises for the quasi-religious, doctrinaire-elevated status they hold in early modern economics. It is striking how little has changed in the 150 years since Marx's facetious summary of attitudes toward wealth and poverty. Perhaps the only major difference is that today's super-elite are anything but frugal, and it is, indeed, in part the visibility of their wealth and conspicuous consumption that fuels protest movements such as Occupy and anti-austerity, which are in turn denigrated as excesses of energy more usefully expended in work. In his ensuing theory of primitive accumulation, Marx claims the reality behind the decoupling of the producer from his own means of production has less to do with inherent personal character than with expropriation, the use of force, and robbery, terms common to the theorists of colonialism and writers of fiction analysed in this chapter.

The assumed separation of the discourse of culture from that of economics makes it difficult to discuss racism as a structuring device that propagates and excuses economic inequality. The common public rejoinder to racism is to dismiss racist claims of the assumed cultural inferiority of the Other. Rather, the bias has been inverted to instead celebrate ethnicity and identity exactly for their different forms of knowledge, social structures, and values. The problem with this neat inversion, as Walter Benn Michaels smartly reveals in *The Trouble with Diversity* (2006), is that the significant work over the past twenty or more years to espouse racial equality does little to remedy the economic inequality that continues to disproportionately affect ex-colonised peoples. In Michaels's words, '[w]e would much rather get rid of racism than get rid of poverty. And we would much rather celebrate cultural diversity than seek to establish economic equality' (2006, 12). The recent shift away from the politics of identity to those of inequality may reinvigorate analysis of racism for its materialist dimensions.

For Immanuel Wallerstein, the mutability of this widespread and long-held cultural explanation for economic wellbeing is closely linked to the changing use of racist discourse that emerged in the colonial era. He defines racism as 'a cultural pillar of historical capitalism' (80), a way of confining, managing, and reproducing a hierarchical workforce. This is not to say that racism is an invention of capitalism or of colonialism, although trans-Atlantic slavery was certainly pivotal in its modern formation. Rather, it developed a very specific meaning in these two interrelated domains. In Wallerstein's configuration:

> Racism was the mode by which various segments of the work-force within the same economic structure were constrained to relate to each other. Racism was the ideological justification for the hierarchization of the workforce and its highly unequal distributions of rewards. (78)

Examples of this relational use of racist judgements about Western superiority and the inferiority of the colonised abound in the historical fiction discussed in this chapter. In each case, the cause of inefficiency in labour and production, and lack of motivation for financial gain and reward, is attributed to a lack of desirable personality traits applied to the ethnic group as a whole.

Stereotypes of natives as animal-like, child-like, or effeminate abound in the fictional portrayals of racist slurs in the fiction analysed in this chapter. In each, racism reflects a hierarchy in which power is measured more by economic wealth than by race itself, making it thus possible for non-whites to wield racial put-downs against other ethnic minorities, or even against poorer members of their own minority culture. In Scott's representation of early colonial Australia, *That Deadman Dance* gives voice to a common colonial view of Aborigines as child-like, a perception that helped justify their role as domestic servants and household labourers: '[t]he native girls they kept now, the servants, might almost be family also and yet one must—as Papa said—impose one's will. They were forever laughing and playing without purpose, and it was almost impossible to get things done' (392). Setting work and play in contradiction, the narrator goes on to criticise the infantile native as lacking a work ethic, 'the necessary discipline to defray one's immediate and short-term gain, and understand self-sacrifice' (392). Across the Pacific and updated to neoliberal times, Davenport's Hawai'ian characters condemn this same perception, as wealthy foreign tourists characterise the locals in the 'benign stereotype of the childlike, tourist-loving, bare-foot, *aloha*-spirit natives' (*Shark Dialogues*, 338, italics in original), while their sovereignty-movement protests are similarly scorned: '[c]ertain groups of wealthy *haole* laughed, calling Hawaiians lazy do-nothings, seeing their all-night vigils as a form of entertainment, their demonstrations as a joke' (312, italics in original). In both examples, Hawai'ians are viewed as incapable of or uninterested in their economic wellbeing, with their assumed spirituality, sexuality, and cultural expressions imagined as existing wholly outside of material daily reality. Furthermore, from colonial Australia to modern-day Hawai'i, work is formulated in rather puritanical terms, as unpleasant and serious and thus incompatible with laughter or fun, which, in making light of work, diminishes its importance or indicates lack of effort or value for money for the employers (in Scott) and customers (in Davenport), who are the conveyors of the above racist attitudes.

In Ghosh's historical fiction, racist judgements against the native working body are framed in even more dehumanising terms, as animals and machines. In The Glass Palace, the Eurasian plantation overseer adopts the role of a 'strict headmaster' and a 'snappish sergeant,' swearing and threatening the Tamil workers in a daily theatrical enactment of their social hierarchy: '[y]ou dog of a coolie, keep your black face up and look at me when I'm talking to you' (231). Challenged over the necessity of such behaviour, the Anglo-Burmese plantation owner's excuse is to describe the working environment as antagonistic, requiring strict control enacted in a simulated fight with reluctant workers and nature alike. Thus, the plantation is 'a vast machine, made of wood and flesh. And at every turn, every little piece of this machine is resisting you, fighting you, waiting for you to give in' (232). Ghosh's chosen vocabulary here purposely evokes Marx's understanding of capitalism's co-option of nature and the labouring body into a machine, a role that extends to labouring animals, in the elephants and their *oo-sis* trainers, traditionally used in religious festivals and ceremonies, now 'made to work for human profit' (74). The idea of a more equal or at least ethical treatment of plantation workers, and of the value of traditional forms of knowledge and systems of value, in the *oo-sis*'s 'hoary wisdom' (75), are rejected in derisive language. Thus are sympathetic characters—and readers—chastised for thinking outside the logic of the persuasive capitalists.

The way that Ghosh's British, Indian, and Burmese capitalists consistently privilege economic use over other social relationships, including family, and cultural functions, such as art and religion, provides a literary embodiment of the well-documented epistemological split in the histories of modern economics and aesthetics. The Romantic-era privileging of artistic value as distinct from commercial value, combined with the gendering of literary output, specifically the novel, as belonging to the cultural sphere of the domestic, the feminine, and the unpaid, establishes art as an easy target of derision for capitalists intent on privileging financial over other concepts of 'value,' 'wealth,' and 'asset.' Ghosh succinctly captures the easy co-option of this gendered cultural judgement to a racist target in River of Smoke, in a heated debate over the future of the opium trade in the Chamber of Commerce meeting of opium traders:

> It is surely apparent to you, is it not, that effeminacy is the curse of the Asiatic? It is what makes him susceptible to opium; it is what makes him so fatefully dependent on the government. If the gentry of this country had not been weakened by their love of painting and poetry China would not be in the piteous state that she is today. Until the masculine energies of this country are replenished and renewed, its people will never understand the value of freedom; nor will they appreciate the cardinal importance of Free Trade. (492)

The gendered language construes the economic sphere as a masculine public domain of entrepreneurial trade, while art and literature reside in a private, feminine space of leisure. Attributing as feminine traits the 'weakness' of opium addiction and dependence on government thus assigns by way of contrast the role and duty of independent and individualistic men in the spread of free-trade capitalism espoused in the new discipline of modern economics, emerging at the time hand in hand with colonial expansion and distancing this modern 'science' from its earlier roots in ethics and theology. Unsurprisingly within the logic of this gendered racism, Charles King's attempts to side with the Chinese Emperor on banning the opium trade result in aspersions of his homosexuality.

In Makereti's *Where the Rekohu Bone Sings*, mid-twentieth-century Maori children, having internalised the racism to which they have themselves been subjected by the Pakeha mainstream, bully their own poorer relatives, landless servants, and labourers who have darker skins and are descendants of a Moriori slave:

When we were kids, we didn't know what a Moriori was. Then they had this book at school – a school journal – it said Morioris were ugly and stupid, that the superior Maori race came to Aotearoa and overpowered them. ... We teased her. Called her dirty, darkie, Moriori slave ... from people who were too ignorant and slow to fight. She was our cousin, but it felt good to have someone lower than us. We had always been the lowest at school. (Chap. 7, Sect. 2, para 8)

The children bully their poorer cousin by framing their taunts not in terms of her current lack of wealth but in reference to a long-past conquest that in their Maori eyes shows their superiority over Moriori. This elision unwittingly traces the history of Moriori impoverishment from their original dispossession from their land and subsequent enslavement by the Maori to multiple generations of landlessness and constant moving for insecure menial work. As these intangible economic motivations and repercussions remain invisible to the children, their racist slurs of dirtiness and lack of intelligence are attached to a perceived Maori heroism in war. The above passage, recalled by an adult by way of apology for discriminating against the Moriori strand of their extended family, attributes to children the overt forms of racism internalised in social and cultural exclusion by several generations of adults. Within the delicate family politics of admitting fault for historical wrongdoing, the memory is framed in such a way as to blame the dominant Pakeha education system for having taught the children such racism, in the school journal article about Moriori. The novel hereby dodges the need to respond to the children's perception of the latent racism practiced within their own Maori community. While the examples from Australian and Hawai'ian contexts firmly attach racism to guilty white parties, the New Zealand example suggests a difficulty for the Maori in naming racism within their own culture, as perpetrators as well as victims of racist ideology that enables and excuses class-like hierarchy of inequality within thier own communities and even families.

Common across these citations are notions of indolence or low intelligence, often coupled with connotations of deviance or criminality. The culture to which they are compared is in each case considered superior by dint of its wealth and power, which permits a dominating role from the wealthier character to teach and discipline the weak, a hierarchy which is clearly condoned in the relationship between employer and employee. Weakness is portrayed as feminine or child-like, and resistance *and* lack thereof are both construed as indicative of inferiority. Non-resistance, by the playful female Aborigine servants, in *That Deadman Dance*, or the Indian indentured labourers, including Kalua the Dalit in *Sea of Poppies*, shows a 'natural' servile will. Resistance is cast as belligerent criminality, to be put down by police or military intervention, such as Bobby's imprisonment for theft in *That Deadman Dance*, police dispersal of Hawai'ian environmental protests, and the British Opium Wars to quash Chinese attempts to staunch the opium trade.

Through the range of cultures exemplified here—Chinese, Burmese, Indian, Hawai'ian, Maori, Moriori, and Aborigine—any possible truth to these racist aspersions cannot be ascribed to cultural specificity. Rather, they are in each case applied to groups who are subordinate in economic terms, a point Sartre also identifies in pan-colonial explications of the native: 'yellow, black or white, they always have the same characteristics: they are lazy, sly, and thieving, live off nothing and understand only force' (143). Responding, here, to Frantz Fanon's critical analysis of the Algiers School of psychiatry, as founded on a conception of the North African as criminal, aggressive, impulsive, and 'incapable of self-discipline' (Fanon 1963, 299), Sartre anchors this colonial mentality in colonialism's profit-driven bottom line. Writing within a Marxist frame of the capitalist logic of exploitation for accumulation, Sartre writes of the Western construction of the native twenty years before Edward Said's *Orientalism* (1978), considered foundational to postcolonial theory.

The above quotes from fiction show the inextricability of culture and economics in engendering racism, which is in each case applied to ethnicities exploited by the dominant national or ethnic group for the former's land, resources, or labour. In the above literary examples, Hawai'ians and Aborigines have been dispossessed from their land, valuable commodities of opium, teak, and rubber are extracted for export, and in all cases except the Chinese the autochthones are exploited for labour: Hawai'ians and imported indentured Indians on plantations, Burmese in forestry, and Aborigines and Moriori as domestic slaves or servants. The correlation between race and economic function concurs with Wallerstein's claim for the ethnicisation of the workforce in historical capitalism (76–77), with the cluster of moral judgements relating to race and to economic output blurring into one and the same. As analysed at greater length in Chapter 4, these representations of historical racism toward the losers of early capitalism have modern-day equivalents. In particular, the US Black Lives Matter campaign against police violence, and the 2011

UK riots during which black youths were disproportionately targeted by police, alongside media misrepresentations of 'feral' gangs and criminals, illustrate the facile blurring of race, poverty, and crime.

The continuity of class-based racism in the core capitalist countries today further illustrates the way that coloniser–colonised relations merely re-enacted socio-economic hierarchies already present at home. Synchronicity with the past is also elaborated by Jeremy Seabrook in *Pauperland: A Short History of Poverty in Britain*, which traces the changing attitudes to poverty throughout the rise of capital social relations since the Industrial Revolution (2013). The changing discourse of poverty evolving in nineteenth-century Britain meant that the British poor were described in similar terms and ascribed similar characteristics as the colonised abroad, as indeed illustrated in Chang's historical examples of Australian and British views of the Japanese and Germans. As Walter Mignolo puts it, in the context of capitalist motivations of colonial racism, 'the very concept of poverty was invented and introduced in the rhetoric of modernity to hide the fact that the poor are indeed lives that are dispensable and as such they are either discarded or when necessary made indispensable as labor force and consumers' (2009, 76). As theories of the modern economy solidified, buoyed by the gathering momentum of the Industrial Revolution and successful expansion into the New World, earlier concepts of social dependence between the classes and the poor's right to Christian charity gave way to a privileging of self-sufficiency, of independence based on work (Lloyd 2001, 118). As Sarah Lloyd summarises, by the turn of the nineteenth century, the pauper was linked in the popular imagination to 'the inhabitants of a foreign land as unfamiliar objects of scrutiny' (114):

> Pauperism was seen as individual moral failure, and parish relief, particularly wage supplementation, was condemned for paralysing moral independence and dissolving social ties. Symptomatic of this economic and moral disorder, the pauper's house was typically represented as dirty, cheerless, indolent, and demoralized. Pauperism chained English labourers to the African negro and Arabian slave; once this link was broken, observers discerned the labourers' pride and contentment in their cottages, gardens, and families. (119)

Lloyd's analysis reveals the easy elision of cultural essentialist categories of race with the overtly economic categories of class. In effect, to call a British pauper a 'Negro' or an 'Arab' was equivalent to a racist insult, which the indigent could escape by demonstrating domestic British cultural values, with cleanliness, cheerfulness in labour, and hard physical work packaged and publically symbolised in a neat front garden. Changing attitudes to poverty culminated in the 1834 Poor Law Amendment Act, greatly influenced by the economic theories of Bentham, Malthus, Ricardo, and Smith, which forced the rural unemployed off parish relief into urban factory work, and increased the role of the workhouse as a last resort for paupers, predominantly children, single mothers, widows, and the elderly. Masculinity, by contrast, was linked to the ability to provide for a family, and connoted prudence, moral virtue, independence, and responsibility (119).

The criminalisation of poverty as 'bad' and 'unnatural' in market terms,[24] was embodied in the workhouse, which was conceived as a penitentiary institution. Its explicit aim to deter pauperism resulted in various correctional measures, including hard labour and religious education (Higginbotham 2012, 263–266). Some inmates, particularly orphan boys, were sent to the colonies as domestic labour (Higginbotham, 92–94),[25] while even married men and women were segregated, both techniques espoused by Malthus in his 1798 *An Essay on the Principle of Population* to reduce population growth among the poor in order to avoid overpopulation. The domestic form of the workhouse and its overseas form in the penal colonies are often indistinguishable for their function, daily organisation, and the type of people enclosed there. To belabour the similarities between British and colonial denigration of the poor, its criminalisation, and 'correction' by penal measures is to underline structural forms of inequality played out in social hierarchy and cultural stereotyping that is common across capitalist spaces and eras.

The problem of what to do with the poor under capitalism and the difficulty of effecting measures to curtail poverty that preoccupied nineteenth-century Britain was even more stark in the colonies, where the indigenous populations held unclear citizenship and did not easily fit into the class or religious hierarchy that structured duties to the poor within British society. Racist discourses thus served to justify unjust and discriminatory practices. The use of indigenous people as domestic labour in settler colonies fulfilled the double function of providing cheap (or free) labour and modelling 'civilised' social, cultural, and religious practices which they were expected to adopt. Despite this rhetoric of improvement that fit the belief in capitalism as development and progress, the biological essentialism of racist discourse ensured that the local population could never work their way out of this economically inferior position. As a way of ensuring a supply of cheap labour, colonial racism was thus as institutional to early capitalism as Wakefield's understanding of the need to keep the cost of land artificially high so as to maintain a class of landless workers.

Indeed, the lack of work rights meshes with a similar lack of living rights. In the Australian context, Buckley and Wheelwright summarise the displacement of Aborigines from their land by squatter settlers: 'racism was as functional for the frontier squatter as the Colt revolver. One cleared the land, the other cleared the conscience' (Henry Reynolds qtd in Buckley and Wheelwright, 3). The most compelling example of this dual method is perhaps the systematic extermination of Tasmanian Aborigines. This practice of dispossession continued well past the initial clearing of the land, spatially embodied in the new colonial city itself, from which the native was commonly excluded or marginalised. In his history of slums, Davis claims:

> [T]he British were arguably the greatest slum-builders of all time. Their policies in Africa forced the local labor force to live in precarious shantytowns on the fringes of segregated and restricted cities. In India, Burma, and Ceylon, their refusal to improve sanitation or provide even the most minimal infrastructure to native neighborhoods ensured huge death tolls from early-twentieth-century epidemics. (Davis 2006, 52)

The colonised body is only minimally accommodated into the infrastructure built on their stolen land and built by their labour. This housing inequality, analysed in the context of modern-day slums in Chapter 4, expresses in spatial and architectural terms the same racist ideology that, as Wallerstein identifies, constrains the rich and the poor within the same economic structure to relate to each other.

Representations of these multiple expressions of racist discrimination against indigenous peoples and local communities are the mainstay of postcolonial fiction and its critique. Focusing on examples of cultural specificity, however, often makes it hard to see the larger pattern and its use under capitalism to create and excuse inequality. By here analysing racism through an economic lens, disparate fictional representations of the colonial era all show racism as a common weapon, a feature not only of imperialism but of the rich over the poor everywhere.

Indeed, as Gavin Jones argues in his study of poverty in American literature from 1840–1945, the issues of poverty grappled with in novels by Herman Melville, Theodore Dreiser, Edith Wharton, James Agee, and Richard Wright map the development of contemporary socioeconomic values in the USA: '[t]his cultural history of poverty matters now precisely because so many of the dominant opinions and legislative policies regarding income inequity repeat beliefs that were formulated, debated, and frequently challenged in past generations' (xv). Exporting this optic to a study of postcolonial historical novels of colonial-era capitalism similarly reveals the pertinence, if not urgency, of recognising the past in our present, a background necessary for understanding the foundations of global neoliberalism and its structures and mechanisms of inequality that were instated deliberately and often by force at its colonial institution.

Notes

1. 2014 statistics from the British Office for National Statistics, 'How important is China to the UK economy?'
2. In a 2015 BBC article on Chinese artefacts stolen by the British during the 1860 sack of the Beijing Imperial Palace, Chris Bowlby reiterates Britain's ongoing refusal to address its historical imperial injustices in China. Chris Bowlby, 'The palace of shame that makes China angry' (2015).
3. For detail of the repartition of British wealth, see Piketty's graph of the history of capital in Britain: http://piketty.pse.ens.fr/files/capital21c/en/pdf/F3.1.pdf.
4. Benita Parry, in her important critique of the culturalist focus of postcolonial studies that ignores materialism, also cites this passage. See Parry, *Postcolonial Studies: A Materialist Critique* (2004, 4). On the Permanent Settlement and famine, see also Anil Seal, *The Emergence of Indian Nationalism: Competition and Collaboration in the Later Nineteenth Century* (1968, 51–55); Rosa Luxemburg, *The Accumulation of Capital* (2003, 350–357); and Amartya Sen, *Poverty and Famines: An Essay on Entitlement and Deprivation* (1981). Updating Davis's argument to the Sahel region in the 1970s, Mohamed Lamine Gakou similarly argues that famines were the engineered outcome of a development-led shift to cash-cropping for export that decimated subsistence agriculture. See *The Crisis in African Agriculture*, 39–66.
5. 80% of the Chinese stock market is capitalised by the state. Other nations doing well out of state-owned corporations include Russia, Singapore, the United Arab Emirates, and Saudi Arabia. See 'The Company that ruled the waves.'

6. In *Bad Samaritans*, Chang cites Toyota, subsidised by the Japanese government for over 25 years with a trade embargo on American cars to further foster home-grown (19–21); Nokia, subsidised for 17 years (210); and Samsung, subsidised for over ten years (210).
7. For a longer list of British protectionism that shows unequal treaties with the earlier colonies of Ireland and America, see also Chang, 'Why Developing Countries Need Tariffs,' 60–61.
8. For an overview of the importance of privately owned land to empire-building, see Dominic Alessio, '"…territorial acquisitions are among the landmarks of our history": the buying and leasing of imperial territory' (2013).
9. See also R. R. Neild on private interests and early public-company structures in Britain's Agricultural and Industrial Revolutions: *Public Corruption: The Dark Side of Social Evolution*, 67–73; 90–95.
10. In *Hul: Cry Rebel*, Bahadur notes as an aside that East India College, a private university established by the Company in 1806 to train its India-bound civil administrators, hired Thomas Malthus to teach political economy, 'which was not yet being taught at Oxford or Cambridge' (Section 'October 1830,' para 21). The import of private business interest in shaping tertiary institutions and their disciplines, which is at issue today in the neoliberal university, is thus seen in early evidence.
11. Indeed, the trading partnership established by Jardine and Matheson continues today as Jardine Matheson Holdings, still operating out of Hong Kong, still predominantly run by descendants of the Keswick brothers tai-pan traders, and still involved in transport, insurance, and property industries. Similar direct lines of wealth have been traced in the recent 'Legacies of British Slave-ownership' project at University College, London, one aspect of which has been to follow the investments made by the predominantly British slave-owners paid recompense by the British government after the abolition of slavery.
12. Pramoedya called the tetralogy the Buru Quartet after Buru Island, where he was imprisoned as a political dissident without trial or sentence from 1965–1979. Banned from writing, Pramoedya narrated his stories orally to his fellow inmates, who later helped him reconstitute them on paper.
13. The Dutch East Indies were controlled by the French by proxy (1806–1811) after Napoleon conquered the Netherlands, and later by the British, who waged a naval battle to hold Java (1811–1816).
14. While postcolonial studies ignores Japan's role in colonial history, the nation itself frames its post-World War Two pacifist rebranding as part of the liberating forces that rid South-East Asia of European colonial masters. See Melissa Kennedy, 'Theoretical Encounters: Postcolonial Studies in East Asia 2013.'

15. In the case of settler colonies Australia, New Zealand, Canada, and South Africa, World War One is often contextualised within the history of nation-building and national independence from the British Dominion. The focus remains, however, on the impacts and outcomes for the colonies, not their role as catalysts that caused the war.
16. Japan, Australia, and New Zealand took over German colonies in the Pacific as mandated dependencies. Understanding Australia and New Zealand as exploitative colonisers in Papua New Guinea, Nauru, the Solomons, and Western Samoa remains underanalysed in postcolonial studies.
17. In an early essay collected in *Colonialism and Neocolonialism*, 'Colonialism is a System' (1964), Jean-Paul Sartre gives similar statistics on French settlement and land appropriation in Algeria: 12 million hectares taken by the French state, 7 million left to the Algerians, and 2.7 million hectares in private European ownership, of which '6000 land owners have a gross agricultural revenue of more than 12 million francs; some of them reach 1000 million' (36). He further states that Europeans owned three-quarters of the prime irrigated land (42).
18. Australia's longitudinal trends accord with Piketty's general argument. Following a low point in the 1950s, income inequality rose steadily, a trend that has accelerated since the 1980s' turn to free-market liberalism. By 2010 the top 10% earned nearly 31% of the national income, a figure approaching that of the 1915 first census. See the World Wealth and Incomes Database for Australia.
19. My point here is to show the similar structures of economic inequality perpetuated in the settler colonies based on the British model of capitalism, and the resulting internal gap between rich and poor within the nation. When comparing poverty rates across countries, on a qualitative level life in the settler colonies may be considered comparatively 'better' than life in Britain in the same period. For example, Buckley and Wheelwright note that the abundance of land, highly-productive rural industry, and scarcity of labour meant that Australian wages were among the highest in the world at the turn of the nineteenth century (9–10). The phenomenon of gross income inequality within the nation, however, remains valid.
20. Scott's choice of career for his character concurs with Buckley and Wheelwright's identification of the large number of surgeons and chaplains in the colonies as the colonial counterpart to industrial capitalists in Britain, which heralded the new possibilities of upward mobility in the emergent middle class (36).
21. The term emerged from Hispanic and Black scholars in the USA to describe race-based inequality in the USA. See Mario Barrera, *Race and Class in the Southwest: A Theory of Racial Inequality* (1979); Peter

Calvert, 'Internal Colonisation, Development and Environment' (2001); Michael Hechner, *Internal Colonialism: The Celtic Fringe in British National Development.*

22. Pramoedya's engagement with US imperial expansion in the Philippines as colonial, and Davenport's portrayal of Hawai'i's subjection to American incursion as economic imperialism invoke the pressing question of the extent to which the USA was and is an imperial or colonial power. For a useful overview of the argument for US imperialism, see Dominic Alessio, '"...territorial acquisitions are among the landmarks of our history": the buying and leasing of imperial territory,' 79–83.

23. The US government officially annexed Hawai'i in 1898 as a strategic military base for the Spanish–American War over the Philippines.

24. On classical economics configurations of the 'good' and 'bad' nature and the 'natural' order of the market, particularly in Smith, Malthus, Hobbes, and Locke, see Ruth L. Smith, 'Order and Disorder: The Naturalization of Poverty (1989–1990).'

25. Peter Higginbotham, *The Workhouse Encyclopedia,* 92–94. The British practice of unburdening children's homes by adopting orphans and guardians of the state to the colonies for domestic labour continued in the post-World War Two era, known as the Home Children in Canada and under the Child Migrant Policy in Australia.

WORKS CITED

Primary

Bahadur, Sanjay. *Hul: Cry Rebel!* New Delhi: Roli, 2013, Kindle Edition.
Carey, Peter. *True History of the Kelly Gang.* Brisbane: University of Queensland Press, 2000.
Clayton, Hamish. *Wulf.* Auckland: Penguin, 2011.
Davenport, Kiana. *Shark Dialogues.* New York: Plume, 1995.
Devi, Mahasweta. *Imaginary Maps.* Trans. Gayatri Chakravorty Spivak. New York and London: Routledge, 1995.
Ghosh, Amitav. *The Glass Palace.* London: Harper Collins, 2001.
———. *Sea of Poppies.* London: John Murray, 2008a.
———. 'Opium Financed British Rule in India,' BBC Interview with Amitav Ghosh, *BBC News,* 23 June 2008 (2008b), http://news.bbc.co.uk/2/hi/south_asia/7460682.stm. 3 January, 2017.
———. *River of Smoke.* London: John Murray, 2011.
———. *Flood of Fire.* London: John Murray, 2015.
Grenville, Kate. *The Secret River.* New York: Canongate, 2005.
Ihimaera, Witi. *The Matriarch.* Auckland: Secker and Warburg, 1986.

———. *Whanau II*. Auckland: Reed, 2004.
Makereti, Tina. *Where the Rekohu Bone Sings*. Auckland: Random House, 2014, Kindle Edition.
Toer, Pramoedya Ananta. *This Earth of Mankind*. Trans. Max Lane. Ringwood, Victoria: Penguin, 1982 [1980].
———. *Child of All Nations*. Ringwood, Victoria: Penguin, 1984 [1980].
———. *Footsteps*. Trans. Max Lane. Ringwood, Victoria: Penguin, 1990 [1985].
———. *House of Glass*. Trans. Max Lane. New York: William Morrow, 1996 [1988].

Speeches

Bernanke, Ben. 'Financial Regulation and the Invisible Hand,' Speech at the New York University Law School, 11 April, 2007, http://www.federalreserve.gov/newsevents/speech/bernanke20070411a.htm. 3 January, 2017.
Bush, George W. Address to the United Nations General Assembly, 14 September, 2005, http://www.state.gov/p/io/potusunga/207566.htm. 3 January, 2017.
Cameron, David. Transcript of Speech at Peking University, 10 November, 2010, http://english.pku.edu.cn/News_Events/News/Global/7328.htm. 3 January, 2017.

Films and Documentaries

Luhrmann, Baz, dir. *Australia*. Twentieth-Century Fox, 2008.

Secondary

Alessio, Dominic. "'…Territorial Acquisitions are Among the Landmarks of our History': The Buying and Leasing of Imperial Territory,' *Global Discourse* 3(1), 2013, 74–96.
Barrera, Mario. *Race and Class in the Southwest: A Theory of Racial Inequality*. Notre Dame, IN: University of Notre Dame Press, 1979.
Beckert, Sven. *Empire of Cotton: A Global History*. New York: Knopf, 2014.
Bowlby, Chris. 'The Palace of Shame That Makes China Angry,' *BBC News Beijing*, 2 February 2015, http://www.bbc.com/news/magazine-30810596. 3 January, 2017.
Buckley, Ken, and Ted Wheelwright. *No Paradise for Workers: Capitalism and the Common People in Australia 1788–1914*. Oxford, UK: Oxford University Press, 1988.
Calvert, Peter. 'Internal Colonisation, Development and Environment,' *Third World Quarterly*, Vol. 22, No. 1 (Feb., 2001), 51–63.

Chamberlain, M.E. *Decolonization: The Fall of the European Empires.* Second Edition. Malden, MA: Blackwell, 1999.
Chang, Ha-Joon. *Bad Samaritans: The Guilty Secrets of the Rich Nations and the Threat to Global Prosperity.* London: Random House, 2007.
———. 'Why Developing Countries Need Tariffs,' Oxfam and The South Centre, 2005.
Chapman, James. 'David Cameron Rejects Chinese Request to Remove 'Offensive' Poppies During Visit,' *The Daily Mail*, 10 November, 2010, http://www.dailymail.co.uk/news/article-1328311/David-Cameron-rejects-China-request-remove-offensive-poppies.html. 3 January, 2017.
Chomsky, Noam. *Profit over People: Neoliberalism and Global Order.* New York: Seven Stories, 1999.
———. *World Orders Old and New.* New York: Columbia University Press, 1994.
Clifford, James. *Routes: Travel and Translation in the Late Twentieth Century.* Cambridge, MA: Harvard University Press, 1997.
Davis, Mike. *Late-Victorian Holocausts: El Niño Famines and the Making of the Third World.* London and New York: Verso, 2002.
———. *Planet of Slums.* London and New York: Verso, 2006.
Fanon, Frantz. *The Wretched of the Earth.* Trans. Constance Farrington. New York: Grove, 1963 [Présence Africaine, 1961].
Higginbotham, Peter. *The Workhouse Encyclopedia.* Stroud, Gloucestershire: The History Press, 2012.
Kennedy, Melissa. 'Theoretical Encounters: Postcolonial Studies in East Asia,' IAFOR Journal of Literature and Librarianship Vol. 2.1 (Spring 2013), 7–16, http://iafor.org/archives/journals/iafor-librasia-journal-volume2-issue1.pdf. 3 January, 2017.
King, Charles. 'The Opium Crisis: A letter addressed to Charles Elliot, Esq., Chief-Superintendent of the British Trade with China.' London: Edward Sutter,1839, https://archive.org/details/opiumcrisislette00king. 3 January, 2017.
Krugman, Paul. 'Why We're in a New Gilded Age,' *The New York Review of Books*, 8 May, 2014, http://www.nybooks.com/articles/archives/2014/may/08/thomas-piketty-new-gilded-age/. 3 January, 2017.
Lenin, Vladimir Ilyich. *Imperialism, the Highest Stage of Capitalism.* Sydney:Resistance Books, 1999 [1917].
Lloyd, Sarah. 'Poverty,' *An Oxford Companion to The Romantic Age: British Culture 1776–1832.* Ed. Iain McCalman. Oxford: Oxford University Press, 2001, 114–125.
Luxemburg, Rosa. *The Accumulation of Capital.* London and New York: Routledge, 2003 [1913].
Luxemburg, Rosa. *The Junius Pamphlet: The Crisis of German Social Democracy.* Trans. Dave Hollis, [1916], https://www.marxists.org/archive/luxemburg/1915/junius/. 2 January, 2017.
Michaels, Walter Benn. *The Trouble with Diversity: How We Learned to Love Identity and Ignore Inequality.* New York: Metropolitan, 2006.

Mignolo, Walter. 'Dispensable and Bare Lives: Coloniality and the Hidden Political/Economic Agenda of Modernity,' *Human Architecture: Journal of the Sociology of Self-Knowledge*, Vol. 7, no. 2, Spring 2009, 69–88.

Muecke, Stephen. *Ancient and Modern: Time, Culture and Indigenous Philosophy.* Sydney: University of New South Wales Press, 2004.

Parry, Benita. *Postcolonial Studies: A Materialist Critique.* London and NewYork: Routledge, 2004.

———. 'What is Left in Postcolonial Studies?' *New Literary History* 43(2), 2012, 341–358.

Porter, Bernard. *The Lion's Share: A Short History of British Imperialism, 1850 to the Present.* Fifth Edition. London and New York: Routledge, 2005 [1975].

Robins, Nick. 'Loot: In search of the East India Company,' *Open Democracy*, 22 January, 2003, https://www.opendemocracy.net/theme_7-corporations/article_904.jsp. 3 January, 2017.

———. *The Corporation that Changed the World: How the East India Company Shaped the Modern Multinational.* London: Pluto, 2006.

———. 'East India Company: The Original Too-Big-to-Fail Firm,' *Bloomberg View*, 12 March, 2013, https://www.bloomberg.com/view/articles/2013-03-12/east-india-company-the-original-too-big-to-fail-firm. 3 January, 2017.

Romein, J.M., and W.F. Wertheim. *A World on the Move: A History of Colonialism and Nationalism in Asia and North Africa from the Turn of the Century to the Bandung Conference.* Amsterdam: Djambaten, 1956.

Said, Edward. *Orientalism.* London: Routledge, 1978.

Sartre, Jean-Paul. *Colonialism, and Neocolonialism,* trans. Azzedine Haddour, Steve Brewer and Terry McWilliams. London: Routledge, 2001 [Gallimard, 1964].

Schirokauer, Conrad, and Miranda Brown. *A Brief History of Chinese Civilization.* Fourth Edition. Boston: Wadsworth Cengage, 2013.

Seabrook, Jeremy. *Pauperland: A Short History of Poverty in Britain.* London:Hurst, 2013.

Seal, Anil. *The Emergence of Indian Nationalism: Competition and Collaborationin the Later Nineteenth Century.* London: Cambridge University Press, 1968.

Sen, Amartya. 'Imperial Illusions: India, Britain and the Wrong Lessons,' *The New Republic*, 31 December, 2007, http://www.newrepublic.com/article/books/imperial-illusions. 3 January, 2017.

Sen, Amartya. *Poverty and Famines: An Essay on Entitlement and Deprivation.* Oxford: Oxford University Press, 1981.

Slade, John. *Narrative of the Late Proceedings and Events in China.* Public Domain E-book, 2007 [1839].

Smith, Adam. *The Wealth of Nations.* London: Penguin Classics, 1999 Edition [1776].

Smith, Ruth L. 'Order and Disorder: The Naturalization of Poverty,' *Cultural Critique* 14(Winter), 209–229.
Sorkin, Andrew Ross. *Too Big to Fail*. New York: Viking, 2009.
Trachtenberg, Marc. 'Intervention in Historical Perspective,' in *Emerging Norms of Justified Intervention*. Eds. Laura W. Reed and Carl Kaysen. Cambridge, MA: American Academy of Arts and Sciences, 1993, 15–36.
Wakefield, Edward Gibbon. *A View of the Art of Colonization: With Present Reference to the British Empire; In Letters Between a Statesman and a Colonist*. Ontario: Batoche, 2001 [1849].
Williams, Mark. 'The Long Maori Renaissance,' in *Other Renaissances: A New Approach to World Literature*. Eds. Zhou Gang, Sander Gilman, and Brenda Deen Schilgen. London: Palgrave Macmillan, 2006, 207–226.
Zahedieh, Nuala. *The Capital and the Colonies: London and the Atlantic Economy 1660–1700*. Cambridge: Cambridge University Press, 2010.
———. 'Overseas Trade and Empire,' in *The Cambridge Economic History of Modern Britain. Volume I: 1700–1870*. Eds. Roderick Floud, Jane Humphries, and Paul Johnson. Cambridge: Cambridge University Press, 2014, 392–420.

Websites

Legacies of British Slave-Ownership, University College, London: https://www.ucl.ac.uk/lbs/. 3 January, 2017.
Office for National Statistics (UK): http://www.ons.gov.uk/. 3 January, 2017.
———.'How important is China to the UK economy?': http://www.ons.gov.uk/ons/rel/international-transactions/outward-foreign-affiliates-statistics/how-important-is-china-to-the-uk-economy-/sty-china.html. 3 January, 2017.
World Wealth and Income Database: http://wid.world/#Database. 3 January, 2017.

CHAPTER 3

Neocolonialism

NEOCOLONIAL INDEPENDENCE

On August 16, 2012, South African police opened fire on striking mine workers at Lonmin platinum mine in Marikana, killing thirty-four protesters, the worst incidence of security-force violence since the end of apartheid. The police action was supported by the National Union of Mineworkers, which had also injured strikers during the week-long standoff. The shooting, filmed live and replayed on news channels around the world, was quickly interpreted in international media as evoking apartheid-era police shootings such as the Sharpeville Massacre. This time, however, the police were black and the strike-breaking action was condoned by the democratically elected African National Congress government. The Marikana protest and shootings were visual, visceral reminders of the economic apartheid that has replaced racial apartheid in South Africa, which is ranked as having one of the highest rates of inequality in the world.[1] Around 50% of the population live below the national poverty line,[2] while the top 10% earn around 50% of total national earnings. Miners, who earn on average €350 per month, drew attention to the mine manager's salary, allegedly €1,000,000 per year, and the National Union of Mineworkers' director, who earns €90,000.[3]

The history of the mining company Lonmin, like that of the Ghazipur opium factory outlined in the previous chapter, illustrates the important role that colonial capitalism played in the establishment of some of today's most successful corporations. The publically listed,

London-based company was established in 1909 as the London and Rhodesian Mining and Land Company Limited (Lonrho). The company emerged out of the late-nineteenth-century scramble for Africa that featured the same combination of aggressive private investment backed by state political and military support as the East India Company's opening of Bengal. In the decolonising era, Lonrho's director, British business tycoon Roland Rowland, famous for his aggressive multinational takeovers, bought up British businesses throughout Africa:

> Rowland cultivated friendships with the leaders of the nationalistic movements and promoted decolonization in order to secure business contracts for Lonrho after independence … befriend[ed] African political leaders through unorthodox methods and meddled in the political affairs of the continent to advance the interests of his company. (Page 2003, 350–351)

The renown of businessmen such as Rowland confirms the argument of historians including Nuala Zahedieh and Bernard Porter, cited in Chap. 2, that colonialism and its aftermath were predominantly led by private business interests. Indeed, updating this argument to the Thatcherite era of deregulation, the four-part BBC documentary *The Mayfair Set: Four Stories about the Rise of Business and the Decline of Political Power* (1999) features Rowland at considerable length. Lonrho is today present in eighteen Sub-Saharan African nations, while its mining division, Lonmin, operates solely in South Africa, with exploration in Canada and Northern Ireland.[4] The trajectory of companies such as Lonmin, from colonial-era founding to contemporary blue-chip investment status, illustrates the importance of colonial capitalism to today's global finance, of which the centre remains in London.[5]

Lonmin and the Marikana incident highlight both the structures of continued capitalism after independence under neocolonialism and the forms of injustice condoned by the state to maintain and support the uneven distribution of capital. The violence against striking miners exemplifies within a national context the same use of law and its enforcement to protect private market interests as practiced under colonialism, described in the previous chapter in Britain's military defence of the opium trade, and the same in the New Zealand Land Wars to subdue Maori unrest at having their land stolen or swindled by private settler land companies such as E.G. Wakefield's New Zealand Company. The sub-standard living conditions and worker poverty that provoked the union action at Marikana similarly followed a common pattern of inequality, discussed at length in regard to slums and the (un)liveable wage in the next chapter. Lonmin is currently under investigation by the World Bank for its failure to provide the social infrastructure of housing, schools, and other facilities promised in its investment plan. The June 2015 release of the official inquiry[6] into the massacre, which attributes no fault for the violence and only makes recommendations to Lonmin for improving working and living conditions, illustrates the uncomfortable complicity between private corporations and national policies that is constitutive of capitalism throughout its history. In particular, the report absolves Cyril Ramaphosa from any official conflict of interest or responsibility for ordering the special armed force's violent resolution to the strike, even though he was at the time both South Africa's deputy president and a member of Lonmin's board of directors. Following the 2015 Marikana Inquiry, media attention continues to focus on the unsanitary living conditions of Lonmin's worker housing and the financial hardship facing the miners' widows in light of lack of legal responsibility from either Lonmin or the government. Highlighting the non-resolution of the Marikana strike, less than two years later, workers at another Lonmin mine also took extended strike action to similarly protest pay inequality.

Examples of gross inequality in extractive industries occur both globally and historically, as miners' low standards of working and living conditions and the often-violent struggle for workers' rights have been synonymous and continuous with industrial capitalism in both developing and developed world-spaces. Such primary industries are not only a common source of entry into capitalism, through primitive accumulation, but also deeply entangled in the invention of the nation itself. As an intrinsically capitalist project, building the modern nation has required harnessing the land to the programme of progress and development. The growth of the nation through capitalist social relations is consistently represented in literature that portrays primary industries. In the British literary canon, historical novels such as Winston Graham's *Poldark* series on Cornish mining (1943–2002) and Richard Llewellyn's Welsh *How Green Was My Valley* (1939) capture early inequalities of class, gender, and race crystallising in the national imaginary. These dynamics are continued in twentieth-century, Northern, working-class mining and industrial settings in writers such as D.H. Lawrence and Alan Sillitoe, and rendered as more overt socio-political commentary in George Orwell's *The Road to Wigan Pier* (1937). Similarly, literature of the nation-building era in white-settler nations South Africa, Canada, Australia, and New Zealand consistently feature writing of taming the land, particularly through hunting and farming. The importance of these writers to their national literary traditions attests to the foundational presence of extractive industries in the nation-state, providing both the economic requisites of nation-building and the cultural need for a national imaginary grounded in local interaction with the land.

Early postcolonial fiction similarly foregrounds extractive industries as the site of both potential national wealth and conflicts of interests that highlight social inequality. Peter Abrahams's *Mine Boy* (1946) depicts gold-mining work and slum living conditions in an informal black settlement and a mining township on the edge of Johannesburg. The novel signals the mapping onto urban space of racial and class segregation that would become policy only a few years later under apartheid, of 'white man's ventures to get the natives and coloureds out of the towns' (95), and of urban drift and immigrant labour: 'they come from the farms and some are from the land of the Portuguese [Mozambique] and others are from Rhodesia. The white man fetched them. And those that are fetched must live in the compounds, it is the law here' (34). In *Mine Boy*, the inequality between miners and executives evident in Lonmin's pay gap and living conditions is evoked in a comparison of abstract profit and its concrete human cost. As 'gold dust streamed upwards to make men wealthy and powerful,' the toxic dust trickles down, causing fatal respiratory illness (107). In one of the novel's numerous examples of the depersonalisation of the human body to the function of labour, a sick worker hides his terminal lung disease in order to work long enough to pay off a debt to a local white landholder so that his family will not be dispossessed from their farm after his death (108).

While the conflict in Abrahams's novel plays out along white–black racial lines, other postcolonial novels reveal closer historical synchronicity with the 2012 events at Marikana in depicting black-on-black violence. Ngũgĩ wa Thiong'o's *Weep Not, Child* (1964) portrays an agricultural labour strike that rejects an idealist sense of budding national unity that imagines '[w]e black people are brothers' (51). The wealthy Jacobo sides with the white landowners and the police, a betrayal that presages the novel's main focus, the demise of the idea of national unity shattered by the partisanship of the Mau Mau uprising. Similar dynamics of state military and police intervention on behalf of the wealthy are also found in the later *Devil on the Cross* (1980), in which the heroine is incited to activism after multiple experiences of persecution from male domination of women in her own culture, including from lovers, her boss, and a prospective employer: 'the black man gave me up to the police, who were black like me' (43). Later in the novel, workers and students are shot at and imprisoned for demonstrating against the meeting of African capitalist 'thieves and robbers.' Rather than a hierarchy of coloniser exploiting the colonised, Ngũgĩ's novels expose a split within the emerging postcolonial nation comprising a local comprador elite who intervene as gatekeepers between a restless working public and foreign business owners.

Reading Abrahams and Ngũgĩ today confronts the reader with the shock of recognition, as the fiction plays out the familiar structures of abuse mediatised in the live news feeds that allow the world to witness the Marikana shootings, and the investigative journalism that exposes the national and international legal battlefields on which private and public responsibilities and obligations are endlessly deferred. Following Rita Felski's phenomenology of shock, the Marikana shootings shock through surprise, betraying expected conventions of peaceful protest in an age of democratic negotiation overseen by the watchful, policing gaze of global media. The violence in Abrahams and Ngũgĩ, by contrast, upsets the reader in part through the emotional closeness that is literature's specificity, as the reader experiences the narrator's pain vicariously. Perhaps more strikingly, however, these texts shock the contemporary reader not with the surprise of newness but with the disappointment of familiarity. As Felski argues, 'texts from the past can interrupt our stories of cultural progress, speak across centuries, spark moments of affinity across the gulf of temporal difference. Their very untimeliness renders them newly timely' (120). Read today, such novels call attention to the lack of progress in African workers' rights despite the rhetoric of development that both private companies and governments celebrate as the gains of independence and globalisation. Both writers use the fictional register to bear witness to experiences of degradation that play out market dynamics on a human scale. They offer to the permanent record subjective testimonies of labouring and living conditions in their respective times and places that reverberate with a contemporary, global readership.

This pattern of internal inequality repeats in more contemporary postcolonial novels on extractive industries. In Helon Habila's *Oil on Water* (2011), about Niger River Delta oil exploration, and Alexis Wright's *Carpentaria*, centred on Australian mining on Aboriginal land, local tribal peoples differently resist or acquiesce to the encroaching private ventures, creating schisms within communities that fracture along economic lines. In both novels, devastation of the environment and of local cultural practices and relationships with the land are represented quite literally as crimes, in suspenseful acts of sabotage and thrilling chase scenes in which big-business private security firms and public policing become indistinguishable in the mayhem. In a different context of public–private collusion in the Indian mining industry, in *The Sound of Water* (2009) Sanjay Bahadur portrays responses to a deadly mining disaster—a fictional account of two Bagdighi mine accidents in 2001. Multiple narrative points of view play out the competitive one-upmanship in which the team leader, foreman, mine owner, workers' union representative, and ministry official all defer blame and dissimulate responsibility for the tragedy. Bahadur, who was himself a director of the Indian Ministry of Coal, highlights the conflict of financial and ethical interests in maintaining a positive public image of this important national industry. The characters reveal various self-interested motivations to maximise profit, play down risks and dangers, and spare themselves unnecessary paperwork—all factors that minimise worker and environmental safety.

These novels, which are not only stylistically very different but are also set in divergent historical periods, political regimes, and in developed (Australia), middle-income (India, South Africa), and developing (Kenya, Nigeria) nations, nonetheless all convey similar structures of investment and labour and the means by which they are enforced. In each storyline, local land and labour practices are subjugated to the demands of multinational corporations beholden to their often-foreign shareholders. The violent struggles for worker's rights portrayed in these texts stake a claim to a particular cluster of socio-economic conditions and relations. The similarities across this historical and global body of mine fiction demonstrate the specific capacity of narrative to bring together interdependent yet disparate socio-economic relations—such as between labour, management, and ownership, and between producer and consumer—that are often difficult to see in the real world exactly because of the spatial and cultural dislocation of owners, workers, and stakeholders.

While it may seem incongruous to liken the Australian mining culture portrayed in *Carpentaria* to that in developing Africa, their synchronicity is borne out in contemporary geopolitics. Less than a month after the Lonmin shootings, one of the world's wealthiest women, Australian mining heiress Gina Rinehart, warned that Australia's mining industry, which accounts for around 10% of the nation's GDP and up to half of its exports,[7] was unable to remain competitive on the global stage because of its miners' high wages and comfortable working conditions. By contrast, she said in a speech to the Sydney Mining Club, 'Africans want to work and its workers are willing to work for less than two dollars per day. Such statistics make me worry for this country's future' (2012, n.p.; qtd in O'Carroll 2012, n.p.). Her solution, which includes importing cheap foreign labour, lowering taxes, softening regulations, and increasing access to bank loans for mining projects, embraces the neoliberal rationale that national wellbeing is prefigured on global economic competitiveness. Rinehart construes the international mining industry as a level playing field on which rich countries, such as Australia, must equally compete with poor countries which offer lower wages, negligible safety measures, and have higher negative environmental impacts than Australian regulations allow. Her solution to reduced Australian competitiveness is drastic cost-cutting in the name of a dubious form of economic common sense derived from analysing the 'statistics' of bottom-line financial reports, a modern-day example of what Noam Chomsky calls 'profit over people.' The 2010 Pike River mining disaster in New Zealand[8] offers a tragic illustration of how the globally calibrated economic competitiveness Rinehart advocates can result in the same chain of government deregulation and corporate negligence that lead to accidents in the developed world as in the developing world.

In a post-apartheid South African example of the social impact of exactly the type of competitive corporate practices expounded by Rinehart, activist journalist Ashwin Desai in *We Are the Poors* (2002) analyses public–private collusion in response to multiple labour struggles. These include prolonged labour strikes at Engen (Exxon) petroleum plant in 2000 against the exploitation of outsourced labourers (110–116), a situation similar to Lonmin, which employs one-third of its miners through labour brokers, and who are thus subject to poorer pay, no living allowance, and lower job security than unionised and permanent workers (Webb 2012, n.p.). During the Engen strikes, the General Manager offered a press report stating the company's position against worker protest: '[t]hat refinery is owned by an American corporation. I will not, repeat not, allow some ridiculous South African laws to override my obligation to make money for Exxon and its shareholders' (Desai, 111). Obligingly, the state sent in the army to end the strike, as it did a decade later at Marikana. In abandoning the civic in favour of the corporate, South Africa's state intervention effectively heeded the threat expressed by such private interests as the Engen General Manager and, in Australia, Gina Rinehart on behalf of the Sydney Mining Club. Like Amitav Ghosh's nineteenth-century Canton Chamber of Commerce opium dealers, these executives see the role of the government, police, and legal system as to facilitate their profit-making obligations to their (often foreign) shareholders and directors, and to manage any civil unrest and social fallout—including worker fatalities—that may occur.[9]

Lonmin and the Marikana shooting exemplify the transfer of power from imperial to national governance through the neocolonial transition period so that the capitalist political economy continues today, now enforced internally by the state rather than from afar under empire. Extraction of natural resources constituted one of the main motivations for colonisation in the past and remains today the backbone of the export economy in many ex-colonial nations, which are encouraged to exploit primary industries in which they have a global competitive advantage rather than to invest in the development of secondary and tertiary sectors. Furthermore, as Lonmin again illustrates, key industries in postcolonial nation-states are often foreign owned and the products are exported rather than consumed locally. Michael Barratt Brown, in his classic text *The Economics of Imperialism* (1974), argues that this transfer of wealth from ex-colonial lands to private businesses owned in developed core countries is the key economic feature of neocolonialism (273, 284). Thomas Piketty's comparison of national ownership offers supporting statistics for this historical and international structure of financial inequality. At the height of colonial rule at the turn of the twentieth century, total foreign ownership in Africa and Asia was between a third and a half of domestic capital and three-quarters of industrial capital (69). Today, a similar figure of 20% of African capital is owned by foreigners, a figure that rises to up to 50% of manufacturing and perhaps even more of extractive industries (68–69).[10] By contrast, foreign ownership of developed nations hovers around 1–2%. Piketty, following other dissenters from neoliberal ideology, argues bluntly that 'capital mobility has [not] been the primary factor promoting convergence of rich and poor nations... . Conversely, countries owned by other countries, whether in the colonial period or in Africa today, have been less successful' (70). As Lonmin's ownership, company structure, and pay scale illustrate, the wealth exported from areas of extraction in the colonial peripheries to the financial core of London is a feature of the uneven profits common to capitalism under colonial, neocolonial, and latterly neoliberal regimes.

Beholden by debt to a structure of 'underdevelopment' (Amin 1990), 'dependent development' (Barratt Brown 1974), or 'archaic' forms of capitalism (Gakou 1987, 33), ex-colonial developing nations continue to be pressured by international bodies such as the International Monetary Fund (IMF), World Trade Organisation (WTO), and World Bank to focus on existing industries often established under colonialism, namely cash crops and extraction of natural resources. While the establishment of the IMF, WTO, and World Bank outwardly appears to mark a shift in global political economy after the end of empire, these financial institutions were established by the core colonial powers before decolonisation, part of the post-World War Two Bretton Woods refinancing.[11] Tellingly, the head of the IMF is always a European, and the president of the World Bank is always American, one feature that leads William Tabb, in *Economic Governance in the Age of Globalization* (2004), to wryly label these institutions 'reminiscent of the colonial civil service and advisors to local rulers sent from the "mother" country. And like the colonial administrators they never seem to go away' (193). Whereas colonialism was driven by Western investors seeking profit in heretofore untouched markets of tradable goods and industries, the debt financing introduced by the IMF and World Bank was driven by Western investors looking to place financial capital with good returns through interest.[12] Arguing the seamless crossover from British colonial empire to what Alice Amsden calls the 'First American Empire' of the post-war period (2009, 1), Walden Bello identifies the IMF and World Bank as key to expanding and enforcing the new era of globalisation, which he defines as the imposition of American economic liberalism on the world stage (1994, 3). Under the political rubric of containment liberalism, development loans to the Third World shored up Western power to thwart the spread of communism and the kind of radical nationalism espoused by Third Way leaders such as Ghana's Kwame Nkrumah, Egypt's Gamal Abdel Nasser, and Indonesia's Sukarno.

The perpetuation of colonial-era financial infrastructure in the neocolonial and neoliberal ages means that the economic structure Fanon identified during decolonisation remains true today, with the national economy still dependent on cash crops and primary industry exported to advance development in the West (1963, 151–152). In his study of 'Africa's economic backwardness,' Samir Amin links African underdevelopment explicitly to Western Europe's post-war growth programme, which used colonial spheres of influence and currency zones to bolster and secure home development:

> [T]he kind of unequal relations renewed in this [neocolonial] framework in no sense represents progress towards the liberation of Africa and development of its peoples, but on the contrary their restriction to obsolete mining and agricultural specializations that are to Europe's advantage. In that sense Europe bears a heavy responsibility for the crystallization of the power of the new local ruling classes and thereby in the continent's economic, social and political disaster. (144)

Amin labels this purposive maintenance of these unequal business relations, in which African countries are considered as markets for Europe rather than national economies in their own right, 'maldevelopment.' Illustrating the importance for Britain of cheap imports from the colonies in the post-war, pre-independence period, Ghanaian (Gold Coast) cocoa and Malayan rubber plantations kept the Sterling Area solvent (Chamberlain 1999, 40), an important line of cash for the near-bankrupt Britain. Post-independence, Amin and Mohamed Lamine Gakou's studies of the rise of cash-cropping across the Saharel provide compelling accounts of neocolonial-era trade imbalances, and the very structures of debt financing that made the previously food-sufficient region reliant on foreign investment, imports, and aid relief. Gakou's claim, in *The Crisis in African Agriculture* (1987), that by the mid-1970s 'famine began to take on the appearance of a structural feature in most African countries' (43) strikingly recalls Mike Davis's argument of colonial-era Bengal famines in *Late-Victorian Holocausts*. The international flow of goods, resources, and profits toward Britain, particularly London, and, in the other direction, the newly independent nation's ongoing reliance on the former colonial centre for finance and imports, demonstrate the capitalist economic structure imposed under colonialism and maintained under neocolonialism.

From an economic perspective, decolonisation was not about national independences in respect of cultural *plurality* but a shift in the form of global capitalism to flows of finance and goods based on interdependent economic *singularity*. Arguing that the demise of colonial empire was motivated by a market rationale, historian of decolonisation Muriel Chamberlain recalls that the end of empire was desirable as long as it could 'leave behind a sufficiently stable political structure to provide a satisfactory trading partner; that after all ... was what the Europeans had been seeking in the nineteenth century; they had only moved into formal political control when they could not find it' (124). The 1944 Bretton Woods Agreement set the agenda for a new form of global connectivity centred on market freedom, which limited national control of import-export tariffs and of monetary policy, including international exchange rates and borrowing criteria. The shift from colonial to financial forms of imperialism as grounds for intervening in world affairs was clearly outlined in the 1947 Marshall Plan, which states that the USA 'should do whatever it is able to assist in the return of normal economic health in the world, without which there can be no political stability and no assured peace' (Torricelli and Carroll 1999, 165). The famous statement implies that the free market, construed as 'normal,' is to be defended by force, a market-led position that echoes Britain's motivation to wage war on China over the opium market.

From the colonial-era civilising mission to the global-market era of the development mission, capitalist expansion underpins the rationale for Western interference overseas. The neocolonial-era integration of these peripheral regions into the global financial market through indebtedness, foreign ownership, and dependence on stock prices, each controlled by the twin financial hubs of London and New York, joins together the past and present ages of colonial and neoliberal globalisation. Although the post-war rebuild in Europe and the decolonisation of the Global South are usually construed as a retraction to more insular national concerns, from an economic viewpoint it was a time of increasing global connectivity of markets, circulation of currency, and a growing number of multinational corporations, such as those partnerships negotiated by figures such as Lonrho's director Tiny Rowland. As Bello points out, early development loans propped up often repressive regimes, such as in Indonesia, Brazil, and the Philippines: '[b]y the late 1970s, in fact, five of the top eight recipients of Bank loans were authoritarian regimes' (Chap. 3, Sect. 1). His point again illustrates capitalism's tendency to work out of sight of the political and social structures that often appear to have quite different ambitions of self-governance and redistribution of capital.

The extensive output of fiction concerned with the time of independence and early nationalism contains numerous portrayals and analyses of the transformation of the capitalist world-system in the middle decades of the twentieth century. Decolonisation, the *raison d'être* of postcolonial studies, gave writers of previously colonised spaces both the national freedom and the international readership to express their cultural imaginaries and their histories from their own perspectives. The emergent new literature labelled postcolonial offers a valuable source of information about the extensive changes taking place, the people's subjective, affective, and emotional responses to decolonisation, and the authors' hesitations, apprehensions, or outright critiques of neocolonialism. As the writers were often highly educated and with experience abroad, particularly in Britain, they held a privileged yet ambivalent position, able to notice colonial continuities despite the strong rhetoric of independence, aware of the connectivity between local and global political economy. The writers' knowledge of the political economy of the period offers a blueprint for postcolonial literary economics, while the openly Marxist positions of several early writers are a timely reminder of the discipline's indebtedness to Marxist, socialist, and more generally leftist social critique that is of value in today's climate of renewed critique of capitalism.

The previous chapter showed how unequal, unjust policies during the colonial era established British colonial settlement and private company extraction and trade in systematically favourable terms and conditions for the coloniser at the expense of the colonised. In the settler colonies, these same techniques of patronage, bullying, monopolisation, and a significant amount of illegal and underhand dealings, in each case reinforced by military and police enforcement, worked to continue British class relations, with colonial land and businesses owned by an elite minority and worked by a large labouring class. This chapter shows the repetition of these same techniques through the globalisation of private corporations in ex-colonial centres and the installation of a native comprador elite in decolonising territories. It is notable that the term 'comprador,' used in postcolonial studies to define the internal elite that emerged during decolonisation, came into the English language through the opium trade; it is a Portuguese term originating in the Canton and Macau trading ports of the colonial era. Across the world, the revolutions and upheavals during decolonisation failed to live up to expectations. Instead of radical change, the majority of new nations established instead neocolonial regimes that maintained capitalism as the economic basis for the new nation-states—although not without struggle. Thus, the same structures of inequality of wealth and income continued, albeit with different, locally inflected dynamics of haves and have-nots, often split along ethnic or sectarian lines. Specific mechanisms of this transfer are closely traced in fiction written in the early postcolonial era, as well as in more recent novels that return to specific national struggles with great awareness of the global geopolitics in which the local and regional was enmeshed.

The period's extensive civil unrest, including revolutions and wars, is inextricable from the search for alternatives to the capitalist–communist split that had made the USA and USSR the two world spheres of power that replaced the colonial form of imperialism. The decisive Bandung Conference of 1955 and the 1961 Non-Alignment Pact provide two windows into the energies of resistance to colonialism and the search for regional connectivity forged during decolonisation efforts. Both events illuminate the importance of areas generally ignored by postcolonial studies, notably South-East Asia, the Near East protectorates of Egypt, Iran, and Iraq, and the Balkan territory of Yugoslavia, which is commonly regarded in European studies as a practice ground for colonialism. India's independence in 1947, well-discussed in postcolonial studies, was two years later than Indonesia's independence, which remains underanalysed. The Bandung Conference also tends to be ignored as a founding moment of postcolonial studies, even though its proclamation was incorporated into the 1960 UN Declaration on the Granting of Independence to Colonial Countries and Peoples (Crawford 1993, 44). In their search for alternatives to capitalism and regional-based alliances that would economically and politically unhitch the ex-colonies from their erstwhile colonisers, the Third Way impetus of the Bandung Conference, the pan-African Congresses, and the Non-Alignment Movement conceived of the postcolonial as structurally as well as ideologically different.

The push for non-alignment quickly lost impetus following Nehru's death and the collapse of non-aligned governments—in several cases backed by British and American military involvement—in Brazil, Ghana, Indonesia, Egypt, and Iraq (Barratt Brown, 272). Following the failure of a third power bloc to challenge the USA and the USSR, the term 'Third World,' coined by Alfred Sauvy in 1952 and quickly taken up by the non-aligned to mean the 'Third Way' alternative to capitalism or communism, became synonymous with underdevelopment and poverty. As the post-war boom in Europe and the USA reduced inequality and saw the rise of a strong middle class in developed countries,[13] the spotlight turned to external inequality in the then-widening gap between the West and the Rest. This split between the 'First' and 'Third' Worlds was incrusted in popular culture by highly mediatised famines in the 1980s and 1990s, and 'one-dollar-a-day' charity slogans that 'reproduce imperial tropes' of exoticism and otherness (Ng 2006, 133).

The difficulty for postcolonial studies to come up with a theory that can encompass the very different cultural experiences of decolonisation in the Middle East, all of Africa, and South and South-East Asia is not unique to the discipline. In the field of history, Ellen Meiksins Wood signals the lack of a bridging theory that can connect the colonial to the neoliberal forms of capitalism through the hinge decolonial period:

> [J]ust as we have not yet seen a systematic theory of imperialism in a world of universal capitalism, we have no theory of imperialism that adequately comprehends a world that consists not of imperial masters and colonial subjects but of an international system in which both imperial and subordinate powers are more or less sovereign states. (152)

Arguably, Wood, in *Empire of Capital*, along with the theorists of the world-systems approach such as Wallerstein, Amin, Gakou, and Giovanni Arrighi, do make significant contributions to presenting a 'systematic theory of imperialism in a world of universal capitalism.' Postcolonial studies, as the discipline dedicated to defining the dynamics between, to paraphrase Wood, imperial and subordinate powers which are sovereign states, is well placed to take up her challenge. To this end, however, decolonisation must be studied for its role in marking the crossover from colonial to neoliberal globalisation.

In a much-undervalued novel that comprehensively registers the ownership of national wealth during decolonisation and its place in global geopolitics, Waguih Ghali's *Beer in the Snooker Club* (1964) describes the end of Britain's protectorate mandate in Egypt in the 1950s, amid the 1956 Suez Crisis and Egypt's struggle for national independence under Gamal Abdel Nasser. Symbolically, along with the 1947 independence of India, the Suez Crisis marks the end of Britain's world hegemony and increasing devolution to a financial rather than territorial era of imperialism. Nonetheless, like Britain's colonial relations in China, Egypt is rarely considered in postcolonial literary studies. Nasser, along with India's Jawaharlal Nehru, Ghana's Kwame Nkrumah, Indonesia's Sukarno, and Yugoslavia's Josip Broz Tito, led the 1961 Non-Alignment Pact, which makes Egypt's Third Way experiment immensely important in analysing the triumph of capitalism amid a concerted search for alternatives. Egypt is also important for being Britain's only declared act of war against a colony, unlike protracted colonial wars fought by France (in Algeria), the Netherlands (in the Dutch East Indies and New Guinea), and Portugal (in Angola and Mozambique). France and Britain's intervention in Egypt was based on financial rather than territorial reasons, justifying their attack on the grounds of stopping Egypt from defaulting on its debts with Europe,[14] as well as in support of Israel. Other than the outstanding loan, Britain's main interest in co-owning the Canal was to ensure access to India, for which purpose Britain had held a military colony in Cyprus since 1878 and troops in Egypt since 1882. Rosa Luxemburg tellingly calls the British military presence in Egypt the result of 'Big Business' (437). The US diffusion of the Suez standoff, by claiming that free trade would ensure ongoing access to the Canal, shows the shift in emphasis away from the protection of territory to the protection of markets.

Ghali's novel, set in Cairo and London in the 1950s, follows rich young Egyptian intellectuals who dabble in communism and protests, and imagine the new Egypt and the new Britain forming in those turbulent early years when the capitalist future of the West and Egypt's place in it was unclear. *Beer in the Snooker Club* does not represent the Suez war or ethnic or class conflict, which all happen off the page and are only alluded to in passing by the idle elite amid their insipid conversations about money and how to spend it. In fact, the protagonist Ram becomes most involved in the Suez Crisis not by joining student demonstrations or, on the front lines, taunting the English troops stationed at the Canal, but comfortably ensconced in a pub in London, where he passionately discusses it with liberal British intellectuals supporting the independence movements and revolutions that swept the world in the post-war period. Indeed, his most radical action is to get himself deported from the UK for joining an anti-Suez street protest in London.

Although the majority of Britain's colonies gained and maintained independence without direct conflict over the fact of colonialism, covert military and political support hid behind partisan claims of nationalist fervour. Western military meddling to protect their business interests in ex-colonial spaces underpins both the Suez Crisis, which Barry Turner labels 'the first oil war' because of the features it shares with the 2003 US invasion of Iraq (Turner 2006), and Britain's 1967 support of federalist Nigeria in the Biafran war of secession to protect their oil interests, British Petroleum and Shell. Collapsing the difference between overt military and covert geopolitical interference, Ghali situates British military intervention in Egypt among multiple other 'Suezes,' which he broadly defines as recurring crises caused by 'the slyness and cruelty of

England's foreign policy. ... Of course the Africans and the Asians had had their Suezes a long time before us ... over and over again' (58). In naming multiple other Suezes, Ghali ties the specific conditions of Egypt's colonial history to repeating patterns of colonial injustice and inequality led by financial interests.

Ghali diagnoses colonialism and its support by King Farouk's monarchy and comprador elite as the mechanism behind ongoing inequality in the nationalising era. He outlines, for example, how Ram's family buy the title of pasha to control land on which impoverished fellaheen tenants work (161). Ram's coming-of-age journey conforms to a common postcolonial trope in which the individual's exploration of his own identity is simultaneously that of the newly independent nation's identity. Guided by a moral compass for fairness that appears to come from outside his social and cultural milieu, Ram is intensely aware of and sensitive to the structures of inequality in Egypt that have created the luxury of his social set: he despises the rich, including himself, yet is pessimistic that Nasser's revolution will effect any change.[15] The target of his critique of unjust inequality, however, extends outside the urban Cairo and national Egyptian field to incorporate imperial British injustices done in the name of colonialism everywhere. Ram thus indicts rich Egyptians for ill-gotten wealth, as well as the further-afield beneficiaries of colonialism, accusing all Britons of their unwitting complicity in the actions of their 'rich relatives': like Ram, the British are born into a position of privilege built on colonial pillage.

Comparing the relative luxury of life in London to poverty in Cairo (90), Ram situates Egypt's 1950s civil strife as a logical outcome of British imperialism. Just as his family's wealth is based on colonial privilege, he urges the British to acknowledge how they passively and often unwittingly share in the prosperity brought by empire:

> 'Some of the richest people on earth are your relatives. All the rich country-house owners and Mayfair-flat occupiers are your relatives. All the Rolls-Royce-transported and unlimited expense-account possessors are your relatives. Isn't it bloody horrible you have so many rich relatives, while half the population in Africa, which you own, is half-starving? Isn't it bloody horrible that your relatives have so fleeced Jamaica of all it possessed that the people there are half-starving?' I was warming up and enjoying myself. 'You are so well informed you know all about the

Egyptian fellah, do you? Do you know anything of the natives in Kenya? in Rhodesia? in Aden? And worst of all, perhaps, in South Africa? Or are you going to tell me South Africa doesn't belong to your rich relatives? It does. If your rich relatives weren't so happy doing business with those filthy rich there, they would have been scared to flog defenceless black women. Don't you know your rich relatives will send you to South Africa in a second if a few white throats are cut by the natives? But it's the fellah you're worried about, is it? He is in his present plight after being ruled by your rich relatives, the Kitcheners and Co. for sixty years. Whatever happens to him now he can't be worse off than when *your* rich relatives were looking after his welfare. (88–89, italics in original)

This long diatribe links British wealth to all forms of British colonialism, from the settler Commonwealth (South Africa) and extractive colonies (Jamaica) to colonies of strategic location (Aden) and administrative protectorates (Egypt). Even though South Africa is an independent dominion, Ram's recognition of ongoing British economic interests, 'doing business with those filthy rich there,' speaks to incrusted neocolonial relations there, as exemplified in the Lonmin mining company and Tiny Rowland.

Offering an overview of combined and uneven development between exaggerated poles of the 'rich relatives' and the 'half-starving' local inhabitants, the passage telescopes between different combinations of internal and external inequality, a technique used to great effect throughout the novel to demonstrate the interdependence of local and global economic disparities. In this entanglement of hierarchies, Ram shows his awareness of multiple levels of inequality, including: the gap between working-class and wealthy Britons; Britain's wealth compared to poverty in the colonies; Egyptian inequality between Ram and the rural fellaheen from whom Ram's family wealth is made; and the elite Ram discussing imperialism with a middle-class Briton in a London pub.

While this passage may be interpreted as a classic condemnation of colonialism specifically targeting the British, Ghali reminds readers that the post-war rise of American power is also structured on similarly imperial structures of inequality. Taking exception to his cousin's excessive praise of the USA and his family's infatuation with the increasing number of Americans joining the Cairo Country Club, Ram counters thus:

[Mounir] didn't know there was any racial discrimination in America. He had never heard of Sacco and Vanzetti, he did not know what 'un-American' activities was. No, he did not believe there were poor Puerto Ricans or poor anyone else in America. Who was Paul Robeson? Red Indians without full citizenship? What was I talking about? I must be mad. (48–49)

Ram here identifies America's own internal colonialism, in which immigrants, African Americans, and the indigenous are excluded from the post-war boom. For the budding revolutionary, the US witch-hunt for communists and the clamp-down on political activism, illustrated in the persecution of Italian-immigrant anarchists Sacco and Vanzetti and black civil rights personality Robeson, are as reprehensible as Britain's colonial strategies of governance. Ghali's passage usefully foregrounds economic inequality in the early boom years of the 'American Century' of prosperity. His critique is not, however, contextualised in the postcolonial terminology of minority marginalisation. Instead of the soft politics of identity familiar today, he recalls the very overt politics and truly violent persecution of the disenfranchised in the name of national security during the Cold War and the Civil Rights Movement.

Ghali's diatribe against multiple forms of British and American meddling during the late-1950s and early-1960s period of decolonisation connects the specific situation of Egyptian and Sudanese nationalisms with the Sub-Saharan independences that are usually privileged in postcolonial studies. This very early postcolonial text is deeply aware of the international geopolitical struggles in which each local and specific narrative is placed, and is particularly attentive to the influence of both British and American power politics in shaping the hopes and aspirations of new nationalisms. In an almost opposite narrative context to the elite Ram's intellectual interest in inequality that he personally never suffers and only rarely even witnesses, Thomas Akare's *The Slums* (1981) is written through the perspective of a Nairobi slum dweller. The novel portrays a spatially constrained life-world of extreme material poverty in which the daily focus is on earning enough to buy one meal a day, an existence that the reader might assume equates with an equally limited narrative view from a cast of characters whose daily struggles eclipse awareness of or interest in politics. On the contrary, Akare portrays slum dwellers as highly informed about and interested in regional independence politics, which is incorporated into the material fabric of the slum. Thus, a long list of international examples of imperial-inflected injustice is tagged on a church wall:

3 NEOCOLONIALISM 117

Under this sign I stopped and looked at the writings and the names on the wall of this church. The names read: Viet Nam, very shiny because the paint was still wet, followed by El Fatah, Black September, Ku Klux Clan, Black Panthers, Black Power, Fu Manchu, Black Sunday, Dracula, The Suicide Commando, CIA, FBI, Peace-Makers, Harlem, Black Ghettos, Cotton Comes to Harlem, Shaft, IRA, Hare Krishna, Mau Mau, Anyanya, Mafia, Frelimo, Che Guevara, Castro, Dr Martin Luther King, Dr Nkrumah, Eduardo Mondlane, Malcolm X, Bangla Desh, Biafra, Mao, Karl Marx, Lenin, Amilcar Cabral, Kennedy, Sonny Liston, Clay, Lumumba, Hippies and many other names which I could not make out or whom they belonged to. (6–7)

Over the following pages, the origins of and connections between these people, groups, movies, and events are explained to the reader, who is unlikely to be familiar with all of them. The narrative interweaves these explanations with details of the daily routine of touting for enough work to buy food, with the tight spatial confines of the slum bringing the narrator into contact with multiple figures who represent different religious, political, and ethnic groups.

Akare's list, rendered in the informal medium of graffiti, is discussed by characters on the streets as they loiter around, waiting for casual work. Scattered among their interests in foreign films, music, and sport, they are articulate about several movements of freedom fighting, namely Arab guerrilla groups El Fatah and Black September, Kenyan Mau Mau, Sudanese Anyanya, and Mozambique's Frelimo, and demonstrate sympathy toward communist leaders and struggles in listing Che Guevara, Castro, Mao, Marx, Lenin, and the conflict in Vietnam. Akare peppers his novel with debates about local and international politics, as well as the cultural tensions within the slum and with the city of Nairobi, without any of them taking precedence to provide any sense of hope for future direction or improvement. In the range of subjects covered, *The Slums* alerts the reader to the undecided position-taking of this early independence period: by the time of Akare's novel, still waiting for strong political leadership to decide Kenya's direction. Within a few years, those decisions would be made for them, by the enforced World Bank and IMF neoliberal remedy most infamously represented by Structural Adjustment Programmes.

In African fiction over twenty years later, the same desire to call attention to the international arena of geopolitical interest and its economic underpinnings during decolonisation is still evident. Just as twenty-first-century postcolonial fiction continues to reflect on colonial history, as discussed in the previous chapter, neocolonialism is still evoked as being of contemporary relevance, even for the next generation of writers, themselves not witnesses of decolonisation. Recalling Nigeria's Biafran War in *Half of a Yellow Sun* (2006), Chimamanda Ngozi Adichie blames British geopolitics for both the war's cause and outcome. Using a technique similar to Ghosh's in the Ibis trilogy, Adichie paraphrases her own considerable research of historical sources in the words of her educated, elite narrators: radical academic Odenigbo, British-educated sociologist Olanna, businesswoman Kainene, and British expatriate Richard. The character of Richard, with his didactic and wooden, frustrated and failed attempts at writing a book and journalism about the war, provides a convenient vehicle for Adichie to smuggle in textbook information about the influence of 1960s geopolitics on Biafra's attempt at secession:

> He writes about Independence. The Second World War changed the world order. Empire was crumbling and a vocal Nigerian elite, mostly from the South, had emerged. … But the British had to preserve Nigeria as it was, their prized creation, their large market, their thorn in France's eye. To propitiate the North, they fixed the pre-Independence elections in favour of the North. (155)

Summarised by Richard but equally expounded by other characters, Adichie identifies British meddling in Nigerian politics in order to maintain influence in burgeoning national markets as the catalyst for the Biafran War of secession. As the non-natural borders imposed by colonial map-makers come up for negotiation within the newly independent state, Western business interests continue to inform the physical shape of the nation as well as its economic shape as a space of global capitalism.

Echoing Akare's technique of listing global simultaneity, Adichie also positions the local within the international to show the specific experiences of new African nation-states as inseparable from global geopolitics. Writing years later, however, her access to secondary resources makes her more able to synthesise the historical moment in narrative form. Again in the guise of Richard's writing, Adichie outlines the different international responses to the Biafran War to demonstrate the shaping force of global spheres of influence and acquiescence:

> He writes about the world that remained silent while Biafrans died. He argues that Britain inspired this silence. The arms and advice that Britain

gave Nigeria shaped other countries. In the United States, Biafra was 'under Britain's sphere of interest.' In Canada, the prime minister quipped, 'Where is Biafra?' The Soviet Union sent technicians and planes to Nigeria, thrilled at the chance to influence Africa without offending America or Britain. And from their white-supremacist positions, South Africa and Rhodesia gloated at further proof that black-run governments were doomed to failure.

Communist China denounced the Anglo-American-Soviet imperialism but did little else to support Biafra. The French sold Biafra some arms but did not give the recognition that Biafra most needed. And many Black African countries feared that an independent Biafra would trigger other secessions and so supported Nigeria. (258)

Adichie's example of the British, American, Russian, Chinese, and other African nations' attitudes toward Nigeria demonstrates the power-brokering between and within spheres of influence. Just as in historical fiction of the colonial era writers such as Ghosh and Pramoedya remind readers of how Europe decided together how best to carve up the world into colonies, Adichie recalls similar practices shaping decolonisation.

Ghali, Akare, and Adichie all include the USA in their lists of colonial power-brokering, making no discernible difference between Britain's direct imperialism and the USA's 'soft' or 'informal' imperialism through control of markets rather than territories. Their position is contrary to postcolonial critical studies' reluctance to engage in the debate across the disciplines over similarities and differences between twentieth-century US global hegemony and the preceding age of European empire, and the discipline's studious discounting of fiction from American indigenous, black, and immigrant writers. Postcolonial fiction has been altogether less squeamish in tracing the crossover from British to American economic imperialism and in underlining the similar use of political pressure and military force to succeed where diplomacy fails. Edward Said's *Culture and Imperialism*, as well as many of his later essays and much of his work on Palestine, works hard to counter this theoretical lacuna. He opens the last chapter of *Culture and Imperialism* by quoting Barratt Brown's claim of the longevity of imperial relations into the present day: 'imperialism is still without question a most powerful force in the economic, political and military relations by which the less economically developed lands are subjected to the more economically developed' (Barratt Brown qtd in Said, 341). Said, in arguing for the American continuation of the European imperial mission, notes that a US 'military intervention in the Third World had occurred every year between 1945 and 1967' (345), setting a precedent for overseas military action based on a nebulous sense of threat to liberal democracy—to which free trade is integral—that in the past twenty years has easily switched focus from communism to terrorism.

Representative of the uneasy cohabitation of postcolonial and American forms of minority discrimination, British Pakistani novelist Mohsin Hamid's *The Reluctant Fundamentalist* (2008) recalls explicitly postcolonial concerns in the context of post-9/11 American foreign policy. Although the novel's action is played out in Lahore, a perfectly postcolonial setting, the target of its scathing critique of discrimination and open racism is the US rather than Britain. Voicing disgust at the US invasion of Afghanistan as a response to the September 11, 2001 attack on New York's World Trade Centre, Hamid's narrator, who calls himself 'a modern-day janissary, a servant of the American empire' (173), offers a list of American wrongdoings in the postcolonial sphere that collapses the different motivations behind each invasion as subservient to world economic supremacy:

> I had always resented the manner in which America conducted itself in the world; your country's constant interference in the affairs of others was insufferable. Vietnam, Korea, the straits of Taiwan, the Middle East, and now Afghanistan: in each of the major conflicts and standoffs that ringed my mother continent of Asia, America played a central role. Moreover I knew from my experience as a Pakistani—of alternating periods of American aid and sanctions—that finance was a primary means by which the American empire exercised its power. (177)

In a by now familiar technique of listing multiple incursions abroad, Hamid, like the other authors analysed above, makes sure historical aggressions from many geographical spaces remain in the public eye. In their fiction's postcolonial positioning alongside the victimised narrator, these writers' lists expand their condemnation of inequality and injustice from the novel's immediate context to a historical and global level.

Attention in fiction to the global political arena in recalling the motivations of neocolonial economics and its place in world politics contradicts the common misconception of the mid-century period as a return to more insular, national preoccupations which only gave way to renewed globalisation in the 1980s. Reading older postcolonial writers such as Ngũgĩ, Akare, and Ghali today draws attention to socialist and communist forms of struggle that seriously challenged capitalism in the mid-century period, rendered obsolete by the 1989 end of communism and its falling out of favour in academia as in politics by the disengagement from political Marxism. Reading younger writers, such as Adichie and Hamid, update these decolonising-era concerns to the present day. Following the post-2008-crash disenchantment with capitalism, it is timely to look back on the energies of non-alignment and the search for alternatives that energised decolonial movements and early independence, which lie at the heart of postcolonial fiction and much of postcolonial studies' early theorisation. Writers in the mid-century period were necessarily influenced by the rhetoric and jargon of communism, and several writers were at various times communist, including Abrahams, Ghali, Pramoedya, Aimé Césaire, Ousmane Sembène, and New Zealand Maori writer Hone Tuwhare. The international attraction to communism, and more broadly to socialism and leftist politics, is important for understanding the energies and disillusions of the post-war era, evident in early postcolonial fiction as well as in British fiction throughout the mid-twentieth century.

In *Beer in the Snooker Club*, Ram joins the Communist Party not while he is a student in Egypt but in England, influenced by middle-class British intellectuals and unionised workers. Ghali's educated Egyptians describe themselves as 'Jimmy Porters in the Egyptian Victorian age' (20), thereby signalling synchronicity between Britain's and Egypt's mid-century 'angry young men': of disillusionment with middle-class values and the attraction of socialist ideals. Ram is impatient to discover Europe because this is where he expects to meet communist miners, fascist policemen, 'something called the "bourgeoisie" and someone called the "landlady"'; 'to win at Monte Carlo and to be down-and-out in London' (55). He reads British literary texts similarly featuring class dislocation and politicisation, including Kingsley Amis's *Lucky Jim*, George Orwell's *Down and Out in London and Paris*, and John Osborne's *Look Back in Anger*, and describes himself and his friends as 'the polished products of the English "Left," lonely and without lustre in the budding revolution of the Arab world' (20).[16] This last phrase has added contemporary relevance in light of the Arab Spring uprisings of 2010–2012, which indeed renewed interest in Ghali's work. The novel was rereleased in the UK in 2010 and has since been translated into Arabic.

Disenchanted with injustices and atrocities committed by both the British and Nasser, as both violently wrest control of wealth only to redistribute it in their favour, Ram blames his liberal idealism on the leftist political energies discovered in his four years in London:

> All this is London I told myself. All this comes of hearing Father Huddleston speak, of knowing who Rosa Luxemburg was, of seeing Gorki's trilogy in Hampstead. It comes of Donald Soper at Speaker's Corner, of reading Koestler and Alan Paton and Doris Lessing and Orwell and Wells and *La Question* and even Kenneth Tynan. Of knowing how Franco came to power and who has befriended him since, of Churchill's hundred million to squash Lenin and then later the telegram; of knowing how Palestine was given to the Jews and why ... of the bombing of Damascus and Robert Graves's *Good-bye*. (36)

Ghali lists key writers and intellectuals as well as political events that were formative in post-war European society and culture, and which gave rise to the New Left that emerged in the 1960s. Ram's internationalism is of his time, principally concerned with new and emerging forms of governance and political economy, of which class structure and socialism were openly contested issues. Ram's Britain of the early 1950s is a hotbed of heady communist, anarchist, and socialist ideals; each of these movements also supported decolonisation. In Ghali's novel, Ram joins this milieu of political engagement to join London street protests against the British military occupation of Suez, which leads him to be deported from the UK. Other novelists also point to British agitation at home against British treatment of Mau Mau nationalists in Kenya, alluded to in Akare and featured in much of Ngũgĩ's fiction and essays, and the international support against Biafra's secession, described at length in Adichie, as well as more famous movements such as the May 1968 Paris student demonstrations and widespread anti-Vietnam War rallies. The particularly postcolonial contexts of agitation in these novels are embedded in a larger context of British, American, and European public engagement with the issues of economic, political, and social inequality and injustice that shaped the post-war period.

Ram's awakening to broadly socialist concerns within the Empire's core in London is a reminder that several early postcolonial leaders developed their political philosophies from the international debates over socialism raging across Europe. Most notably, Nehru studied with Fabian and leftist economists in London, Nkrumah was involved in the Harlem Renaissance in New York and joined African revolutionary groups in London, and Aimé Césaire became a communist in Paris. Timothy Brennan further cites the importance of London as a gathering point for African American and Caribbean figures C.L.R. James, George Padmore, W.E.B. Du Bois, and Sylvester Williams, as well as for Indian reformers Rajah Rammohun

Roy, Shyamaji Krishnavarma, and Cornelia Sorabji, 'leading to the founding, on British soil, of the Indian Congress itself' (Brennan 1989, x–xi). Indeed, in a 1975 report castigating the rising tide of anti-US sentiment throughout the newly independent post-colony, the staunchly anti-communist US ambassador to India and the UN Daniel Patrick Moynihan diagnoses 'British socialism' as the pernicious root of 'Third Worldism':

> What the civil service began, British education completed. Has there ever been a conversion as complete as that of the Malay, the Ibo, the Gujarati, the Jamaican, the Australian, the Cypriot, the Guyanan, the Yemenite, the Yoruban, the sabra, the felaheen to this distant creed? The London School of Economics, Shils notes, was often said to be the most important institution of higher education in Asia and Africa. (1975, n.p.)

As well as Nkrumah and many later African leaders, London School of Economics alumni include the first president of Kenya, Jomo Kenyatta, and of Togo, Sylvanus Olympio, and Barbados's first prime minister, Errol Barrow. While Moynihan's aim is to unfavourably contrast British state interventionism with American liberalism, his argument also draws attention to the extent to which post-war Britain's new welfare socialism offered policy models for independence governments in Sub-Saharan Africa and South Asia. As Brennan argues, echoing Stuart Hall and Paul Gilroy, the presence in Britain of this significant body of intellectuals from the colonies is, 'if not the starting point, at least the most graphic occasion and opportunity for any theory of British alternative culture' (xi).

Ghali's central sequence in *Beer in the Snooker Club* of Ram's London introduction to British academic socialists and working-class communists is a reminder of the strength of these social movements in capitalist centres such as New York, Paris, and London. Britain's much-vaunted invention of the welfare state was a significant concession to socialism, in effect a '"middle way" between the extremes of laissez-faire capitalism and paternalistic communism' (Mishra 1993, 31).[17] To recall that Britain's post-war Labour government left-wing voice advocated a controlled economy with very little private capital (Joan Robinson qtd in Nasar 2012, 432), and that the USA's top individual tax rate was *reduced* to 70% during the 1950s–1970s boom period, belies these countries' later advocacy of market self-regulation under Thatcher and Regan. The high level of state intervention and social policy in the UK and USA at this time exposes the double standards of Anglo-American Cold War political pressure, trade embargoes, and military interventions against similarly left-leaning governments across the newly independent postcolonial world. The reduction of internal inequality at home corresponded to increasing inequality between home and abroad, increasing the gap between the First World and the Third World through systemic structural underdevelopment. Thus, renewed attention to the neocolonial economics of the decolonising period illuminates the continuation of colonial-era power dynamics by which the Global North continues to shape the South for its own profit. Despite the obfuscating discourse of newness surrounding decolonisation and the new post-war world order, the shift from colonial to neoliberal capitalism was a relatively smooth transition.

Internal Inequality and the Neocolonial 1%

If neocolonialism is constituted on the one side by foreign ownership, investment, and debt financing of ex-colonial nations, its other defining feature is the comprador native elite that continues colonial inequality within an independent nation-state. Fanon's early definition of neocolonialism is scathing of this local middle management, whose 'mission has nothing to do with transforming the nation; it consists, prosaically, of being the transmission line between the nation and a capitalism, rampant though camouflaged, which today puts on the masque of neocolonialism' (152). Ngũgĩ, who is perhaps the most overtly Marxist postcolonial writer and critic, brings together the two sides of external financial structures and their necessary facilitation by an internal elite. Neocolonialism, for him, is:

> [A] situation where a client indigenous government is ruling and oppressing people on behalf of American, European and Japanese capital. Such a regime acts as a policeman of international capital and often mortgages a whole country for arms and crumbs from the master's table. It never changes the colonial economy of development and uneven development. (1981, 119–120)

Ngũgĩ's 1981 definition, which he updates in his 1997 re-edition of *Writers in Politics*, is identifiable in the South African government's role of the state as 'policeman of international capital' in its condemnation of the 2012 Lonmin striking workers.

The comprador native elite that facilitates ongoing structures of colonial capitalism bears out Fanon's prescient predictions that 'nationalization quite simply means the transfer into native hands of those unfair advantages which are a legacy of the colonial period' (152). As Neil Lazarus points out, nationalist indignation at decolonising-Africa's push for self-governance as the means to owning national wealth is not directed 'at the fact of colonial capitalist exploitation, but at the fact that no indigenous class is profiting from it' (1990, 8). As Ngũgĩ puts it sarcastically, in the mouth of one of the 'modern thieves' in *Devil on the Cross*, 'how can you allow the imperialists to milk their country and yours? Don't we have people of our own who can milk the masses?' (168). This neocolonial understanding of national independence set within a larger political economy driven by globalised finance poses neither a challenge to capitalism nor aims explicitly to redress the economic inequality that has historically characterised it. Amin's study of post-independence growth in the African region indeed finds ongoing inequality: 'the fruits of growth are appropriated by between 1% and 15% of the population.... This development, described as "neocolonial," warrants the name in so far as it continues colonial exploitation and is satisfied to associate with it a local elite' (46). When Ram, in *Beer in the Snooker Club*, labels the Egyptian elite the '[l]ess than 1% of the population [who] have the urge to, can, or have to leave the country,' in comparison to the 80% of the population he claims are 'half starving' (57), Ghali, like Amin, prefigures the language of inequality percentiles made popular by Piketty and Occupy. The novelist's intuitions are borne out by historical tax data from India, South Africa, Argentina, and Indonesia, which show similar levels of inequality in these colonies as in contemporaneous Britain, with the top 1% earning around 20% of national income in the period 1910–1950 (Piketty, 326).

The difficulty of coming to grips with the term 'neocolonialism' and the new-independence period resides in the open and unresolved tensions between the desire for newness and difference conflicting with continuous structures of the political economy and the social hierarchy that maintains it. Many early postcolonial novels express alternately great pride and optimism for independence and change, and great disillusion and pessimism for the lack of change, an oscillating stance that represents the contradiction of autonomy and dependence, and the lack of concrete strategies for independent or Third Way governance. These incongruities are often embodied in an ambivalent narrator, such as in Ayi Kwei

Armah's *The Beautyful Ones Are Not Yet Born* (1968), and Chinua Achebe's *A Man of the People* (1966) and *No Longer at Ease* (1960). In *Xala*, Ousmane Sembène represents equivocating attitudes in consecutive paragraphs: '[w]hat are we? Mere agents, less than petty traders! We merely redistribute ... the remains the big men deign to leave us'; '[w]e are independent now. We are the ones who govern. ... So stop all this empty, stupid talk about foreign control' (83). This paradox, larger than the specific Senegalese context of Sembène's novel, registers in its contradiction—though fails to coherently articulate in plain words—the tendency for the global flows of capital to hide behind social and cultural explanations, expectations, and norms.

The literary focus on ongoing foreign meddling in new neocolonial nations is interwoven with a significant amount of information on the comprador elite. Novels that portray the characteristics of the rich, the ways they have made their money, and their strategies for retaining it, suggest parallels with and continuation of colonial mechanisms of wealth accumulation, including abuse of power, violence, and corruption. The protagonist of *Xala* puts it most succinctly: '[t]he colonist is stronger, more powerful than ever before, hidden inside us, here in this very place' (84). The ominous tone of this comment recalls Fanon's eloquent description of the cause of black-on-black violence in the struggles of early neocolonialism:

> For a long time, I believed that the men of Africa would not fight each other. Alas, black blood is being spilled, black men are spilling it, and it will be spilled for a long time to come. The whites are leaving, but *their accomplices are among us, armed by them*. The last battle of the colonized against the colonizers will often be that of the colonized among themselves. (Fanon qtd in Sartre, 157, my italics)

Although Fanon was speaking in the context of the Congo Civil War of the early 1960s, which removed Patrice Lumumba's Third Way vision in favour of the American-supported dictator Mobutu Sese Seko, his comment today evokes the more recent example of black-on-black violence in the Lonmin Marikana shootings.

Through narrators and protagonists who embody Sembène's colonist from within, a number of novels set during the turbulent years of early nationalism offer close studies of the internal inequality caused by a minority elite having access to a share of the foreign transfer of wealth out of the country. The lifestyle of the comprador elite often has more in common with the West than with the vast majority of its own country's inhabitants, through access to education, a house (or more than one), and bank accounts not only at home but often also in Western centres of wealth. In Ghali's novel, Ram's politicisation enables him to see the biases of his European-educated family's wealth, based on bought titles, land rent, and overseas stock-market investments. His world, he claims, is significantly different from that of the majority: '[i]t is rare, in the milieu in which I was born, to know Egyptians. ... Cairo and Alexandria were cosmopolitan not so much because they contained foreigners, but because the Egyptian born in them is himself a stranger to his land' (53). These wealthy Egyptians cannot speak Arabic and are educated in French and English schools to become the next generation of pro-European leaders 'to rule in Britain's favour' (59). Registering Ghali's condemnation of this national separation, Ram is at his most outrageous and sarcastic at the exclusive Cairo Country Club for the Egyptian elite and white foreigners. Leila Aboulela's *Minaret* (2006), which chronicles the life of the Sudanese elite before a fictional coup resembling Omar al-Bashir's 1989 takeover, similarly portrays the narrator's awareness of her inherited privilege: 'I was an aristocrat, yes, from my mother's side with a long history of acres of land and support for the British and hotels in the capital and bank accounts abroad' (37–38). In her daily circuit, from her gated luxury house to the university and back, her only connection with Sudanese workers is noticing the gardeners and gatekeepers as she looks from the window of her room, her car, and her classroom.

The ability to travel abroad is a significant symbol and feature of the wealth recorded by these characters. Ghali's narrator jokes about a clever aunt who sends money every month to a fictitious son studying in Switzerland, money she spends herself on an annual holiday in Lausanne (213). Najwa's family, in *Minaret*, spend their summer holidays in London, 'as if they had every right to be there. Money did that. Money gave us rights' (94). Money also bestows the privilege of being able to flee to England during the Egyptian revolution in *Beer in the Snooker Club*, during the Sudanese political coup in *Minaret*, and during the Nigerian civil war in *Half of a Yellow Sun*. Recounted in reproachful tones from the loyalists to Biafra who stay, Kainene and Olanna only briefly mention their rich parents fleeing to London, where they pay token donations to the Save Biafra campaign there (387), before returning at the end and bribing their high-ranking friends to forge ownership papers to take back property they owned before the war (533–534). By centring on narrators and related characters representative of the ruling class, these writers critique the mechanisms of uneven wealth accumulation that create and maintain structures of social and economic inequality.

The literary portrayal of the postcolonial elite's international cosmopolitanism recalls Fanon's class-inflected charge against 'The Pitfalls of National Consciousness' that 'the bourgeoisie does not hesitate to invest in foreign banks the profits that it makes out of its native soil' (1963, 155). His accusation is even more evident in today's extensive globalisation that takes for granted the international mobility of money and its owners, although his category 'bourgeois' is today more likely to be called an 'entrepreneur' or an 'investor.' Mobility of money and of the elite few who possess it is common throughout the history of capitalism, with the financial institutions established during the colonial era simply used by the comprador elite in a pattern of neocolonial mimicry in which the new takes after the old. The haemorrhage of profit away from its source of production and into world centres of capitalism—particularly London—for the benefit of a few is by no means restricted to the African sub-continent or to the neocolonial period. Piketty claims, in his critique of the lax laws of international money transfers, controls on its provenance, and its taxation, that '[i]n Africa, the outflow of capital has always exceeded the inflow of foreign aid by a wide margin,' a 'pillage' he pins jointly on foreign companies, overseas stockholders, and the African elite (539). Indeed, following the 2008 financial crisis's exposure of the fallibility and misconduct of large financial institutions, the international banking system has been subjected to greater scrutiny. In particular, increasing pressure on banks to release information about foreign account holders and to name the beneficial owners of shell companies, particularly since the 2016 Panama Papers leak, is directly relevant to the kind of wealth ownership depicted in postcolonial novels. Testimony to the historical practice of exporting colonial wealth to core capitalist countries, Britain and its crown dependencies and territories, along with the USA, topped the 2011 World Bank Stolen Asset Recovery list of opaque corporate ownership (van der Does de Willebois et al. 2011), and a 2010 study found that the UK was the easiest location in which to set up an offshore company without declaring the beneficial owner (Sharman 2010).

The novels analysed in this chapter offer close studies of internal dynamics between the elite and poor of the same country, while the coloniser's role remains minor, again hidden in the economic mechanisms on which the nation's finances are run. A focus on the neocolonial period, in which the dominant relationships occur within the nation, necessarily emphasises internal colonialism, thus shifting attention away from the external inequality of coloniser–colonised relations. Postcolonial fiction, written within the frame of the independent nation, portrays gross levels of internal inequality through close attention to the enormous differences in lifestyles and opportunities between the rich and the poor within the same community, culture, and nation. These same dynamics have only belatedly appeared in Western media, particularly since the 2008 crisis which brought to mainstream attention the increasing profits for the very rich amid ongoing austerity measures and stagnating wages for an increasing majority. Piketty claims that inequality 'is a far greater domestic issue than it is an international one. Inequality in the ownership of capital brings the rich and the poor within each country into conflict with one another far more than it pits one country against another' (44–45). In support, Ben Jackson and Paul Segal write, '[i]n the developed world, inequality is more important than per capita GDP in determining the living standards of the poor' (2004, 5). Looking back on the decolonising-era dynamics of internal inequality thus fits today's post-crisis focus on the gap between the rich and the poor. In amplifying the gross material differences and daily conflict between rich and poor individuals of the same community, postcolonial fiction has long been engaged in mapping the domestic structures and analysing the social and cultural repercussions of economic inequality.

The ways in which the elite makes its money in fiction set in the new-independence period models under neocolonialism the same techniques of wealth accumulation identified in the colonial period and discussed in the previous chapter. Access to capital, patronage, and useful contacts ensures that the rich stay rich and protect their interests against competition. The creation of a comprador native elite by the colonial administration and foreign trading companies is paramount, a point often emphasised by postcolonial writers. The family history Adichie gives to her central characters, Kainene and Olanna Ozobia, corroborates the historical record of colonial-era privileges bestowed on Igbo. Their father, Chief Ozobia, 'owns half of Lagos' (59), including hotels, farms, industries, and oil interests (31). Adichie only hints at the possibility that Ozobia is a warrant chief, a title bestowed by the British under the rule-from-afar colonial apparatus that used locals to act as tax collectors, a lucrative, sought-after job despite its stigma as immoral thievery (97). The position is more strongly played out in Achebe's *A Man of the People*, which juxtaposes the public's social exclusion of the comparatively minor gain-getting of Odili's father, an interpreter for the local tax collector chief, with their gullible admiration of the self-titled Chief Nanga's blatant moral and financial corruption. Sembène, in his later novel *The Last of the Empire* (1981), closely details the family background of the post-independence businessmen, bankers, and politicians who take the reins after the colonial regime. All his leaders are from wealthy families which have transferred their high rank in traditional society to that in colonial and neocolonial society. For example, the Minister of the Interior, whose aristocratic lineage dates back to the time of the first trading posts (49), and the Minister of Finance, son of a *chef de canton* under the colonial administration and 'heir to a famous name, enriched and renewed' from one generation to the next (54). The comprador mentality that Fanon identifies as '[t]he psychology of the national bourgeoisie is that of the businessman, not that of a captain of industry' (1963, 150) is most clearly represented in *Xala*'s protagonist, an opportunistic petty trader dabbling in many businesses. Fredric Jameson summarises the character as 'not an industrialist, that his business is in no sense productive, but functions as a middle-man between European multinationals and local extraction industries' (1986, 81). In such characters, all of this diverse fiction diagnoses the foundations of the new postcolonial nation as not based on production and development but on the management of already-circulating financial flows.

While the cultural contexts that engender these elite family dynasties are specific to each nation, the paths to wealth outlined in these texts are by no means unique. The global financial crisis's attention to the 1% top income and wealth strata provides a relevant frame for analysing how wealth is generated and circulated by the comprador elite of newly independent nation-states. Factors such as the faster growth of personal than national wealth (Piketty), wage stagnation (Reich 2012), and the limits of meritocratic education (Stiglitz 2015; Brown et al. 2011) identified under neoliberalism dispel the myth that increased productivity necessarily entails prosperity for all in boundless upward mobility. Rather, the statistical evidence today uncomfortably meshes with the examples in these early postcolonial novels: wealth tends to generate more wealth, inheritance is still key, and an individual's educational level and place in the job market is strongly coterminous with his or her parents' socioeconomic standing. Early postcolonial fiction mines exactly this disjunction between the popular rhetoric of opportunity celebrated during decolonisation and the ingrained inequalities experienced on the ground. When Joseph Stiglitz proclaims the American dream 'a myth reinforced by anecdotes and stories, but not supported by the data' (2012, xlv), he disconcertingly identifies a similar discord between fact and fiction in the world's richest country.

Several novels delineate the way in which neocolonial business is run, at all levels dependent on foreign currency, banks, credit, and businesses, a dependency culture particularly blatant in British and French ex-colonies, which retained the imperial currency until the late 1960s and so were reliant on the colonial core for the hard currency they needed to trade abroad. National dependence on and profit-making from global finance is evocatively illustrated in Ngũgĩ's *Devil on the Cross* and Sembène's *The Last of the Empire*, two satirical novels from the early 1980s which both name and shame these institutions' unfair lending practices and blindness to internal corruption. One of the entrepreneurial 'thieves' in Ngũgĩ's text outlines the process of a city council taking a development loan from 'the American-owned World Bank, or from European and Japanese banks, to finance the construction of cheap houses for the poor' (1982, 115–116). A slum is demolished, an Italian bank extends the credit and wins the construction contract, and the councillor pockets the bribes from prospective tenants.

Such dependence on international finance, however, is not restricted to public spending on infrastructure projects, which also benefits the intermediary brokers. Many neocolonial political economies became heavily reliant on World Bank and IMF loans for civil emergencies, such as disasters, including famine. In Sembène's *The Last of the Empire*, the Finance Minister negotiates French credit to buy the President a Boeing plane for his personal travel, 'to attract investment,' while simultaneously calling for international aid for famine relief (31). The scene illustrates how the internal political economy relies on international finance for support at both ends of the economic scale: personal loans for the richest, and disaster relief for the poorest. Giving figures to this dependency culture, Amin claims that, by the 1980s, the Sahel region paid more in debt-servicing than it earned in export of primary products (16), with three-quarters of African countries relying on foreign aid to pay for even essential imports (17; see also Mittelman 2000).

In *Xala*, Sembène's protagonist illustrates how the stratum of elite Senegalese businessmen was created. With the increasing difficulties, after independence, for foreign-owned and -operated corporations, international companies maintained their business foothold by brokering through local middlemen. Thus, El Hadji is paid 'to act as a front,' put on the board of directors of several companies (3), and entrusted as broker between import companies and the national distribution of key products, such as rice (55). Deflating the impression that these African entrepreneurs are either important or powerful, Sembène comments in an authorial aside:

> [A]ll these men who had given themselves the pompous title of 'businessmen' were nothing more than middlemen, a new kind of salesman. The old trading firms of the colonial period, adapting themselves to the new situation created by African Independence, supplied them with goods on a wholesale or semi-wholesale basis, which they then resold. (55)

By setting his novel in a context of businessmen and the politics of the Chamber of Commerce, Sembène makes a case for understanding the coloniser–colonised relationship as one of business transactions, thereby revealing the commercial motivations of empire and its neocolonial aftermath. Sembène's portrayal of Senegalese business is echoed in Ngũgĩ's *Devil on the Cross*, in a passage narrated as a neocolonial version of the Bible parable of the prodigal son, the characters recast as British 'lord' and Kenyan 'loyalist slaves and servants':

> 'My lord and master, you left me with capital of 500,000 shillings. I have doubled it.' And the lord was truly amazed, and he exclaimed, '100 per cent profit? *A fantastic rate of profit*. You have done well, you good and faithful servant. You have proved that you can be trusted with a little property. I shall now make you an overseer of many enterprises. Come and share in your lord's happiness and prosperity. I shall make you *managing director* of the local branches of my banks here and I shall appoint you a director of certain companies. You will also acquire a few *shares* in the same companies. From today I shall not let my face be too visible. You will represent me in this country.' (84, italics in original)

The bombastic biblical language combined with italicised business jargon satirises the worship of money, a critique which is intensified by the covert reference to the biblical parables of the prodigal son and the dishonest manager (Luke, 15–16) that explicitly teach against collecting interest on investment.

The structure of ownership, management, and the open expectation of profit-making expounded in Ngũgĩ's parable are far from fictional, describing the inherent inequality of the capitalist economy, in which the greatest benefits go to the owners and shareholders, with diminishing rates of return lower down the hierarchy—often from those who do proportionately more of the actual work. In counterpoint to Ngũgĩ's sharp satire, Adichie approaches the foreigner–comprador relationship from a position that accepts this unequal affiliation as mutually beneficial, portraying the social interaction between the wealthy expatriates and their elite Nigerian counterparts. Mixing in expat circles, characterised by 'mostly English, ex-colonial administrators and business people from John Holt and Kingsway and GB Ollivant and Shell-BP and United Africa Company' (53), Chief Ozobia is offered deals to sell land to expatriates at an inflated price (33) and Kainene fosters business networks with both foreign and Nigerian businessmen, meeting 'company people negotiating deals, government people negotiating bribes, factory people negotiating jobs' (78). These Senegalese, Kenyan, and Nigerian literary examples of post-independence economics illustrate how the comprador elite join and expand the existing business structures established under colonial capitalism.

The above adumbration of how fiction outlines the mechanics of transfer of capitalist structures from colonial to neocolonial hands demonstrates how postcolonial fiction can be read as corroborating the few socio-economic studies on the period dedicated to individual nations. Read together, perhaps under the category of African fiction or Heinemann publications, for example, such works expose regional economic patterns and tendencies that individual studies miss. More compellingly, however, fiction's unique perspective through characterisation shifts the focus from merely diagnosing capitalist structures and financial circuits to emphasising human interaction and the personal and social cost of unequal economic structures. Each of these novels outlines the political economy merely as background context. They are each principally concerned with representing and critiquing the compradors' exploitation of their fellow countrymen. They condemn illegal or immoral acts of internal colonialism by which characters cheat, steal, and use violence to appropriate wealth or wrest it from others. Among the multiple forms of violence caused by greed in *Xala*, El Hadji's ejection from the Senegalese Chamber of Commerce for '[u]nderhand dealings. Embezzlement. Moral harm' (83) hides an earlier theft. In the novel's climax, an unnamed homeless beggar, unnoticed and ignored by El Hadji throughout the narrative, claims retribution for being cheated and dispossessed of his land, swindled by El Hadji, who falsified the land title and used his family's money and power to bribe the courts. In a cathartic ending, El Hadji is humiliated by the poor, who spit on him and speak their grievances: '[p]eople like you live on theft,' 'exploit the poor,' and have built wealth 'by cheating. You and your colleagues build on the misfortunes of honest, ordinary people' (100). In giving voice to those characters who have been literally stepped over and pushed aside throughout the narrative, Sembène quite literally speaks truth to power.

Adichie's liberal sociologist, Olanna, articulates the same injustice when she finds her mother humiliating a servant for stealing a handful of rice to feed his family:

> My father and his politician friends steal money with their contracts, but nobody makes them kneel to beg for forgiveness. And they build houses with their stolen money and rent them out to people like this man and charge inflated rents that make it impossible to buy food. (221)

Subjected to the common problematic of low wages and high rent, the servant is caught in the poverty trap and risks falling further if he loses his precarious job. Although Olanna finishes by posing a rhetorical question, 'does inequality have to mean indignity?' (221), the example seems to provide an affirmative answer. Narrating the incident through Olanna, a British-educated sociologist, allows Adichie to align her reader with the narrator's Western judgement that condemns social inequality as an aberration of the human-rights discourse that assumes basic human equality. From this point of view, Adichie invests great power in words, in naming injustice and speaking up on behalf of the servant. However, actual solutions rather than verbal platitudes are thin on the ground, and Olanna's own complicity with and role in Nigeria's elite remains, problematically, unexplored.

Similar stories of the rich wielding their influence to punish those lower on the social scale frequently occur in postcolonial novels as anecdotes or background information that establish the pervasiveness of inequality within which the narrative takes place. *Beer in the Snooker Club* adumbrates multiple efforts by the rich to maintain their wealth and prestige at the expense of the poor. Ram's rich aunt sells off a million pounds' worth of land to small landowners before it can be nationalised, ostensibly gifting it to the fellaheen tenants who work it, 'selling cheap and pretending to the government she was giving the land to the poor' (13). Ram's wealthy family continually search for new ways to extract money from their fellaheen tenants (169), while another rich merchant has a fellah imprisoned for having a relationship with his daughter (107–108). In *Minaret*, Najwa recalls her Ethiopian maid was fired for receiving a gift from her (48), a situation of unfair dismissal later repeated when Najwa, now herself maid to a wealthy Sudanese family in London, is fired for falling in love with her employer's son (264). The postcolonial narrative perspective that aligns the reader's sympathy with the victims of such injustice critiques the rich persecution of the poor to varying degrees, from open chastisement, as in Olanna confronting her mother, to latent parallels of character experience, as in Aboulela's text. The narrative power of these critiques is, however, mitigated as such storylines play a minimal role, existing as short anecdotes while the dramatic focus remains on the complex character studies of Ram's and Najwa's conflicted identities, and, in *Half of a Yellow Sun*, on the psychological and physical ravages of war.

The form of internal colonialism that gains the most publicity in discourse about development is not the insidious, small-scale expressions of inequality that largely go unnoticed and unprosecuted, but the more visible and blatant corruption. Certainly, many novels about decolonisation portray instances of financial and political corruption among the comprador elite. Broaching this topic exposes a tension between fiction's ability to identify and critique injustice, yet its difficulty in performing narrative scenarios that respond to or resolve corruption. This problematic, however, may have more to do with the contradictions of capitalism than any assumed clash in fiction between the real and the imagined. In *Half of a Yellow Sun*, Adichie portrays Kainene as nonchalant towards corrupt practices, such as paying bribes, appealing to Igbo favouritism to deal only with other Igbo (81), donating money to the Biafran government to ensure preference for later contracts (180), and 'profiteering from the war' as a supply contractor (343). Several African writers diagnose the epicentre of national underdevelopment as residing in lack of leadership, often symbolically characterised in fiction by corrupt politicians and details of election rigging, perhaps best illustrated by Ngũgĩ's *Wizard of the Crow*. Achebe, for example, in his collection of essays *The Trouble with Nigeria* (1983), claims the lack of leadership as the reason that Nigeria is 'disorderly,' 'corrupt,' and 'inefficient' (9): 'Nigerians are what they are only because their leaders are *not* what *they* should be' (10, italics in original). Achebe illustrates his claim in his fiction in the character of Chief Nanga in *A Man of the People*, who engages in profit-skimming at every level, from cheating his constituents to brokering deals with foreign companies.

The issue of corruption offers a clear example of the neocolonial difficulty of accounting for the continuity of unequal colonial capitalism under the guise of independence. In each of the above texts, the writers condemn Western stereotypes about African cultures as pre-modern, 'living according to feudal customs,' negligent, incompetent (Sembène 1976, 82), and 'not quite so ready to rule themselves after all' (Adichie, 53). In these citations, economic failure is again construed in racist terminology, as argued in Chap. 2. Although such aspersions on the national character are often written with irony or personified in unsympathetic characters, the writer's acknowledgement of these internalised colonial cultural judgements generates considerable discomfort in the text and in the reader. The writers all take a critical stance against such injustice. The novels work hard to expose the moral reprehensibility of corruption and thereby refute the inferred undesirable cultural traits such as backwardness and barbaric unfairness. Olanna chides her sister for her lack of scruples; the curse of impotence on El Hadji and his expulsion from the Chamber of Commerce are satisfying punishments for his greed; and Armah's *The Beautyful Ones Are Not Yet Born*, Achebe's *A Man of the People*, and Ngũgĩ's *Devil on the Cross* are simultaneously poignant and excoriating for their protagonists' defeat at the hands of the corrupt. And yet, from an economic perspective, attacking corruption with recourse to morality and culture fails to engage with the root of the problem: like racism, corruption is endemic to capitalism, not to any particular culture or political regime.

Corruption is found in both highly regulated economies, such as in China, and in overly deregulated states: in both the UK and the USA, corporate corruption has increased dramatically under neoliberalism (Neild 2002; Stiglitz 2003), as publicised following the 2008 financial crisis, as well as in developing nations (Chang 2007, 167–181). Corruption also occurs across the economic scale, practised by the poor in the absence of welfare services and a living wage, and by the rich in countries where government and the judiciary turn a blind eye to white-collar corruption. For economists George Akerlof and Robert Shiller, corruption is a natural element of capitalism: '[i]f we wish to understand the functioning of the economy, and its animal spirits, we must also understand the economy's sinister side—the tendencies toward antisocial behaviour and ... economic activity that, while technically legal, has sinister motives' (2009, 26). The fickle social barometer of acceptability ensures that the shape of corruption, its names, and its disguises continually change. The propensity, however, is always there. David Harvey is even more forthright in his insistence that there is no structural difference between legal and illegal means of accumulating profit: 'I think it is time we overthrew this convenient but profoundly misleading fiction promoted by the economics textbooks and recognise the symbiotic relation between these two forms of appropriation' (2014, 53). Empirically, illegal parts of the economy, including the informal economy, undeclared labour, cartels, monopolies, trafficking, and insider trading, play significant roles in world trade, although they are often ignored in policy and omitted from official statistics and financial calculations.

Corruption, such as embezzlement, money laundering, bribery, fraud, insider trading, informal inducements, and tax evasion, is coterminous with the history of capitalism. Just as the current neoliberal promotion of low trade tariffs forgets the importance of a long history of protectionist tariffs practiced by the now-core capitalist countries, discussed in the previous chapter, the contemporary definitions of and attitudes toward corruption conceal its usefulness in advancing economic interests. Ha-Joon Chang's study of eighteenth- to-twentieth-century British and American corruption illustrates the long history of public–private and political–commercial entanglements. He documents the use of political power for promoting and facilitating business deals, bribery, and vote-buying in the electoral process, and the use of insider knowledge for stock-market speculation to argue that economic development is not dependent on clean governance. Chang does not condone corruption, but surmises it is typical of early economic development, and featured as much in the history of now-developed countries as it currently does in developing nations. As the predisposition to corruption thus appears common to capitalism—a point which indicates the desirability of state intervention to mediate market tendencies—he argues that penalising developing countries for practices common throughout economic history is unfair. The World Bank, for example, punishes developing nations with high levels of corruption by reducing aid (2007, 161), and the naming and shaming of the annual publication of the Transparency Index discourages investment from those countries lower on the list.

Chang gives two examples of historical corruption that are striking to today's readers for the openness with which famous politicians acknowledge and accept the presence of corrupt practices. Accused of corruption in 1730, the first British prime minister, Robert Walpole, defended the sale of public offices and the use of public funds to acquire personal property: 'having held some of the most lucrative offices for nearly 20 years, what could anyone expect, unless it was a crime to get estates by great office' (2007, 162). In the early 1880s, US statesman Theodore Roosevelt 'lamented that the New York assemblymen, who engaged in the open selling of votes to lobbying groups, 'had the same idea about Public Life and Civil Service that a vulture has of a dead sheep' (163). Akerlof and Shiller offer neoliberal-era examples of the same, claiming in regard to the US recessions of 1990–1991, the dotcom crash of 2001, and the 2008 sub-prime crisis, that '[e]ach of the past three economic contractions in the United States ... involved corruption scandals ... and its lesser counterpart, bad faith' (29–30). While the site of corruption has shifted to the finance industry, today's shady deals share with those of the past corporate influence in politics, the strong public personalities of fraudsters,[18] and the aggressive or predatory targeting of the poor and uninformed.

Set alongside these historical and contemporary examples of corruption from developed nations, the African examples read as typical rather than exceptional. Achebe's indignant stance against President Awolowo's forthright proclamation 'to make all the money that is possible for a man with my brains and brawn to make in Nigeria' (Booth qtd in Achebe 1983, 11), and Armah's negative judgement that a school official 'regarded his job as an opportunity he had won for making as much money as he could as quickly as he could' (109), are misplaced. These fictional and real entrepreneurs are merely articulating the point of capitalist accumulation, using the means made available to them to achieve the maximum profit possible. Certainly, corruption is damaging and undesirable, but its historical presence displaces the culture-centred argument which contains negative stereotypes about the capacity of underdeveloped nations to progress, commonly deploying the same racist aspersions as those discussed on an individual level in the previous chapter. As Chang argues, the common development-discourse stance that corruption hinders economic growth is often used as an excuse for the failure of neocolonial and latterly neoliberal capitalist policies. Rather, he claims, Third World development strategies and policies 'have failed because they were wrong, not because they have been overwhelmed by local anti-developmental factors, like corruption or "wrong" culture' (161). Having survived the shift from colonial to independent national structures of governance, the ongoing presence of corruption is a litmus test indicating the successful crossover of capitalism from past to present.

SATIRE AS RESPONSE TO CAPITALISM'S CONTRADICTIONS

The difficulties and disappointments of decolonisation and its aftermath, of ongoing poverty alongside the increasing visibility of great wealth in those nations, underpin the West's perception of postcolonial developing nations as different from the developed capitalist core countries. The tendency to label the causes of the gap between the First and Third Worlds as cultural, social, and the fault of poor leadership indicates the hidden mechanisms of capitalist maldevelopment that further forgets the similar histories of uneven and unfair economic development in the West. The impression of instability in developing regions similarly contributes to the discourse of difference, while forgetting the role of Western interference in creating that instability, which includes financial and military support of undemocratically chosen leaders, including dictators. Whereas capitalist core nations grew into capitalism and democratic nationhood over several hundred years, which were marked by great turbulence, revolutions, famines, imperial expansionist as well as civil wars, pogroms, and radical policy about-turns, the process forced by decolonisation has been compressed into mere decades. Splitting developing-world history into two seemingly discrete phases of before and after independence divorces postcolonial nations from the *longue durée* world interconnectivity of the first (colonial) and second (neoliberal) eras of globalisation. This split makes it difficult to account for underdevelopment as an integral, necessary part of global capitalism, or to imagine any way forward except by following the formula practiced by the capitalist core countries.

The voice of impasse is common to commentators on the African situation in particular. Following Fanon's poignant essay, 'La mort de Lumumba: Pouvions nous faire autrement?' (1961), Sartre expresses disappointment, anger, frustration, and sadness at the failure of Lumumba's ambitions to achieve Congolese independence from the Belgian Empire in a unified, anti-tribal, centralised nation. He reflects on the reasons for Lumumba's failure, deposed by a coup from his own party, imprisoned, and executed:

> He was unaware that the old mother countries wished to entrust nominal power to 'natives' who would govern, more or less consciously, according to colonial interests. ... He wished to give back to the subhumans of colonial exploitation their native humanity. Of course, this could not be done without a reworking of all the structures: his training prevented him from seeing this. ... The important thing, at any rate, was that he placed his class in power and then set about governing against it. Could it have been any different? No: during the last years of colonization, the proletariat did not do a single thing that would have made these petty bourgeois accept it as a valid interlocutor. (175–176)

Sartre's review of Congolese politics summarises the tensions of neocolonial dependency explored in this chapter. Although his communist-inflected terminology of the 'proletariat' and 'petty bourgeois' today reads as outdated, his distressed tone is compelling in that it registers the difficulty of imagining, to paraphrase Fanon, how history could have played out differently: of what, exactly, 'a reworking of all the structures' would entail, and around what the (undefined) proletariat would rally. The geopolitical pressure from foreign interest groups (Belgium, Britain, the USA, and the USSR) casts further doubt on the power of a more astute Lumumba or better-organised proletariat to effectuate change.

In more familiar postcolonial language, Lazarus expresses similar disappointment in the context of early Ghanaian independence portrayed in Armah's novel *The Beautyful Ones Are Not Yet Born*:

> I remember being haunted by the question [Armah] asked in the middle of chapter 6: 'How long will Africa be cursed with its leaders?' ... He was already beginning to compare the post-independence leaders with the older collaborationist or elitist forms of leadership that he saw as being the blight of the continent—and that was very difficult for me to get my head around. In the anti-apartheid movement in South Africa the future was always viewed in a very positive sense, and yet here was a writer from elsewhere on the continent who was arguing that the future had come and that it was a graveyard. (Gunne 2012, 1)

3 NEOCOLONIALISM   141

Referring to early postcolonial texts by Armah, Ngũgĩ, and Achebe, Lazarus finds 'a widespread sense that the great expectations of independence, as I called them, had been replaced with the morning/mourning after' (1). Lazarus reiterates Sartre's frustration with the great gap between the positive ambitions of the independence movement and the disappointing outcomes of neocolonialism. Both commentators lament the inability—of themselves as much as of African leaders and writers—to anticipate the problems and conflicts independence would bring, the most pressing of which was in underestimating the shaping influence of foreign geopolitics and of capitalism itself.

While Sartre's comment, published in 1964, and Lazarus's thoughts during the anti-apartheid movement of the 1970s, might appear to mark historical moments, as late as 2005 Nicholas Brown censures the same cluster of problems in a voice that similarly betrays frustration and sadness:

> In the light of the general squalor and disappointment of the neocolonial situation, where nominal political independence masks a crippling economic dependence and a crushing subservience to the demands of the First-World-dominated multinational capital, and when mainstream economists can paint a rosy picture of the world system only by finding excuses for leaving Africa out of the reckoning altogether, is there any way to conceive contemporary African history in a way that does not contribute to the very cynicism and disappointment that characterize much of contemporary African literature's representational raw material? (2005, 150)

Posed as a question, Brown, like Sartre and Lazarus and the African leaders and writers they discuss, is no closer to suggesting a way out of the impasse. Furthermore, Brown suggests, the economists are similarly stuck. Speaking in 2012, Lazarus's 'haunted' consciousness of the postcolonial paradox continues to inform his understanding of 'the unbroken project' of imperialism from the nineteenth century until today (Gunne, 10).

Each of these quotes is evocative and emotional, registering the author's own frustrations, a sense of powerlessness and an inability to suggest—to think of—Africa differently. This incoherence, however, describes not only African economic history since the mid-twentieth century and its representations in literary fiction. The difficulty of conceptualising capitalism as anything other than structured by the inequality of combined and uneven development through accumulation by dispossession is of pressing concern to present-day thinkers, writers, and critics of neoliberalism. The question of how to think outside of capitalist social relations is of global concern, with the difficulty of doing so played out in the utter discombobulation of European, British, and American politics (particularly the left) and its representation in the media in 2016. Faced with increasingly blatant media lies and policy contradictions that have recently been labelled the era of 'post-truth,' farce and satire rise to the surface.

In his influential essay 'Third-World Literature in the Era of Multinational Capitalism' (1986), Jameson discusses African literary uses of satire to expose and comment on capitalism's debasement of pre-contact cultural traditions and its suppression of any other guiding principle with which to organise social relations. For Jameson, the dilemma of 'bearing a passion for change and social regeneration which has not yet found its agents' is also:

> ... an aesthetic dilemma, a crisis of representation: it was not difficult to identify an adversary who spoke another language and wore the visible trappings of colonial occupation. When those are replaced by your own people, the connections to external controlling forces are much more difficult to represent.... One is led to conclude that under these circumstances traditional realism is less effective than the satiric fable. (81–82)

No longer overtly controlled by an external power with clear-cut roles of exploiter and exploited, novelists are faced with the difficulty of criticising victimisation from within. This is also the difficulty of revealing the hidden structures of economic inequality which underlie forms of exploitation integrated into and accepted by social and cultural norms.

Caught in a bind of intellectual awareness yet constrained by relative political powerlessness, many postcolonial writers of neocolonialism offer satire as a mitigated form of critique, which is directed as much at their own ideals and those of other middle-class liberals as those of society at large. Satire, indeed, is a common mode of postcolonial expression, a wittier version of the pathos of victimhood conveyed in the great body of work written as social realism. As a discordant mismatch with reality, satire embodies discomfort, frustration, antagonism, conflict, and a sense of hopelessness—those same sentiments expressed melancholically by Sartre, Lazarus, and Brown. Faced with inconsolable gaps in development, in social discourse, and in literary representation, satire has emerged as a common mode through which to expose and criticise the excesses and privations of economic inequality. Farce exposes and castigates capitalism's contradictions, illustrating in its focus, form, and function the same tendency that Harvey finds in contemporary neoliberal responses: there is 'no such thing as a non-contradictory response to a contradiction' (2014, 279). Confused, vacillating, inconsistent, comedic, satirical, and wildly imaginative responses to economic injustices and inequalities appear not only in fiction but also in many recent critiques of neoliberalism in the past decade, a *rapprochement* between two forms of discourse both attempting to make sense of a naturalised economic system that is as difficult to define as it is to think outside of.

African neocolonial- and neoliberal-era satires that turn into farce capitalism's contradictions and hypocrisies join a long history of satire as response to economic inequality. In eighteenth-century England, Walpole's public flaunting of corruption was the target of fictional satires, in Daniel Defoe's pamphlets, Jonathan Swift's *Gulliver's Travels*, and Gay's *The Beggar's Opera* (1728). Bertolt Brecht and Kurt Weill's *The Threepenny Opera* (1928) updates Gay's work to a socialist critique of the Roaring Twenties, and Soyinka's version of it, *Opera Wonyosi* (1981), attacks political corruption amid Nigeria's oil boom. As a literary form of historical periodicity, satire illuminates the international breadth and historical longevity of the capitalist world-system, along with its sustained critique, constant across time and space. Study of the intertextuality between the three operas offers a literary map of socio-economic inequality at key periods of concentrated wealth and widespread immiseration. Brecht's famous line, 'What is the burgling of a bank to the founding of a bank?' (Act III:iii, 222) is thus reformulated to suit different contexts. Soyinka rephrases it in the last lines of *Opera Wonyosi*: 'What we must look for is the real beneficiary/Who does it profit? ... Who really accumulates and exercises/Power over others?' (83). In the wake of the 2008 financial crisis, Brecht's play has enjoyed a revival on the German stage, with theatre reviews consistently referencing the play's timeliness.

Soyinka's use of earlier eras of economic inequality that he feels chime with his local and specific Nigerian context exemplifies textual inter-reference common in other postcolonial satires. In 'Africa Kills Her Sun' (1989), another Nigerian writer, Ken Saro-Wiwa, links colonial to neocolonial relations and white to black violence. The narrator likens his fellow death-row robbers to European heroes of colonial endeavour—'[i]n another time and in another country, they'd be Sir Francis Drake, Cortés or Sir Walter Raleigh. They'd have made empires and earned national honours' (216)—as well as to Nigeria's postcolonial leaders: 'Sazan would have made a good Army General any day, possibly a President of our country, in the mold of Idi Amin or Bokassa' (215). Scale is the salient difference between the robbers fêted as national heroes and those killed before a firing squad: the poor narrator is a criminal on death row, whereas the government official who steals seven million naira goes unpunished (215). The story is all the more effective for its self-deprecating tone of gentle parody rather than the pathos of poignancy or rage of searing indictment. Outside of the text, Saro-Wiwa's arrest and 1995 execution, a response to government pressure by petro-giant Royal Dutch Shell, gives lie to the fictional medium in which he writes. If money speaks louder than words, as Saro-Wiwa himself claims in his short story, then Shell's 2009 multimillion-dollar settlement of a court case against them for human-rights violations pertaining to the execution of activists, including Saro-Wiwa, is adequate testimony of the company's acknowledged complicity.

Saro-Wiwa's claim that '[i]n every facet of our lives—in politics, in commerce, and in the professions—robbery is the base line' (217), like Brecht's line on the foundational principles of banking or Gay's professional thief, Macheath, indicts a system that is inherently unequal and unfair. Both Brecht's and Saro-Wiwa's stories highlight the injustice of this inequality by portraying disproportionate punishment of crimes by the poor, while white-collar criminals are fêted as empire-builders (Saro-Wiwa) or upstanding members of society (Brecht). The indictment is even clearer in Gay's original opera, in the character of Bob Booty, a thinly disguised Robert Walpole, who is portrayed as a customer and friend of Peachum and Macheath's criminal syndicate. Peachum offers a wry yet apt summary: '[a] rich Rogue now-a-days is fit Company for any Gentleman; and the World, my Dear, hath not such a contempt for Roguery as you imagine' (Act I:i, 17). Making the colonial aspect of the period's unethical money-making even clearer, Gay's sequel, *Polly* (1729) is set in the West Indies.

The blatancy of the unfair and often illegal practices that have generated great wealth is a rich seam mined by parody and farce. Satire deploys the fantastic and the hyperbolic to mark a break between fiction and reality, offering preposterous scenarios that could not possibly happen. And yet, breaking down this assumed divide, Achebe, in his collection of essays *The Trouble with Nigeria*, offers multiple newspaper examples of similarly outrageous, highly creative corruption scandals that suggest truth is stranger than fiction. On the playbill for *Opera Wonyosi*, Soyinka twists the usual caveat of fictionality to claim the opposite: 'the characters in this opera are either strangers or fictitious, for Nigeria is stranger than fiction, and that any resemblance to any Nigerian living or dead, is purely accidental, unintentional and instructive' (Lindfors 1981, 31).

Similarly showing that often the truth of the past can only be imagined as fiction in the present, New Zealand Maori writer Patricia Grace writes in the satirical mode a contemporary update of colonial-era land theft. Her short story 'Ngati Kangaru' (1994), a wordplay on 'kangaroo' referring to the Maori living in Australia, depicts a Maori business initiative to bring home impoverished relatives living in Australia by settling them on underused land. As in many of the novels analysed in this chapter, as well as in the above-mentioned satires, Grace centralises an anti-heroic protagonist whose seriousness about his dubious profession generates the parody through which to critique the 'robbery' of capitalist appropriation. Billy, an unemployed Maori, reads the history of the New Zealand Company: '[o]ut-and-out crooks, liars, cheats and thieves, these Wakefields. He felt inspired' (Sect. 1, para 6). Aided by his un- and underemployed family, Billy applies Wakefield's colonial techniques in the 1990s, repossessing empty luxury waterfront holiday homes to resettle Maori who have failed to prosper in Australia and who want to come home. The force of Grace's satire is located in her appropriation of early settlement reasoning for the purposes of reverse colonisation: '[i]t's a "wasteland." They're waste homes. They're all unoccupied. ... "Reclaiming and cultivating a moral wilderness," that's what we're doing, "serving to the highest degree" that's what we're on about, "according to a deliberate and methodical plan"' (Sect. 4, para 1). The *terra nullius* argument of colonial settlement is here repurposed to reference the moral wasteland of capitalist accumulation for no social use function.

In Grace's modern-day setting, the wealthy absentee landlords rather than the financially marginalised Maori are cast as the inferior people requiring re-education: 'they're simple people who know nothing about how to fully utilise their properties and they can "scarcely cultivate the earth." But who knows they might have a "peculiar aptitude for being improved." It's "high and holy work," this' (Sect. 5, para 9). In paraphrasing and quoting Wakefield's language in the mouths of 'geezers,' 'derros,' and 'park benchers'—the losers and homeless who populate the contemporary inner city recruited for the project—Grace's reverse colonisation is as much linguistic as land based, debasing colonial bombast by housing it in a Maori idiom shared by all the story's active agents. Thus, as well as a damning critique of exorbitant inequality between the rich who own empty beach-front holiday houses and the poor who live in crowded state housing or sleep on the streets, Grace normalises and heroises Maori cultural norms of community and sharing. While the gesture is certainly symbolically empowering, it remains distanced from expectations of realism by the satiric mode. As farce, the Maori cultural precepts that reject capitalist values and offer a practical solution to Auckland's current housing crisis remain in the realm of wishful thinking.

The use of historical inter-reference by the above writers connects colonial to neocolonial and neoliberal examples of the contradictions of autonomy and dependence that are constitutive of capitalism itself. The farcical Chamber of Commerce meeting in *Xala*, cited earlier, reads as parody because the characters seem unaware of the contradictions they tout, posturing alternately as powerful and powerless to protect their self-interest. The neocolonial Senegalese scene resonates with the similar hypocrisy expressed with such earnestness by the colonial-era opium traders in Ghosh's *River of Smoke*, quoted at length in the previous chapter. At the Chamber of Commerce meeting to discuss the crisis of the Chinese embargo on opium, the traders expound the virtues of the free market while calling for British military support to force this so-called freedom, and lambast the Chinese for being alternately child-like imbeciles and shrewd businessmen.

Crisis situations, such as those portrayed in Sembène's and Ghosh's novels, expose many levels of contradictions inherent to capitalist business structure, exposed by critics of neoliberalism in texts including Chang's *Twenty-Three Things They Don't Tell You about Capitalism*, Terry Eagleton's *Why Marx Was Right*, and Harvey's *Seventeen Contradictions and the End of Capitalism*. The alternating bull and bear market confidence and jerky flows of supply and demand lead to radical ups and downs in cyclical booms and busts that are mirrored in equally schizophrenic social, cultural, and political attitudes and positions. Wall Street even has a way to measure investor confidence, in the volatility predictor known as the 'fear index.' The inconsistencies constitutive of the free market create instability and lead to crisis, which the 2008 financial meltdown and its subsequent return to business as usual for the financial institutions and the increasing profits of the super-rich reveal have not been resolved or tamed. Satire registers the human dimension of the boom-and-bust, wave-like, or cyclical economic volatility of the market, capturing the psychology of capitalism which is everywhere riven by contradictions.

Responses to the 2008 financial crisis similarly take a disbelieving, farcical tone when describing incidences of exorbitant greed, crass materialism, and shady, corrupt, and illegal practices. In several pop-economics books, the incredulous, often mocking tone of neoliberal absurdity is tellingly similar to African satires on the blatant lies of neocolonial misrule. Chrystia Freeland begins her book about conspicuous consumption, *Plutocrats: The Rise of the New Global Super Rich* (2012), with an anecdote from guests at a dinner party who lament the problem of having an annual income of 20 million dollars: '"You know, the thing about twenty is ... twenty is only ten [after taxes]." And everyone at the table is nodding' (2).[19] Michael Lewis, in *Boomerang: Travels in the New Third World* (2011), portrays as outrageous, even ridiculous, supposedly authoritative figures of the financial crisis. These include Texan rancher and provincial hedge-fund manager Kyle Bass, who predicted both the sub-prime crash and the fiscal collapse of Iceland and Greece; the Icelandic fisherman turned untrained hedge-fund manager overnight; and the Greek government insiders who openly tell the journalist about the creative accounting and 'epidemic of lying, cheating and stealing' that masked Greek debt (55). In the humorously titled *Griftopia: Bubble Machines, Vampire Squids, and the Long Con That Is Breaking America* (2011), journalist Matt Taibbi uses bad language and colourful imagery to lampoon tycoons, politicians, and institutions such as Goldman Sachs, which he describes as 'a great vampire squid wrapped around the face of humanity' (209). In a chapter entitled 'The Biggest Asshole in the Universe,' detailing Alan Greenspan's career, Taibbi explores the absurdity of appointing a life-long promoter of laissez-faire state non-intervention to head the nation's most powerful regulatory body, the US Federal Reserve. David Graeber, in *Debt: The First 5000 Years* (2011), calls the IMF 'the world's debt enforcers,' 'the high-finance equivalent of the guys who come to break your legs' (2). Jordan Belfort, author of *The Wolf of Wall Street* (2007), subtitles his memoir 'Stock Market Millionaire at 26, Federal Convict at 36, I Partied like a Rock Star, Lived like a King, and Barely Survived My Rise and Fall as an American Entrepreneurial Icon.' In foregrounding sex, drugs, and orgiastic parties,

Belfort's memoir reads so much like fiction that many viewers of its 2013 film version, starring Leonardo DiCaprio in another Gatsby-like role as conspicuous consumer, are unaware it is based on fact. In the face of such texts' revelations of absurd behaviour and outlandish actions, Achebe's early comment in his essays that '[o]ne of the commonest manifestations of underdevelopment is a tendency among the ruling elite to live in a world of make-believe' (1983, 9) takes on a global resonance. While unethical and duplicitous practices might be easier to see in underdeveloped nations, illusion, it would appear, is endemic to the global rich everywhere. Whether applied to fact or fiction, satire mines these disjunctions.

Notes

1. Data compared against other nations ranked by Gini coefficient based on 2011 statistics collated in the World Bank's 2014 'Development Indicators: Distribution of Income or Consumption.'
2. 2011 statistics according to the World Bank's relative poverty measures.
3. Piketty, 39–40; Martin Plaut, 'South Africa's Lonmin Marikana mine clashes killed 34' (2012); Justice Malala, 'The Marikana action is a strike by the poor against the state and the haves' (2012).
4. See Lonrho company website.
5. The role of London as centre of both colonial and financial world trade is discussed in Chap. 4.
6. See the Marikana Commission of Inquiry.
7. Statistics from the Australian Bureau of Statistics. See also Anne Garnett, 'Australia's "five pillar economy"': mining' (2015).
8. In November 2010, explosions at Pike River in New Zealand killed 29 miners in a private coal mine on a gaseous seam already responsible for three previous disasters in 1896, 1926, and 1967. The ensuing investigation found the mine lacked several safety features and had ignored earlier safety breaches, under pressure from management to increase output in the face of company deficit and low returns during the global financial crisis. The government was indicted for lack of safety regulations, inspection, and monitoring, as such services had been progressively rolled back since market deregulation in the 1980s. The company's ensuing bankruptcy and the lack of corporate manslaughter laws in New Zealand have meant very little compensation for miners' families. Meanwhile, the coal seam, like the site of the 1967 disaster, continues to burn underground, in a long-term ecological disaster. See Rebecca Macfie, *Tragedy at Pike River Mine: How and Why 29 Men Died* (2013).

9. In fact, the idea that a company's only responsibility is to its shareholders and profit rather than to society as a whole is relatively recent, expressed in the 1970s by Milton Friedman, one of the most influential exponents of laissez-faire liberalism that came to dominate political economy from the 1980s.
10. British investment in white-settler colonies such as Australia, New Zealand, and Canada, mostly in mines, natural resources, and trade infrastructure, was also around 20% in 1910 (Piketty, 157). For more specific data on African industry, agriculture, and development in the post-independence years, see Barratt Brown, *The Economics of Imperialism*, 266–272; on the Sahel region, see Amin, *Maldevelopment*, 36–46; and on Mozambique, see James Mittelman, *The Globalization Syndrome: Transformation and Resistance*.
11. The IMF and World Bank were established during the Bretton Woods Agreement of 1944. The WTO, founded in 1994, is a revamped form of the earlier General Agreement on Tariffs and Trade (GATT), founded in 1947.
12. In particular, Walden Bello argues that, from the 1970s, private banks awash with petro-dollars invested in Third World loans because there was little demand for credit in their home economies (Chap. 3, Sect. 2).
13. Piketty argues that this drop in internal inequality is an exception in the history of capitalism, caused by the loss of wealth by the rich due to the 1929 crash and two world wars, and the concomitant rise of the poor to create a large middle class that had never existed before, due to the invention of the welfare state and strong government regulation that more evenly distributed the profits of the dynamic growth period of the 1950s–1970s (11–17).
14. Long subject to unequal treaties with Britain and France (Chomsky, *World Orders Old and New*, 116–118), in the 1920s Britain foreclosed on the loans to the puppet Egyptian monarchy so that Egypt owned no part of the Suez Canal it had become indebted to build. See Rosa Luxemburg, *The Accumulation of Capital*, 429–439, and Sylvia Nasar, *Grand Pursuit*, 179–184.
15. On wealth and worth in Ghali, see Annie Gagiano, *Dealing with Evils: Essays on Writing from Africa* (2014, 249–257).
16. For analysis of Ghali's interpretation of the British 'Angry Young Men' movement, see Deborah Starr, 'Drinking, Gambling, and Making Merry: Waguih Ghali's search for cosmopolitan agency' (2006, 275).
17. On Britain's significant socialist movements, see Selina Todd, *The People: The Rise and Fall of the Working Class, 1910–2010* (2014).
18. In the three recent crises, personalities include Michael Milken in 1990 (junk bonds); Enron executives in 2001 (see Akerlof and Shiller, 30–36);

and in 2008 Bernie Madoff's Ponzi scheme and Stephen Green's leadership of HSBC, charged with money-laundering and tax avoidance.
19. Another example of a writer with a strong economics background, Freeland was deputy editor of the *Financial Times* and is currently the Canadian Minister of International Trade.

Works Cited

Primary

Abrahams, Peter. *Mine Boy*. Oxford: Heinemann, 1989 [1946].
Aboulela, Leila. *Minaret*. London: Bloomsbury, 2006.
Achebe, Chinua. *A Man of the People*. Oxford: Heinemann Educational, 1988 [1966].
———. *No Longer at Ease*. Oxford: Heinemann Educational, 1987 [1960].
———. *The Trouble with Nigeria*. Oxford: Heinemann, 1983.
Adichie, Chimamanda Ngozi. *Half of a Yellow Sun*. London: Fourth Estate, 2006.
Akare, Thomas. *The Slums*. London: Heinemann, 1981.
Armah, Ayi Kwei. *The Beautyful Ones Are Not Yet Born*. Oxford: Heinemann Educational, 1968.
Bahadur, Sanjay. *The Sound of Water*. New York: Atria, 2009.
Belfort, Jordan. *The Wolf of Wall Street*. New York: Bantam, 2007.
Brecht, Bertolt, and Kurt Weill. *The Threepenny Opera*, in *Three German Plays*. Harmondsworth: Penguin, 1963 [1928].
Gay, John. *The Beggar's Opera and Polly*. Oxford, UK: Oxford World's Classics, 2013 [1728, 1729].
Ghali, Waguih. *Beer in the Snooker Club*. London: Serpent's Tail, 1987 [1964], Kindle Edition.
Grace, Patricia. 'Ngati Kangaru,' in *Sky People*. Auckland: Penguin, 1994, Kindle Edition.
Habila, Helon. *Oil on Water*. Harmondsworth: Penguin, 2011.
Hamid, Mohsin. *The Reluctant Fundamentalist*. Harmondsworth: Penguin, 2008.
Llewellyn, Richard. *How Green Was My Valley*. London: Penguin Classics, 2001 [1939].
Ngũgĩ wa Thiong'o. *Devil on the Cross*. Oxford: Heinemann, 1982 [1980].
———. *Weep Not, Child*. Oxford: Heinemann, 1987 [1964].
O'Carroll, Sarah. 'Australia is too Expensive for Business Says Gina Rinehart,' September 5, 2012, http://www.news.com.au/finance/business/australia-is-too-expensive-for-business-rinehart/story-fndalbsz-1226465315817. 3 January, 2017.

Saro-Wiwa, Ken. 'Africa Kills Her Sun' [1989], in *Under African Skies: Modern African Stories*. Ed. Charles Larson. New York: Farrar, Straus and Giroux, 1997, 210–221.
———. *Xala*. Trans. Clive Wake. Oxford: Heinemann Educational, 1976 [Présence Africaine, 1974].
Sembène, Ousmane. *The Last of the Empire*. London: Heinemann, 1983 [1981].
Soyinka, Wole. *Opera Wonyosi*. Bloomington: Indiana University Press, 1981.

Films and Documentaries

Curtis, Adam, dir. *The Mayfair Set: Four Stories About the Rise of Business and the Decline of Political Power*. BBC, 1999.

Secondary

Akerlof, George A., and Robert J. Shiller. *Animal Spirits: How Human Psychology Drives the Economy and Why It Matters for Global Capitalism*. Princeton: Princeton University Press, 2009.
Amin, Samir. *Maldevelopment: Anatomy of a Global Failure*. Tokyo: United Nations University, 1990.
Amsden, Alice H. *Escape from Empire: The Developing World's Journey through Heaven and Hell*. Cambridge, MA: MIT Press, 2009.
Barratt Brown, Michael. *The Economics of Imperialism*. Harmondsworth: Penguin, 1974.
Bello, Walden. *Dark Victory: The US, Structural Adjustment, and Global Poverty*. London: Food First, 1994, Kindle Edition.
Brennan, Timothy. *Salman Rushdie and the Third World: Myths of the Nation*. London: Palgrave Macmillan, 1989.
Brown, Nicholas. *The Political Horizon of Twentieth-Century Literature*. Princeton and Oxford: Princeton University Press, 2005.
Brown, Phillip, Hugh Lauder, and David Ashton. *The Global Auction: The Broken Promises of Education, Jobs and Incomes*. Oxford: Oxford University Press, 2011.
Chamberlain, M.E. *Decolonization: The Fall of the European Empires*. Second Edition. Malden, MA: Blackwell, 1999.
Chang, Ha-Joon. *Bad Samaritans: The Guilty Secrets of the Rich Nations and the Threat to Global Prosperity*. London: Random House, 2007.
Crawford, Neta. 'Decolonization as an International Norm: the Evolution of Practices, Arguments, and Beliefs,' in *Emerging Norms of Justified Intervention*. Eds. Laura W. Reed and Carl Kaysen. Cambridge, MA: American Academy of Arts and Sciences, 1993, 37–61.

Desai, Ashwin. *We Are the Poors: Community Struggle in Post-apartheid South Africa*. New York: Monthly Review, 2002.

Fanon, Frantz. *The Wretched of the Earth*. Trans. Constance Farrington. New York: Grove, 1963 [Présence Africaine, 1961].

———. 'La mort de Lumumba: Pouvions nous en faire autrement?' [1961], *Pour la Révolution Africaine: Écrits Politiques*. Paris: Redécouverte, 2001.

Freeland, Chrystia. *Plutocrats: The Rise of the New Global Super Rich*. Harmondsworth: Penguin, 2012.

Gagiano, Annie. *Dealing with Evils: Essays on Writing from Africa*. Second Edition. Stuttgart: Ibidem, 2014.

Gakou, Mohamed Lamine. *The Crisis in African Agriculture*. London and New Jersey: Zed, 1987.

Garnett, Anne. 'Australia's 'Five Pillar Economy': Mining,' *The Conversation*,30 April, 2015, https://theconversation.com/australias-five-pillar-economymining-40701. 3 January, 2017.

Graeber, David. *Debt: The First 5000 Years*. New York: Melville, 2011.

Gunne, Sorcha. 'Mind the Gap: An Interview with Neil Lazarus,' *Postcolonial Text*, Vol. 7, No. 3 (2012), 1–15.

Harvey, David. *Seventeen Contradictions and the End of Capitalism*, Oxford: Oxford University Press, 2014.

Jackson, Ben, and Paul Segal. *Why Inequality Matters*. London: Catalyst, 2004.

Jameson, Fredric. 'Third-World Literature in the Era of Multinational Capitalism,' *Social Text*, No. 15 (Autumn, 1986), 65–88.

Lewis, Michael. *Boomerang: Travels in the New Third World*. London and New York: Norton, 2011.

Lindfors, Bernth. 'Begging Questions in Wole Soyinka's *Opera Wonyosi*,' *Ariel*, Vol. 12, No. 3 (1981), 21–33.

Macfie, Rebecca. *Tragedy at Pike River Mine: How and Why 29 Men Died*. Auckland: Awa Press, 2013.

Malala, Justice. 'The Marikana Action is a Strike by the Poor Against the Stateand the Haves,' *The Guardian*, 17 August, 2012, http://www.theguardian.com/commentisfree/2012/aug/17/marikana-action-strike-poor-state-haves.3 January, 2017.

Mishra, Ramesh. 'Social Policy in the Postmodern World,' in *New Perspectives on the Welfare State in Europe*. Ed. Catherine Jones. London: Routledge, 1993, 16–35.

Mittelman, James. *The Globalization Syndrome: Transformation and Resistance*. Princeton, NJ: Princeton University Press, 2000.

Moynihan, Daniel Patrick. 'The United States in Opposition,' *Commentary*, 1 March, 1975, https://www.commentarymagazine.com/articles/the-united-states-in-opposition/. 3 January, 2017.

Nasar, Sylvia. *Grand Pursuit: The Story of the People Who Made Modern Economics.* London: Fourth Estate, 2012.
Neild, R.R. *Public Corruption: The Dark Side of Social Evolution.* London: Anthem, 2002.
Ng, Edgar. 'Doing Development Differently,' in *Internationalising the Postcolonial: Working to Change the Way We Are.* Ed. Phillip Darby. Honolulu: University of Hawai'i Press, 2006, 125–143.
Ngũgĩ wa Thiong'o. *The Writer in Politics.* London: Heinemann Educational, 1981.
Orwell, George. *The Road to Wigan Pier.* London: Penguin Classics, 2001 [1937].
Page, Melvin E. *Colonialism: An International Social, Cultural and Political Encyclopedia,* Vol. 2. Ed. Melvin E. Page. Santa Barbara: ABC-CLIO, 2003.
Plaut, Martin. 'South Africa's Lonmin Marikana Mine Clashes Killed 34' *BBC News,* 17 August, 2012, http://www.bbc.com/news/worldafrica-19292909. 3 January, 2017.
Reich, Robert. *Beyond Outrage.* New York: Vintage, 2012.
Sharman, J.C. 'Shopping for Anonymous Shell Companies: An Audit Study of Anonymity and Crime in the International Financial System,' *Journal of Economic Perspectives,* Vol. 24, No. 4, Fall 2010, 127–140.
Starr, Deborah. 'Drinking, Gambling, and Making Merry: Waguih Ghali's Search for Cosmopolitan Agency,' *Middle Eastern Literatures,* Vol. 9, No. 3, December 2006, 271–285.
Stiglitz, Joseph. *The Roaring Nineties.* New York: Norton, 2003.
———. *The Price of Inequality: How Today's Divided Society Endangers Our Future.* New York and London: Norton, 2012.
———. *The Great Divide: Unequal Societies and What We Can Do About Them.* New York: Norton, 2015.
Tabb, William K. *Economic Governance in the Age of Globalization.* New York: Columbia University Press, 2004.
Taibbi, Matt. *Griftopia: Bubble Machines, Vampire Squids, and the Long Con That Is Breaking America.* New York: Spiegal and Grau, 2011.
Todd, Selina. *The People: The Rise and Fall of the Working Class,* 1910–2010. London: John Murray, 2014.
Torricelli, Robert, and Andrew Carroll (eds.). *In Our Own Words: Extraordinary Speeches of the American Century.* New York: Washington Square Press, 1999.
Turner, Barry. *Suez 1956: The Inside Story of the First Oil War.* London: Hodder and Stoughton, 2006.
Van der Does de Willebois, Emile, Emily M. Halter, Robert A. Harrison, Ji Won Park, and J.C. Sharman, *The Puppet Masters: How the Corrupt Use Legal Structures to Hide Stolen Assets and What to Do About It.* The International Bank for Reconstruction and Development and The World Bank, Washington, DC, 2011, https://star.worldbank.org/star/sites/star/files/puppetmastersv1.pdf. 3 January, 2017.

Webb, Chris. 'History of South Africa's Cheap Labour Economy: The 1946 Miners Strike and the Marikana Massacre,' *Global Research*, 21 August, 2012, http://www.globalresearch.ca/history-of-south-africa-s-cheap-labour-economy-the-1946-miners-strike-and-the-marikana-massacre/32431. 3 January, 2017.

Websites

Lonrho: http://www.lonrho.com/. 3 January, 2017.
Marikana Commission of Inquiry: http://www.marikanacomm.org.za/. 3 January, 2017.
The World Bank, 'Development Indicators: Distribution of Income or Consumption,' 2014: http://wdi.worldbank.org/table/2.9. 3 January, 2017.
The World Bank, 'Poverty and Equity,' 2011: http://povertydata.worldbank.org/poverty/country/ZAF.

CHAPTER 4

Global Neoliberalism

THE NEOLIBERAL CITY

Following the 2008 bankruptcy of the Lehman Brothers, Fannie Mae, and Freddie Mac, stories soon emerged of bank-foreclosed homes trashed by enraged and humiliated homeowners, who defiled their properties with rubbish, excrement, and graffiti, who abandoned pets, stole fixtures and fittings, and vandalised the homes they were forced to leave (Phillips 2008). In the opening of his novel *Sunset Park* (2010), Paul Auster summarises such aggressive behaviour as 'an eruption of violence and anger, a parting rampage of capricious vandalism … impulsive acts triggered by the rage of the dispossessed, disgusting but understandable statements of despair' (4). The bank repossession of between five and ten million American homes has been one of the most visible signs of the fallout from the 2008 financial meltdown. In contrast with the deliberately confusing financial-sector talk of credit default swaps, sub-prime lending, and shadow banking, stories of home repossession are altogether easier for the reading public—often also middle-class homeowners—to understand. That such destructive, anti-social demonstrations of rage could be middle-class behaviour from the world's number one economy, from the nation held up as the apogee of democracy, freedom, and opportunity for a First World life, is shocking, no less so in newspaper journalism than in Auster's examination of housing and employment precarity among the young and educated. Both the sympathetic voice of journalists reporting on the booming trash-out business, as well as Auster's fictional narrators, interpellate the reader, who is often herself middle-class and comfortably housed. Most of us, the writers imply, can imagine what it might feel like to lose the homes into which we invest time, money, and emotion.

That we can imagine ourselves failing and falling out of the economic system within which we live and work is testimony to the pervasiveness of the precarious, fluctuating, capitalist world-system to influence our lives, behaviours, and emotions. Capitalism's cyclical volatility and tendency to crises are felt on a social level, in cultural attitudes, community cohesion, and in individual emotion and behaviour. George Akerlof and Robert Shiller's behavioural economics, based on 'animal spirits' such as confidence, trust, greed, rivalry, and fear, are informative for the analysis of literary portrayals of inequality in the contemporary world. More precisely, the economic understandings of people's reactions to financial instability account for the similar depiction of emotions and patterns of behaviour found in much postcolonial and black British literature that portrays the economically marginalised and impoverished. As the behaviour of dispossessed homeowners attests, anger, violence, and criminal and anti-social acts do not belong to any particular culture or class. Rather, these appear to be the responses of the dispossessed, disenfranchised, voiceless, and powerless everywhere.

Like the contradictory components of neocolonialism, the term for the contemporary form of capitalism, 'neoliberalism,' contains unreconciled tensions which make it difficult to define or comprehensively grasp. As Jamie Peck summarises, in regard to confusion surrounding the term, its multiple definitions and usages 'may be telling us something about the tangled mess of neoliberalism itself' (2010, 15), with its unattainable goal of a market that is frictionless and stable: '[r]ather than the goal itself, it is the oscillations and vacillations around frustrated attempts to reach it that shape the revealed form of neoliberalism as a contradictory mode of market governance' (16). Perhaps because of the term's inherent contradictions and conflicts, neoliberalism is more usually defined by its critics than by mainstream economists, who focus on the mechanisms of the markets rather than their underlying ideology. The tendency for critics to emphasise the term's foundational political and institutional beliefs make neoliberalism rather like the term 'modernism,' a catch-all category that simultaneously signals and critiques a hegemonic and systemic world view that intersects all aspects of social practice.

The 2008 financial crisis and the flurry of economic analysis that followed revealed the shakiness, even fallacy, of several tenets of neoliberalism heretofore widely accepted by the mainstream as much as by politicians. Exposure of the financial industry's creative invention of ways to package debt showed that the 'invisible hand of the market' is man-made and self-serving, while the very occurrence of a global economic meltdown to rival that of 1929 discredited economists' self-congratulatory claims that they had solved the cyclical instability of the market. Technological advances in data processing also exposed as false several assumptions about the nature of the market. Evidence of widening inequality debunks the notion of the trickle-down effect of wealth distribution and the idea that growth benefits all. Revelations of stagnating rather than rising wages, limited upward mobility, the importance of inheritance, and the proportionally higher growth of earnings from invested wealth than from salary debunks belief in the ability of the market to selflessly self-regulate. From the dubious legality of overleveraged speculative finance, credit default swaps, and zombie mortgages to the outright fraudulence of Bernard Madoff's Ponzi scheme, it is becoming increasingly apparent that capitalism is run by belief systems rather than natural laws. In shining a light on myth as underpinning assumed truths, and drawing attention to emotion as the motor of market confidence, several economists focusing on inequality have rediscovered human subjectivity as the heart of their discipline. In thinking of economics as social narratives that reflect and support cultural norms and expectations, literature and its analysis has a role to play. In particular, the knowledge of and attention to economic inequality that I claim as a constant theme in postcolonial fiction again emerges as overt in the neoliberal era.

The principles of that which critics call neoliberalism and economists call the theories of the free market are based on highly selective readings of the liberal philosophers whose work shaped modern economics. The most notable misinterpretation may be today's over-reliance on Adam Smith's 'invisible hand of the market,' a term he used only three times in all his writings to refer to accidental benefits from individual selfish actions, and which goes against his advocacy of moral justice and social equality created by a close relationship between state and economy. And yet, in the late 1970s, Margaret Thatcher in the UK and Ronald Reagan in the USA claimed that their laissez-faire, non-interventionist model of political economy was inevitable, no-nonsense, and *anti*-idealist common sense. Their response to the 1970s' slowing growth, unpredictable inflation, and solidifying Cold War polemics was to deregulate the market and minimise state intervention under the premise that the market's natural self-regulation was more efficient, objective, and devoid of political ideology. In the mid-twentieth century, decolonisation secured the continuation of the Western imperial political economy and social structures of capitalism brought by imperialism under the new frame of nationalism, which ensured that colonial powers could enjoy ongoing profits from decolonisation. By the end of the century, the rebranding of Labour in the UK under Tony Blair and of the Democratic Party in the USA under Bill Clinton away from their historical socialist leanings to embrace neoliberal policies ensured the continuation of the neoliberal model of laissez-faire capitalism by instilling neoliberal beliefs on both sides of the political spectrum. Thatcher early on defined her view of the new liberal political economy as 'a man's right to work as he will, to spend what he earns, to own property, to have the State as servant not as master: these are the British inheritance. They are the essence of a free country and on that freedom all our other freedoms depend' (Thatcher qtd in Hall 2011, 706). Her terms of economically actuated freedom echo those expounded by the comprador elite under neocolonialism, who revel in the money-making possibilities opened to them by independence, and mirror the attitudes of colonial speculators on their rights to land and trade, parodied in Amitav Ghosh's rapacious opium traders. Indeed, the conflation of individual freedom and market freedom wrapped in such a triumphalist tone attests to the coterminous historical development of liberal democracy and classical economics; the one is unthinkable without the other.

It is notable that the field of modern economics often cites as foundational the free-trade principles of Smith's (1776) *The Wealth of Nations*. And yet, Smith's theory, which was in any case not applied for almost another century, was only made possible by the already-strong trading platforms nurtured through a long history of British mercantile protectionism, as described in Chap. 2. Furthermore, the International Monetary Fund (IMF) and World Bank's advice and loans to developing countries to specialise in primary production, including of extractive industries, replicates British colonial policy, which likewise frowned upon the development of industry in the colonies, and in some cases banned it outright, such as the Indian cotton industry. The fostering of such reliance on tertiary goods and services from core capitalist countries actively hinders development and propagates the uneven global distribution of wealth. Current efforts through the World Trade Organisation (WTO) and the Trans-Pacific Partnership treaty to reduce developing nations' import trade tariffs on agricultural goods, which will allow cheap food and materials to be exported from the richest nations, mean that poor countries will be dependent on the developed world even for basic sustenance. Ha-Joon Chang claims the proposed low tariff of under 5% is 'a level that has not been seen since the days of the "unequal treaties" in the nineteenth and early twentieth centuries' (2007, 78). As Chang puts it elsewhere, the move is redolent of colonialism: '[i]n the name of development, the WTO is in danger of re-introducing precisely the trade rules employed by the imperial powers to stifle the development of poor countries' (2005, 62). In short, the developed world's championing of free trade under neoliberalism displays a strategy of selective historical amnesia that forgets the historical importance of protectionism in creating the wealth of today's core countries. As Chang summarises, 'historically, trade liberalization has been the *outcome* rather than the *cause* of economic development' (2007, 74, italics in original).

The spatial embodiment of capitalist political economy and the enactment of its structures of inequality, which are easiest to see in the historical period at its moment of introduction in the colonies, are most evident in their neoliberal expression in the global city. The financialisation of urban space and the body that inhabits it allows for comparison across world urban centres that reveal similarities between core and peripheral spaces. The trope common to postcolonial fiction of the move from close, traditional rural community to the impersonal, individualistic city is, within this *longue durée* optic, merely the twentieth-century inscription of a trend in human movement that dates back to the displacement of the British agricultural revolution. Urban drift has been a direct response to the emergence and pressures of capital relations on land privatisation and the job opportunities of industrialisation across time and space. The land deals in the settler colonies that displaced indigenous peoples took their legal cues from the concomitant British Enclosure Acts passed throughout the first half of the nineteenth century, which legally ratified the appropriation of common land irrespective of previous traditional usage.

Today's proliferating gated communities for the rich are built, serviced, and secured by the poor, who live in social housing enclaves, in impoverished suburbs on city outskirts, or in neighbouring slums. Mike

Davis's *Planet of Slums* outlines the origins of these invisible structural dynamics of ownership, employment, and spatial separation in the colonial-era regulation of native rights to the city in British and French colonies and its multiple later expressions at moments of massive social upheavals leading to urbanisation in the post-war rebuilds of the 1950s, more recently in Vietnam, Turkey, Egypt and Iran, China since the 1980s, South Africa after 1994, and the ex-USSR since 1990 (Davis 2006, 51–54). Each of these moments is marked by consolidated gentrification and displacement that recalls Walter Benn Michael's reminder of David Brooks's pithy statement: today 'the rich don't exploit the poor, they just out-compete them' (Brooks qtd in Michaels, 10). The pervasiveness of this pattern inscribes the postcolonial trope of the shift from traditional rural realm to the alienating city within an even larger dynamic, thereby calling for analysis of each unique cultural form of dispossession and formulation of the labouring body to be understood in a world context.

The city of London offers one of the starkest examples of uneven internal development. Its configuration of incredible wealth alongside high levels of relative poverty reflects its historical role as the centre of the British Empire as well as its contemporary role as a hub of global finance. In 1933, a contradictory moment that was both the height of the Empire and the inter-war slump following the Great Depression, John Maynard Keynes wrote that 'London is one of the richest cities in the history of civilization, but it cannot "afford" the highest standards of achievement of which its own living citizens are capable, because they do not "pay"' (1933, 764). His comment, which does not sound outdated today, registers the affront, the embarrassment, and the shame of visible inequality in the Empire's centre. For geographer Doreen Massey in *World City*, finance has replaced empire as the global capitalist hegemony, of which London's supremacy gives it a 'new imperial role' (2007, Preface n.p.). Inequality is integral to this achievement, both a sign of and a reason for its success, combining cheap labour endlessly supplied by an international form of urban drift from migrants from poorer nations at one end of the socio-economic scale, to high executive salaries and elite trans-nationals at the other (Massey, 62). Indeed, the fact that the 1930s and the 2010s are moments of historical peaks of internal inequality brings into close proximity Keynes's and Massey's comments. Despite changing political regimes, from imperialism to nationalism, and throughout different forms of capitalism, from colonial to neoliberal economies, great similarities call for closer scrutiny of the structures and mechanisms of the political economy that updates the past in the present.

London, which contains the widest equality gap of any region in the UK (Wilkinson and Pickett 2014), provides a local illustration of the combined and uneven development of urban space. Inequality within London is enacted in the city's geography as well as in its core–periphery relationship to the nation's other regions—that which Michael Hechter labels internal colonialism (Hechter 1999). The pattern of poverty in London's East End from the Industrial Revolution to today provides a snapshot of the fallout from the capitalist world-system. While the sociological demographics have changed in the last 150 years, the patterns have not. The East End has housed successive waves of immigrants, from Chinese, Indian (lascar) sailors, Irish, and Ashkenazi Jews, to today's Pakistani and Bangladeshi immigrants. Opium has made way for heroin and crack cocaine, and civil unrest has changed from the 1889 London Dock strikes to the 2011 London riots and attention to the labour conditions of Bangladeshi women garment workers. When Charles Booth mapped London poverty in the 1890s, he calculated that 30% of Londoners lived in subsistence-level poverty, with precarious jobs closely linked to sub-standard housing. Today, based on different measures of poverty relative to the national median wage, London has a 42% rate of child poverty—one of the highest in the country—which expands to 70% of Bangladeshi children, the poorest immigrant community. The East End state-housing development of Tower Hamlets, which houses one of the largest proportions of immigrants of the London boroughs, regularly scores as the worst location in London for poverty, unemployment, and life expectancy.[1]

The patterns of these sociological demographics have been recorded in London fiction, of which Charles Dickens's *Bleak House* (1853) and Monica Ali's *Brick Lane* (2003) provide convenient bookends. Earlier works include Dickens's portrayals of East End slum dwellers, the international labour of the shipping trade central to Joseph Conrad's *oeuvre*, the opium dens Oscar Wilde calls 'the sordid shame of the great city' in *The Picture of Dorian Gray* (1993, 135), and the changing jobs for day labourers recorded in James Greenwood's (1867) *Unsentimental Journeys*, Jack London's *People of the Abyss* (1903), George Orwell's *Down and Out in Paris and London* (1933), and Simon Blumenfeld's *Jew Boy* (1935). Postcolonial-era black British fiction includes Sam Selvon's portrayal of the Windrush generation of Caribbean immigrants, contemporary portrayals of the informal garment industry in Ali's *Brick Lane*, and criminality in East End estates in Dreda Say Mitchell's thrillers. South London is equally well represented, notably in Gabriel Gbadamosi's portrayal of post-war Irish and Nigerian tenement families in *Vauxhall* (2013), and Alex Wheatle's Brixton novels. Regardless of the time of writing or the community portrayed, recurrent experiences, including child poverty, school drop-outs, gangs, addiction, and overcrowded and precarious living arrangements, as well as unemployment, underemployment, and exploited and underpaid illegal workers are common in over 150 years of London fiction.

The fiction provides a snapshot of the uneven development of urban space described by geographers as being impacted everywhere by capitalist dynamics. The need for on-hand cheap labour to build and service the city created ghettoisation in London just as it did in the colonies—a reminder that colonial structures were commonly patterned on those already at home. Keynes's position on unethical urban development in the 1930s Depression era updates Engel's descriptions of the spatial layout of Manchester nearly one hundred years earlier in *The Condition of the Working Class in England* (1845). Even the system of building and running Britain's workhouses at a profit in the 1930s, described by George Orwell in *Down and Out in Paris and London*, is accepted as commonsense market logic to a contemporary readership. The drive for profit, growth, and investment opportunities leads to constant urban renewal and beautification plans that displace the poor from city centres concomitant with the suburbanisation of the wealthy. Booth's 1898 Poverty Maps of London show both of these features already at work, long before the current neoliberal form of late capitalism. The inner city streets register mixed social strata from the abject poor to the upper-middle class. Often, the road-frontage façade of respectable commerce hides tenement buildings for the labourers in the back, and slum streets encircle factories while the upper-middle and upper classes encircle parks. Danny Dorling's *The 32 Stops: Lives on London's Circle Line* (2013) offers a cross-sectional slice of the same phenomena in 2011, tracing demographic patterns in the 100 years since the 1911 opening of this line of the London Underground. Stark disparities of ethnicity, age, and income are apparent from one stop to the next. For example, Liverpool Street Station, at the heart of the financial district of the City, with its six- and seven-figure salaries, is followed directly by Bethnal Green, the site of one of the East End's most notorious slums at the turn of the nineteenth century, and today dominated by the high-rise council housing of Tower Hamlets, the poorest borough of London and also the most ethnically diverse.

In her outline of the neighbouring Canary Wharf, Massey summarises the capitalist registration of urban development. The top salaries and share dividends of the 1% are facilitated by the minimum-wage builders and cleaners, while the architectural display of wealth and luxury of the business hub contrasts starkly with the area's other high-rises of Tower Hamlets. Describing a 2004 demonstration for a 'living wage' by the Canary Wharf Cleaners' Union, Massey opines:

> The response that one should not 'interfere in the market to pay cleaners more' ... from an organisation which within less than twelve months would appoint a director on £35 million has a telling ring about the operation of 'market forces', as does the geography of the trajectories that were meeting up here in Canary Wharf: the director was from the USA, the cleaners from a wide range of countries in the global South and in Eastern Europe. (139)

Massey's example illustrates the unevenness of the capitalist world-system that connects all regions in an interdependent relationship, recalling parallels with the London-based ownership behind the Lonmin strike and Gina Rinehart's 2012 comments on Australian miners, cited in the previous chapter. In Canary Wharf, the inequality between the First and Third Worlds is enacted at the local level, where geography and salary are still closely connected even at the very core of global power.

Such a local and specific manifestation of global inequality does not appear suddenly in the era of neoliberalism; rather, it is merely the most recent expression of this local site's involvement with the forces of globalisation. The modern financial district was Thatcher's first experiment with devolution, in the public–private quango of the London Docklands Development Corporation. Similarly, its historical predecessors, the East India Docks and West India Docks, were symbiotically financed at the turn of the nineteenth century by the imperial government and speculative merchants, predominantly the East India Company. Today there is neither physical trace of nor memorial to the Company, despite its instrumental role in the history of London, an absence that Nick Robins claims fosters 'a sense that the current era of business dominance is somehow unique' (2003, 79). Docklands history today is reduced to a few streets named after exotic spices, including the wharf itself, named after the Canary Islands, a colonial Spanish trading hub and important source of cash-crop imports to Britain. Canary Wharf is a physical centre of both colonial and neoliberal capitalism, with the trade in world finance today mirroring the trade in New World commodities over one hundred years ago, in each case contributing to London's status as global centre of commercial transactions and economic migration.

Stuart Hall's oft-quoted comment on British ethnic multiculturalism contains further, embodied ghostings of the economic geography of Canary Wharf, described in spatial terms by sociologists and geographers such as Dorling, Massey, and Saskia Sassen:

> People like me who came to England in the 1950s have been there for centuries; symbolically, we have been there for centuries. I was coming home. I am the sugar at the bottom of the English cup of tea. I am the sweet tooth, the sugar plantations that rotted generations of English children's teeth. There are thousands of others beside me that are, you know, the cup of tea itself. ... This is the symbolization of English identity ... That is the outside history that is inside the history of the English. There is no English history without that other history. (Hall 1997, 48–49)

For Hall, the 'outside history' integral to Britain's national identity includes the slave trade and plantation industries: both are characterised by global movement driven by import and export, of which post-war immigration is just one manifestation. That the arrival of the *HMS Windrush* in the London docks at Tilbury represents the symbolic beginning of this era of migration in the popular imaginary attests to the centrality of a world shipping network to constructions of Britishness.

It is exactly this collapsing of the layers of historical time and place accentuated by Hall that narrative fiction best captures. Docklands and the London wharves often feature in historical fiction. Conrad's *oeuvre* revolves around merchant shipping, his nineteenth-century lascar (Southern Indian and Bengali) sailors docked at Canary Wharf, and the casual dockside labourers reported by Greenwood, London, and Orwell offloaded the goods there. These writers, who are central to the national English literary canon, directly represent a nation structured by the shipping industries propelled by colonialism: as Hall would put it, their work was aware of the imbrication of inside and outside histories well before the invention of the postcolonial. In more recent British fiction, Iain Sinclair's peripatetic, fragmented novel *Downriver* (1991) keeps alive the memory of the aforementioned London writers.

Capturing the successive flows and waves of migrants, industry, and property ownership, the novel examines the flotsam, jetsam, and detritus of the Thames and the East End. Both real and fictional historical figures and events, including Conrad, Dickens's Magwitch, Jack the Ripper, and Pocahontas, and other exotic specimens—the characters from Lewis Carroll's *Alice in Wonderland*, shipwrecks, empty warehouses, Spitalfields, Gravesend, and Execution Dock—all surface and sink during the neoliberal reincarnation of Docklands.

The contemporary fiction that most consistently maps the dynamics of neoliberal London is by black British and immigrant writers. In a series of novels set across four generations of black Londoners in Brixton, Alex Wheatle's oeuvre, *Brixton Rock* (1999), *East of Acre Lane* (2001), *The Dirty South* (2008), and *Brenton Brown* (2011), portrays a recurring set of compounding social factors that maintain multigenerational poverty, un- and underemployment, and violence. The novels, set in 1979, 1981, 2006, and 2002 respectively, cover the inception and outcome of Thatcher's neoliberal regime, and hark back to the conditions of the first generation of Jamaican migrants of the 1960s. The novels depict an almost identical cluster of material conditions in the state-housed, predominantly single-parent black and South Asian 'ghetto' of South London. The youth narrators of each book eschew family pressures to succeed in education and employment in favour of lives of crime, predominantly stealing and dealing in drugs to provide for the consumer goods they desire. Their parents almost all work in the kinds of low-skilled, minimum-wage, and often demeaning jobs typified in Massey's Canary Wharf example. These jobs include checkout operator, fast-food restaurant worker, cleaner, and casual and contract worker in construction. By recycling characters from one novel to the next, Wheatle implies continuity rather than change across three generations of London's black British communities. The source of this intergenerational bond, however, is not an active sense of shared culture or faith but of shared and familiar socio-economic conditions. This is charted, for example, in the protagonist of *The Dirty South* following in his father's footsteps—the protagonist of the earlier *East of Acre Lane*—as a drug dealer involved in intergang fighting which leads to murder, and the grandmother's return to Jamaica, claiming she has nothing to show for her forty years in London but unskilled jobs and state housing (154). The novels paint a bleak picture of London lives that contrasts starkly with the opportunities acclaimed of the multicultural, metropolitan London as a leading world city.

Postcolonial fiction, as in black British writing such as Wheatle's, articulates several features of urban inequality, focalised through the losers of capitalism, who are intensely aware of the wealth they see everywhere around them but feel unable to reach. At the same time, the wealthy typically fail even to see the poor amongst them, a point Engels lambasted in nineteenth-century industrial Manchester (Engels, 1872), and which Benjamin Disraeli, author of *Sybil, or The Two Nations* (1845), called 'two nations … the rich and the poor' (Book 2, Chap. 5). The profit to be made out of housing the poor offers one recurring theme useful for exploring the divide, its construction, and its maintenance. The buying of land and construction of housing aimed to house the poor creates oases of bounded poverty for the many and profit for a few. In New Zealand Maori writer Alan Duff's *Once Were Warriors* (1990), the social housing 'dumping ground for [the city's] human rubbish' (14) inhabited principally by Maori is built on land bought by the council from a wealthy farmer, whose large house and fields lie just over the estate's back fence. The visibility of this wealth is the catalyst for Beth's bitterness and anger against her own community's underachievement, and the desire for the neighbour's middle-class lifestyle which leads her daughter to commit suicide in his garden. J.K. Rowling in *The Casual Vacancy* (2012) describes a similar tension between the social classes in her fictional North England town. Pressed into expanding the council estate, the city 'colonize[s]' (55) scrub land on the town's margins, sold for a good price by the local lord of the manor house. The presence of the council estate and its inhabitants infuriates the middle class, who try to pass on the problem of social inequality to another borough.

These literary examples support both Dorling's and Massey's examples of London's City penthouses and council estates, as well as David Harvey's analysis of high-prestige gated communities next to run-down areas in downtown Baltimore (2012, 141–148). Serge Latouche recognised the same proximity in the early 1990s: '[t]he wounded and the victims of development are before our doors; there is no need to go and search for them in the outer suburbs of the West, we run into them in our own backyards' (1993, 235–236). As Phillip Brown, Hugh Lauder, and David Ashton put it in their study of the spatial mapping of labour inequality on the global market, '[w]inners and losers live side by side, creating first and third world conditions in both first and third world countries' (Brown et al. 2011, 129). Their claim, which identifies inequality in education, jobs, and salaries within and between developed and developing countries, in a comparative study of the USA, UK, Germany, China, India, Singapore, and South Korea, finds the internal inequalities of each nation repeated and replicated on a global scale.

Brown et al. identify similar dynamics in the uneven development of Third World cities in which 'winners and losers' coexist. Their example of well-secured, high-tech companies surrounded by slum dwellings in India and China leads to the claim that 'the preindustrial and the postindustrial share the same zip code' (62). In particular, they describe the pattern of '"oasis operations" – high tech factories, offices, and research facilities – in low-spec neighbourhoods that leave the rest of society largely untouched by their existence' (64). More precisely, the poor who live in the surrounding informal housing only have access to such sites in undesirable or unacknowledged roles: the example these writers give is of scrap dealers carting precariously large loads on bicycles. The presence of such people is integral to the city's functioning, yet they are predominantly ignored. Marie-Sophie Laborieux, the slum-tenant narrator of Patrick Chamoiseau's *Texaco* (1992), describes their invisibility thus: '[w]e shoved our way about next to City, holding on to it by its thousand survival cracks. But City ignored us' (1997, 316). The imagery of a tenuous but resolute grip is a leitmotif in this novel, a historical epic in which this shaky foothold is embodied in consecutive forms of makeshift housing, with historical time registered in the changing building materials, from 'the age of straw' following slave franchise, to ages of iron, asbestos, and finally brick in the modern-day slum.

Davis's study of world slums offers an approach to urban poverty that, in its global scope, bypasses the postcolonial fixation on only those spaces previously colonised. However, he identifies slums as colonial creations which emerged out of the transfer of a capitalist urban logic onto newly colonised spaces. In a chapter revealingly titled 'Haussmann in the Tropics,' Davis describes how colonial segregation has been maintained by 'postcolonial elites [who] have inherited and greedily reproduced the physical footprints of segregated colonial cities. Despite rhetoric of national liberation and social justice, they have aggressively adapted the racial zoning of the colonial period to defend their own class privileges and spatial exclusivity' (96). The global city's physical mapping of power relations, described by Davis in the building of colonial cities, certainly remains evident in the urban planning and laws of civic rights in such postcolonial cities as Mumbai and Lagos, but it is also reproduced in the use—and abuse—of immigrant labour in other global cities without a colonial past. In the uneven development of privately financed, capitalled globalisation, economic migrants occupy illegal, precarious, or substandard housing in most global cities, in which they are either forcibly contained or constantly under pressure of eviction, including in Dubai, Abu Dhabi, Bangkok, Seoul, Shanghai, and Beijing.

Although slum dwellers are spatially excluded from the city space, they are crucial cogs in the capitalist economy, which simultaneously ignores and depends on them. Katherine Boo, in her journalistic narrative non-fiction *Beyond the Beautiful Forevers* (2012), describes exactly this contradiction in describing common public attitudes to the slum: 'while some international businessmen descending into the Mumbai airport eyed the vista of slums with disgust, and others regarded it with pity, few took the sight as evidence of a high-functioning, well-managed city' (42). Annawadi, built on a swamp by Tamil labourers brought in from the countryside to expand the international airport (5), deters potential investors who fail to appreciate the crucial role played by this thriving informal economy.[2] From providing cheap labour for construction, to its free service to the city council in cleaning up the city's prodigious waste in the informal garbage-sorting industry, Annawadi helps create the very conditions for the investment success that makes Mumbai the nation's finance capital. Like Canary Wharf and Tower Hamlets, Mumbai International Airport and the adjacent Annawadi slum illustrate the close proximity of economic inequality registered in urban planning and its architecture.

While the rich may ignore the poor, those at the lower end of the scale are intensely aware of the wealth they see around them, which their undervalued work helps generate, but the rewards of which they feel shut out from. Describing this acute awareness of the lifestyle that seems to lie just out of reach, Mohsin Hamid in his satirical 'self-help' novel *How to Get Filthy Rich in Rising Asia* (2013) claims the poor today have 'greater familiarity ... with the rich, their faces pressed to that clear window on wealth afforded by ubiquitous television,' resulting in 'a rising tide of frustration, anger and violence' (205–206). In *Reservation Blues* (1995), Sherman Alexie describes the same feelings of lack on an American Indian reservation: '[h]e turned on his little black-and-white television to watch white people live. White people owned everything: food, houses, clothes, children. Television constantly reminded Thomas of all he never owned' (70). Chris Abani's young narrator of *GraceLand* (2004), Elvis, describes a similar kaleidoscope of wealth and poverty looking out from the Nigerian slum of Makoko (also spelled Maroko), Lagos to the city's adjacent area, Victoria Island, which is also its wealthiest: 'he stared at the city, half slum, half paradise. How could a place be so ugly and violent yet beautiful at the same time? he wondered' (7). Despite their very different contexts, each writer aligns the reader's sympathies with these characters, who are drawn as the underdogs, striving to attain access to the lifestyles and opportunities they see all around them. Indeed, the story arcs of all these narratives are driven by the protagonists' ambitions for wealth and recognition, with the characters' experience and acute awareness of the presence of inequality and injustice providing both the dramatic tension and the political message of the works.

Hammering home his message of structural disadvantage, Abani slips into the narrator's viewpoint a thinly veiled macro-view of Nigeria's political commentary that the youth would be unlikely to make:

> Elvis had read a newspaper editorial that stated, rather proudly, that Nigeria had a higher percentage of millionaires—in dollars, not local currency—than nearly any other country in the world, and most of them lived and conducted their business in Lagos. The editorial failed to mention that their wealth had been made over the years with the help of crooked politicians, criminal soldiers, bent contractors, and greedy oil-company executives. Or that Nigeria also had a higher percentage of poor people than nearly any other country in the world. (8)

In this authorial interlude, Abani fills in information on the terrain of Lagos's political economy, adding a capitalist dimension to the imagery of the 'ugly and violent yet beautiful' city, and foreshadowing the coming confrontation with that violence later in the narrative, in both the human-trafficking trade and slum clearance for private development. Abani's quote succinctly registers all three interconnected levels of local, national, and international unevenness. The global level of inequality, on which multinational oil companies exploit Nigerian oil resources, is facilitated at the national level by internal inequality, such as the great concentration of wealth in Lagos. As the nation's city of capital (and formerly its capital city), Lagos is the interface with global finance and the point of access to the foreign currency dollars that exacerbate local inequality. In the urban development that demolishes the slum to make way for waterfront high-rise apartments financed by petro-dollars, the global ousts the local without any need for contact between them.

Abani's novel may be read as a sustained critique of inequality, its attendant violence, and the injustice of both. In its subjective and limited narrative perspective, tracing one character's interaction with the city and its poor, *GraceLand* offers the inside lived perspective on the impersonal facts and statistics of Davis's case study of the city. Lagos is one of the most radical examples of post-independence, developing-world urbanisation, growing from 300,000 inhabitants to 13.4 million from 1950 to 2004 (Davis, 4). A 1990 Moroko slum that evicted 300,000 people holds the dubious honour of appearing on Davis's list of 'Famous Slum Evictions' (102) under beautification politics.[3] This event forms the novel's dramatic climax, in which Abani again uses his slum-dwelling characters as mouthpieces through which to explain to the reader the economic mechanisms behind the politics of removal and to articulate resistance to them:

> I am not leaving dis place. We just managed to buy dese few rooms we own, and now dey want to come and destroy it. Why? So dat dey can turn dis place to beachside millionaire's paradise? No! And den we will all move to another location and set up another ghetto. Instead of dem to address de unemployment and real cause of poverty and crime, dey want to cover it all under one pile of rubbish. (248)

Contained in this speech is awareness of the structural feature of constant urban development that translates for the poor into constant harassment that is unlikely to stop after one eviction. The character's belligerence is not born of a refusal to participate in the free-market economy: he has worked hard to buy 'dese few rooms we own' but cannot compete with the 'millionaires.' Abani thus exposes the ultimate injustice of the government's coldly calculated sacrifice of the dispensable people at the bottom of the wealth pile in order to appeal to the national and international elite for whom a beach-side 'paradise' is likely only one of many properties they own. In this passage as elsewhere in the novel, Abani takes pains to expose the multiple levels at which the government skims profit. While the slum dweller is proud to 'own' his hut, he bought it illegally from crooked city officials and their various middlemen; instead of direct taxes, he pays the state in the form of bribes to ward off several earlier eviction attempts.

In arguing the purposeful development of underdevelopment under a neoliberal political economy, Davis outlines the negative impact of the World Bank- and IMF-led Structural Adjustment Programmes of the 1980s and 1990s, which caused an increase in poverty in Nigeria from

28% in 1980 to 66% in 1996, with gross national product (GNP) being lower in 2003 than at independence in 1960 (156). In the neoliberal setting of Abani's novel, Elvis is *less* likely to rise out of the poverty trap than the protagonists of neocolonial-era Nigerian fiction, even though writers such as Achebe and Soyinka already wrote with deep pessimism about postcolonial prospects. Indeed, the narrative twist that allows Elvis to trade orphan child homelessness for family in the USA is not a rags-to-riches success story of talent and hard work but one of profiteering from his unwitting role in the cross-border trafficking of children sold for organ transplants. Capitalist success here, as in Hamid's satirical *How to Get Filthy Rich in Rising Asia*, occurs not along the touted lines of progress and development but through corruption, violence, and the black market.

The violent climax of Abani's novel is typical of the clash between wealth and poverty that often drives postcolonial slum narratives. In Vikas Swarup's *Q&A*, the *chai wallah* Ram from the Dharavi slum is apprehended by the police for daring to play as an equal competitor on a middle-class television show. In Aravind Adiga's *The White Tiger* (2008), Balram the lowly chauffeur is physically barred from the modern shopping mall, just as he is spatially contained in his employer's luxury apartment in the domestic servant's domain of garage, kitchen, and basement. Vishnu, in Manil Suri's *The Death of Vishnu* (2001), lives in the no man's land of an apartment building stair landing; the tenants' diverse feelings of responsibility toward him catalyse the violent denouement played out as class, caste, and gender conflicts. In *Behind the Beautiful Forevers*, a high wall covered with an advertisement for Italian floor tiles (slogan, 'Beautiful Forever') separates the gleaming new Mumbai International Airport from the Annawadi slum dwellers who first built the airport and now glean their livelihoods from the airport's detritus. The wall and the main road to the airport are not only symbols but also silent characters with which each person has a particular relationship. The street is a border between rival rubbish-picker gangs, as well as a liminal space where inside and outside meet to conduct shady business, including informal deals, prostitution, and bribes.

Boo's focalising of the material conditions of slum living through eye-witness accounts adopts a stance similar to postcolonial fiction: evidence of the wavering border between narrative non-fiction and social-realist fiction. Whereas Abani's authorial interjection of journalistic information into his characters' stream of consciousness jars in the fiction, reinforcing the novel's purpose as political message as well as aesthetic representation, Boo's narratorial interludes read as expected background research from the reporter, whose critique of poverty in Mumbai openly targets neoliberal economic practices. It is in this role, for example, that she informs readers of the process and repercussions of Mumbai local government's subcontracting of Annawadi slum clearance to a private management consortium, GVK.[4] The South African-based company has been hired to '[s]ecur[e] the airport perimeter' (41) from incursions from the adjacent slums, reclaim the land for high-rise development—including for GVK's own hotel chain—and promote the image of Mumbai as an attractive global city, of which the wall advertising 'Beautiful Forever' Italian tiles is a convenient symbol. Abani's authorial interludes and Boo's journalism explicate the close relationship between public politics and private business in the geography of the neoliberal city. The structure of narrative, which telescopes between long-shot overviews and close-up representations of individual lived experience, illuminates the web of relations between rich and poor: the invisible lives and motivations that embody in building materials the urban architecture of inequality.

Urban beautification programmes may be understood as capitalist 'solutions' to the uncomfortable—and unsightly—proximity of rich and poor. They are not, however, only a short-lived development phase affecting unsanitary slums in the Third World. Rather, today's slum clearances belong to a long history of Western displacement of the poor from the inner city in the name of modernisation. Harvey names Baron Haussmann's radical redesign of Paris in the mid-1800s (2012, 60) as a model subsequently continued in capitalism's core spaces, such as the post-World War Two rebuild, the post-war boom in the USA (9), and the European social housing developments of the 1960s–1970s. Fiction that represents this period includes Gbadamosi's recounting of the demolition of pre-war tenement housing in London's Vauxhall to make way for offices and government buildings of a fast-gentrifying area, and Azouz Begag's portrayal of the same period, of the movement of Lyon's Algerian immigrant community from informal bidonville to state-housing Habitation à Loyer Modéré (HLM) in *Le Gone du Chaâba* (1986). The shift from social housing to neoliberal user pays has not halted the process. New York mayor Rudy Giuliani's draconian campaign against the homeless in the 1990s, and Baltimore's ghettoising displacement practices described by Harvey in 2000 repeated, were more recently in previous London mayor Boris Johnson's initiative to relocate beneficiaries from high-rent London to the provinces.[5] Far from a solution to London's housing problem, the move displaces the poor rather than addressing the underlying causes of the inequality that makes London one of the most unaffordable cities in the world.

In many postcolonial novels, the dynamics of urban dislocation are background settings and contexts for stories of inequality and poverty. The trope of urban displacement is almost as important as the related narrative of rural dislocation and ensuing arrival in the city. Paulo Lins's novel *City of God* (1997) describes the 1960s Brazilian state housing project Cidade de Deus, built on swampy agricultural land on the outskirts of Rio di Janeiro. Similarly to the migration history of London's East End, the 1960s development replaces an earlier generation of immigrants, Portuguese farmers, with a new wave of migrants who are part of the urban drift of casual labourers for the city's construction industry (2006, 45). Built to rehouse people from the inner-city favelas as part of city gentrification, the development exemplifies the ex-centrification of poverty that, despite being touted as an improvement in the quality of accommodation, recreates the same structures of poverty in new locations. The two-room concrete dwellings quickly become overcrowded with multiple generations under one roof (39); water and electricity amenities are switched off when the bills are not paid (13; 31); the relocation of peoples from different favelas breaks up old family and community groups while fostering new resentments and mistrust (22); and workers now have a long commute to places of work (19). Precarity of place, of family structure, and of employment combine to create material and emotional stress, a humiliation that Lins's characters try to solve with crime.

In South Africa, the racial inflection of economic inequality, in which blacks are significantly poorer than whites, has not significantly changed in the post-apartheid era, despite the dismantling of formal rules of segregation. In *Mother to Mother* (1998), Sindiwe Magona, like Lins, argues that the poverty trap underpins the violence and crime of modern-day South Africa, which continues to be deeply racially inscribed. The apartheid-era spatial discrimination, represented in Magona's portrayal of the 1968 forced removals from designated white areas to concrete tract housing on the outskirts of Cape Town (28–34), leaves a legacy of contemporary crime and violence perpetrated by inhabitants against each other. Whereas '[w]hite people live in their own areas and mind their own business,' the grieving mother claims, '[w]e live here, fight and kill each other' (3). Yet her neat, racially inflected spatial split is undermined by the story's narrative arc, as her son is involved in killing a young white woman. The storyline is based on the 1993 killing of American student Amy Biehl. This particular incidence of inter-racial violence represents a broader level of unequal relations between white and black, allowing Magona to depict how the fabric of everyday black lives, which *looks* to be contained within a black-only community, is everywhere shot through with interactions that exceed its socially constructed boundaries. For example, the mother has a long daily commute to her job as a white woman's maidservant, and there is a lack of public transport, housing, schools, and hospitals exactly because these scarce public resources are distributed elsewhere, predominantly in white, middle-class districts. Magona's novel challenges the popular understanding of Biehl's murder as a crime of race hate. Rather, she vividly portrays how young black lives are constrained by lack of access to opportunities that divide up the city with unpoliced borders, keenly felt by those who live there, yet easily trespassed upon by foreigners, like Biehl, to whom they are invisible.

Boo, Lins, Magona, and Abani show keen awareness of the political economy behind the urban planning of their respective Indian, South American, and African postcolonial cities. Their work portrays the poor as keenly aware of the mechanics of spatial inequality, which they perceive as injustice, and how these factors impact on daily lives, ambitions, attitudes, and behaviour. Focalising their narratives through perspectives of marginalised characters whose economic situations are almost always equally an ethnic and gender issue, economic inequality is seen as a complex and multifaceted issue. The poor of these texts are neither passive nor simply victims of their restricted circumstances, but are intensely aware of and implicated in the competitive capitalist economy. Reading these narratives as sources of information about neoliberal political economies in specific sites around the world reveals a consolidated singular voice that condemns economic inequality as a moral and illegal crime against citizens who strive and fail to participate in the neoliberal nation. Such novels argue that poverty is a form of injustice that must be of central concern to postcolonial literature, joining cultural, social, and gender issues of marginalisation as the discipline's core focus.

Critical attention to structures of economic marginalisation in the fiction reveals the ways in which space is used for living and labouring. The material lives of many characters challenge readers' conceptions of home and notions of work, illuminating the rich and complex societies of people uncounted in censuses, living in blank spaces on city maps, and working in jobs that do not officially exist. In Mumbai, where Boo claims

50% of Greater Mumbai lives in makeshift housing (42) and where 85% of Indian workers are part of the informal economy (6), the poor get by making money where the wealthier might not even see an opportunity. Chang addresses this point in *23 Things They Don't Tell You about Capitalism*, a pop-economics book that debunks common assumptions about the logic of economic success and failure. Many forms of informal economy entrepreneurship are invisible to the Western eye and also to the middle class in general, who propagate a widespread, manifestly false conception of the slum dweller and the indigent as lazy and unintelligent, a contemporary update of the economically driven racism explored in Chap. 2. It is exactly against such stereotypes that slum narratives write, centralising those characters that middle-class readers, whether foreign or local, are most likely not to notice in the street.

In *The Death of Vishnu*, for example, Vishnu may look like a caricatural homeless bum—elderly, rural migrant, drunk, beggar—and yet, far from having opted out of the capitalist labour economy, he is very much a part of it, having competed for his spot on the landing and negotiated his tenancy with the building's middle-class tenants to provide them with an unpaid general lackey to run their errands (10). Furthermore, gaining access to his thoughts allows the reader to modify assumptions about how and why people sleep on the street, as well as to consider the disjunction between Vishnu's impoverished material circumstances and his rich sense of self, particularly concerning religion and faith. As Davis clarifies further, in developing-world cities street sleepers may not be the poorest of the poor and may often have families elsewhere; they sleep on the street to be close to employment. This fact is corroborated in fiction, including the construction workers sleeping at the site in both Lagos, in Abani's *GraceLand*, and Rio, in Lins's *City of God*. Literally sleeping on the job is also common to drivers, such as the family chauffeur in Adiga's *The White Tiger* and one of Ram's jobs in *Q&A*. Thus, the importance of space and place to concepts of identity, the analysis of which has been a mainstay of postcolonial literary critique, is seen to have a strong economic aspect.

The complex and multilayered relationship of the poor to property ownership offers one important example that illustrates their entrepreneurial dexterity while dispelling the myths that any space is free and that the poor help each other. As the privatisation of land is the underlying material on which capitalism is based, the poor are as involved in real estate as the rich investors whose demand drives urban development.

The point is made by Davis in uncovering the multiple layers of ownership and insecure tenure of many modern-day slums:

> [P]etty landlordship and subletting are major wealth strategies of the poor, and that homeowners quickly become exploiters of even more impoverished people. Despite the persistent heroic image of the squatter as self-builder and owner-occupier, the reality in Korogocho and other Nairobi slums is the irresistible increase in tenancy and petty exploitation. (44)

Here, Davis draws attention to hierarchical stratification among the people commonly lumped together under undifferentiating labels such as the homeless or slum dwellers. In this way, Davis is careful to attribute agency to the poor at the same time as refusing to allow them to occupy a simple victim status. That the poor exploit the poor is evident in the financialisation of public spaces, such as the sidewalk, which is rarely free (Davis, 36), a point also often made in fiction of the homeless. In *GraceLand*, Elvis pays to secure a place on the beach to busk for tourists through a well-networked friend (26). In *The Death of Vishnu*, Vishnu pays for the privilege of living on the stairwell landing with a multi-level web of 'I Owe You's and shrewdly calculated profit rates between other impoverished stakeholders' (4–10). In K. Sello Duiker's *Thirteen Cents* (2000), a child orphan pays protection money to various gangs in his search for a safe place to sleep.

In *Behind the Beautiful Forevers*, Boo outlines with journalistic detail the multiple levels of corruption and cheating in an Annawadi relocation project and subsequent slum clearance. Profit-making motivations exist at every level, a phenomenon also evident in slum housing costs in Abani's *GraceLand*. One of Boo's informants, Asha, an upwardly mobile slum dweller:

> ... had identified an opening in land speculation, of which there was much at Annawadi lately. The apartments promised to displaced airport slumd-wellers would be tiny—269 square feet—but would have running water, which made them a valuable asset in a city starved of affordable formal housing. Hence overcity people had been buying up shacks in the slums and concocting legal papers to show that they were longtime Annawadi residents.
>
> Most of the speculators intended to use the rehabilitation flats as rental or investment properties. 'The flat I'll get will be worth ten times what I paid for this place,' said the businessman who bought Abdul's storage hut. A

small-time politician named Papa Panchal had secured a large block of flats by the sewage lake on behalf of a major developer, hiring thugs on commission to persuade the occupants to sell. (225)

In *Texaco*, Chamoiseau describes the exact same chain of formal and informal deals in the context of the bidonville slums surrounding Martiniquan capital Fort-de-France (193). As in Boo's example, Chamoiseau describes the development as a local government response to pressure from the wealthy to get rid of the unsightly slum. Instead, however, corruption among city councillors joins with cheating from wealthier slum inhabitants with ambitions of upward mobility to become middlemen subletting even further down the poverty chain. In the multiple layers of ownership and tenancy, it is impossible to tell which of the agents that Boo and Chamoiseau name have legal titles and rights, which are in any case instable concepts, liable to change along with the next administrative shift in city government. The hierarchy of wealth is in each case built on the exploitation of people lower down the chain of tenants, an illustration of the mechanics of the informal city unprotected by the state or law that Davis calls 'where Darwin beats Keynes' (46).

The novels discussed in this chapter generate significant narrative tension by illustrating how every decision has economic as well as social, cultural, and relational outcomes. Indeed, when one has so very little, any gain or loss is amplified, which makes for vivid, often poignant portrayals of the psychology of lack and of failure, analysed later in this chapter. As in case studies and field research carried out across the social sciences, the individual perspectives provided by literature argue for the need to factor in social costs to economic calculations of poverty and distribution of wealth inequality. In the detailed representation of the material reality and daily lives of the economically marginalised, postcolonial fiction is an important source of information about the daily negotiation and calculation of opportunity costs made by the poor. While literary critics often recoil from the idea that fiction can ever be 'about' the world or interpreted as information, many of the foundations of the economic considerations of poverty are measured by relative and subjective bases that are exactly the stuff of fiction. Amartya Sen's foundational work on social inclusion and relative poverty is particularly important. An economist whose Anglo-Indian background and humanist approach to the ethics of inequality marks him as an overlooked forefather of postcolonial studies, Sen's calculations are used by the World Bank, the United Nations, and most national poverty measures.[6]

Sen defines inequality as a lack of freedom for individuals to pursue the level of wellbeing and quality of life normative to their culture and society. This privileging of relative and subjective understandings of lack is a perspective shared by fiction's narrative bias. His dictum that '[*r*]*elative* deprivation in the space of *incomes* can yield *absolute* deprivation in the space of *capabilities*' (1992, 115, italics in original) supports the world-systems collapse of an assumed split between developed and developing worlds by focusing on the lack of opportunities and positive outcomes that stem from economic deprivation. The formula helps make sense of the striking similarities of experiences of economic inequality described in a significant amount of postcolonial and minority literature, from both the peripheries and the core capitalist countries. Sen's capabilities approach helps explain how the improved living conditions of today's poor relative to the past, and of the poor from developed countries relative to those of the developing world, have by no means eradicated the social, behavioural, and emotional repercussions of immiseration. The inequality of Dickens's London is recognisable in Wheatle's novels, and Wheatle, Duff, Lins, Boo, Magona, and Abani all knowingly label their settings 'slums.' While the postcolonial emphasis on cultural specificity might condemn the way the Manila slum setting of Andy Mulligan's young-adult novel *Trash* (2011) was shifted in the film version to Rio's favelas, or Duff's Rotorua setting of *Once Were Warriors* was moved to Auckland, the interchangeability of settings speaks not only to the homogenising forces of mainstream cinema but also to the global likeness of impoverished urban spaces. Although one would expect the material conditions that constitute poverty to be radically different in developing world slums than in welfare-state UK or New Zealand, many postcolonial novels document a similar mapping of poverty on the urban landscape and register similar social problems and ostensibly 'bad' economic choices likely to propagate or even worsen the characters' financial situations, and thus their place in society.

The Economics of Lack

Although not originally envisaged as a favela, Lins applies the term to Cidade de Deus (216), just as Duff calls the Rotorua state-housing area Pine Block a 'slum' (7) and Wheatle calls Brixton a 'ghetto' (*The Dirty South*, 2). While their loose use of these heavily connoted terms might be objectively refuted, these writers employ the words knowingly. The terminology of abject poverty registers an extreme level of inequality in these societies, in which the poorest live in indecent conditions and circumstances *in relation to* the standards expected by the mainstream. From Dickens to Wheatle, Lins to Duff, a surprisingly consistent cluster of material conditions and responses to them accompany the poor at every time and place. To analyse characters' responses to constrained economic situations through Sen's capabilities approach brings a subjective, human dimension to Piketty's data that shows the bottom percentiles have not profited from the phenomenal development and growth of the twentieth century. In absolute terms, the poor in developed nations today certainly live 'better' lives than the poor of the past: they have smartphones, may receive social benefits, and rarely die of contagious diseases which have been stamped out by national vaccination schemes. Relatively speaking, however, the poor have less access to the opportunities of education and employment, suffer disproportionately higher morbidity, and continue to live in material conditions radically different from the national mainstream. In the physical inscription of poverty on living space, the fiction commonly describes settings that contain rubbish, shit, dirt, graffiti, broken public amenities, and uncared-for accommodation. These indicators of both physical and psychological lack of care combine with overcrowding, illness, stray animals, loitering children, and the unemployed, along with addiction, petty crime, vandalism, and violence, to create a constellation of signifiers of poverty. Characters' rough treatment of their living space and the general air of neglect and abuse of their local settings recall the fury of the American homeowners who trashed their houses when they were repossessed by banks for defaulted loans. In both cases, the radical inequality of modern cities is registered physically on the environment through acts of violence and crime that are the accompanying social ills of inequality: the rage of humiliation at feeling unable to have what others have. The reader is invited to understand that an impoverished physical environment impacts on the emotions, behaviour, and actions of its inhabitants.

These similar patterns of urban inequality cannot be contained by assumptions about cultural practices or values, such as of cleanliness, pride, or expected women's roles of childcare and housework. They are first and foremost economic indicators of relative lack and must therefore be analysed in materialist rather than culturalist terms, even though the history of capitalism's uneven development has always been coterminous with the unequal treatment of women, children, the elderly, ethnic minorities, indigenous peoples, and immigrants. To focus on similarities of economic marginalisation across time and space rather than on differences of culture and identity in each community brings together literary periods and genres usually kept apart, to better amplify the singular global political economy that connects them all.

The tendency for postcolonial interest in cultural identity to obscure urgent debate about material inequality can be illustrated in two well-known and contested novels portraying postcolonial minorities in the developed nations of New Zealand and the UK. *Once Were Warriors*, Duff's novel of an urban New Zealand 'slum' in the 1980s, the decade of the neoliberal turn, is a powerful account of social, cultural, and economic brokenness in a deracinated Maori family. Acclaimed by both Maori and Pakeha readers and critics, the novel was accepted as a sobering yet necessary counterbalance to the congratulatory mood of Maori devolution and the state-led national biculturalism of the 1980s. The novel is by no means unique in describing Maori poverty: this is a staple theme dominant in Maori literature from the early 1970s to today. Duff writes of the social ills disproportionately affecting the Maori, including low education and employment, and high rates of ill health, single-parent families, domestic and child abuse, rape, incest, imprisonment, drug abuse, and alcoholism. In journalism and interviews, he openly situates his work as fictionalised versions distilled from his own personal experience of addiction, underachievement, violence, and crime, an alignment of writer with writing common across the postcolonial genre, which encourages the reader to interpret the text to some extent as real and true.

The singularity of Duff's novel in the Maori literary genre is his trenchant rejection of traditional Maori culture as a panacea for these social problems. Instead, in the spirit of the new neoliberal times in which he writes, particularly in his journalism, Duff proposes individualist and competitive 'self-help' (1993, 166), by which he means Western education and motivation for employment rather than culturalist revivalism. In his polemical newspaper editorial, Duff asks:

> Will a haka explain the financial position of a company to a board of directors? Will an ancient waiata persuade a bank to invest in a business venture? Will learning the traditional flax weaving arts, the carving skills, give its students an in-depth knowledge of financial global affairs? Will a long-winded speech in Maori do anything to assist a massive Futures trade on the New York stock exchange? (1993, 52)

In naming international finance and business as a way out of Maori poverty, Duff buys into the national excitement of the radical, Thatcherism-inspired market liberalisation brought into New Zealand in 1984, fêted as heralding the nation's competitive entry into the global market. Duff agrees that the underlying cause of Maori underachievement is colonialism: in a direct address to the Pakeha reader, the female protagonist in *Once Were Warriors*, Beth, claims that the warrior spirit of Maori was 'what we lost when you, the white audience out there, defeated us. Conquered us. Took our land, our *mana*, left us with nothing' (47, italics in original). Duff directly indicts his Pakeha reader as complicit in the cultural, political, and economic subjugation of the indigenous people. Certainly, Maori impoverishment relative to the white mainstream began with colonial dispossession from their land, restricted access to education until the mid-twentieth century, and the racism that condemned the Maori to poorly paid and irregular employment. More than Pakeha, however, Duff claims that the responsibility for contemporary Maori impoverishment lies in the Maori community itself. He blames Maori-on-Maori violence, a 'loser' mentality, and social delinquency rather than national structural inequality.[7]

Duff's strident voice is unique and problematic to the Maori sovereignty movement, which construes the Maori as the victims of Pakeha discrimination, and proposes the solution of rekindling respect for Maori culture and pride in traditions, and revalorising Maori social practices. The strong reaction against Duff's position from the Maori community usefully animates fundamental problems with the emphasis of postcolonial and indigenous studies on cultural identity as the locus for material poverty and psychological dis-ease. In New Zealand public discourse, addressing social problems through culture means the inherently unequal political economy goes unchallenged and thus unchanged. Indeed, as in other developed nations, it took the 2008 financial crisis and prolonged recession to turn New Zealand public attention once again to economic rather than cultural factors as underpinning inequality.

In modern British literature, Ali's *Brick Lane*, and the critical responses to it, similarly highlight the tendency to split culture from economics in the analysis of the Bangladeshi heroine Nazneen's immigration to and negotiation of space in London. Reminiscent of the negative Maori reaction to Duff's portrayal of the Maori, some members of the London Bengali community were indignant about Ali's version of life around Brick Lane. In their protest about filming the movie in the street, and the highly mediatised war of words over the conflict between Germaine Greer and Salman Rushdie, the very particular dynamics of the world-system unevenness that created the London community of predominantly Sylheti Bangladeshi was lost.[8] It is tempting to read Nazneen's love affair and entry into paid employment as a seamstress as emancipation from her preordained social reproduction function as wife, mother, and domestic labourer. This focus on gendered and cultural self-fashioning, however, smooths over the material conditions of her role in the London garment industry and as a single working mother. A non-unionised pieceworker working from home, Nazneen's income is insecure and she could easily become a target of unethical practices and exploitation. As an uneducated, unskilled, solo parent lacking fluency in English, it is unlikely she will ever earn enough to leave the Tower Hamlets social housing, or to live independent of social welfare benefits. In other words, she fits the demographics that make Tower Hamlets one of the poorest boroughs in the UK.

However much *Brick Lane* attracts interpretative focus on ethnic and gender relationships, Ali wrote her book with London Bangladeshi economic issues in mind. In her Acknowledgements, Ali cites Naila Kabeer's *The Power to Choose: Bangladeshi Women and Labour Market Decisions in London and Dhaka* (2000) as her inspiration for the novel (Ali 2003, 429). As indicated in its title, Kabeer, a social economist, deploys culture only insofar as it is relevant to employment opportunities and conditions in the two global cities. Nonetheless, her study demonstrates the complex entanglement of social and economic factors through the constant slippage of assumptions about culture into her British informants' views on Bangladeshi labour, saving, and consumption. In the course of her research in London in 1985, she explains:

> I was struck by the very contrasting discourses of 'culture', on the one hand, and 'economics' on the other, which came into play in discussions about different categories of British workers. The notion of 'culture' rarely figured when the labour market behaviour of white workers, whether male or female, was under discussion. Instead, the discussion focused on such issues as relative skills, wage differentials, costs of childcare, trade union membership and collective bargaining power. However, in conversations about Bangladeshi workers, and workers from other Asian communities within the UK, a highly racialized discourse of difference almost invariably crept into the conversation: '*they* always stick together', '*they* don't pay tax'; '*they* keep their women at home'.

White employers complained that they could not compete with Asian factory owners who employed people from their own communities and exploited them through various 'feudal' practices, such as paying a single wage for husband and wife, or by using unpaid family labour. (217)

In the very specific context of a study on women's agency in labour market decisions, Kabeer's fieldwork exposes conflicting regards of the commonly assumed split between the spheres of economics and culture. On the one hand, her white participants discuss their own labour practices as if they are devoid of cultural and social influence, an absence that reveals the internalisation of certain capitalistic norms and values. On the other hand, they construe Bangladeshi women's relationships to work as wholly shaped by culture, which they identify precisely because they are different to their own: communal rather than individual labour time; preferential rather than meritocratic employment criteria; and controlled by a patriarchal order rather than free labour. In pitting a capitalistic against a presumed non-capitalistic work and business ethic, her informants' 'racialized discourse of difference' contains clear echoes of the nineteenth-century racism outlined in Chap. 2.

Kabeer's study indicates that postcolonial writers and literary critics are not alone in the tendency to underestimate the extent to which economic considerations are factors of cultural production and thus deeply involved in expressions of inequality enacted through ethnic and gender discrimination. Quoting Zillah Eisenstein that 'racialized, sexualized and gendered labor contributes to capital accumulation and structures the inequality that emanates from it' (Hyman 2014, Sect. 2, para 4), feminist economist Prue Hyman reminds us that 'women and ethnic minorities are overrepresented among those most disadvantaged in the real world. Gender, race and class are at the heart of inequality but are only implicit in most economic writings' (Sect. 2, para 1). It is exactly against such a trend that postcolonial economics must work, by centring the material and by placing the specificity of particular communities in the larger context of capitalism's multiple terrains of inequality.

In yet another economic situation in which culture-specific class relations at work in London's immigrant communities are all but invisible to Western eyes, both V.S. Naipaul in *A Bend in the River* (1979) and Leila Aboulela in *Minaret* (2006) allude to wealthy Arab immigrants bringing their servants with them. The twenty-five years that separates these novels suggests that the shift from neocolonial to neoliberal political economies that continues to attract the elite from the ex-colonies to the colonial centre has not changed this phenomenon. Aboulela's Sudanese narrator spells out forms of economic inequality within and among Middle-Eastern societies to her unaware Western readership in seemingly offhand comments about the close-knit London Sudanese community. Najwa mentions that rich Sudanese bring their maids with them to London, where they further continue their domestic employment practices from home by employing maids from Ethiopia (141) and the Philippines (221), and, in one case, a Sri Lankan nanny from Saudi Arabia for a Lebanese second wife of a Saudi businessman (72). The matter-of-fact tone of Najwa's revelations reminds readers that social practices such as polygamous family models and labour relations of servitude that are non-Western, and thus unfamiliar, are nevertheless present in multicultural London.

In the classic postcolonial text *A Bend in the River*, Naipaul describes rich Arab immigrants to London bringing their 'house-born slaves' with them (1989, 233). His deliberate use of the word 'slave' usefully shocks the Western reader into thinking through modern-day practices of an extreme form of unequal labour relationship. Whereas Naipaul condemns as unjust the forced power relations of the colonial era, when indigenous slaves were colonial chattels, the patina of free-market labour relations renders the same inequality acceptable in London's postcolonial, free-market economy. Naipaul's character Nazruddin explains:

> In the old days, they made a lot of fuss if they caught you sending a couple of fellows to Arabia in a dhow. Today they have their passports and visas like everybody else, and walk past immigration like everybody else, and nobody gives a damn. (242)

When Salim sees a 'house-slave' leaving Waitrose supermarket, 'his little white cap on and his plain white gown, proclaiming his status to everybody … walking the regulation ten paces ahead of his mistress' (241), he instantly recognises a social hierarchy that remains hidden to passers-by of other nationalities, including the British. As indicated by the ironic nod to British (and, presumably, many Western readers') ignorance of the social hierarchy that to Nazruddin is so evident, the passage critiques contemporary forms of colonial hypocrisy. Translocating past colonial relations into the present postcolonial era, Naipaul makes a sly dig at the British proclamation of equal opportunity despite many inequalities. These include discrimination against immigrant entrepreneurs such as Nazruddin, and its inability to see blatant forms of inequality replicated in immigrant societies that ignore the host country's rhetoric of multiculturalism and equality. Kabeer's, Ali's, Aboulela's, and Naipaul's indications of radical economic inequality passing under the radar in neoliberal London because it is disguised by unfamiliar cultural practices are further amplified by the findings of a 2014 European Commission report on modern slavery, in which one of the featured categories is domestic labourers (Eurostat 2015).

Ali's portrayal of internal friction in the Bangladeshi community, and Aboulela's of the immigrant Sudanese group, are less strident and overtly critical than Duff's scathing critique of Maori underachievement, yet both British novels give multiple examples of cultural discrimination based on the main characters' socio-economic marginalisation. Set almost entirely within their respective immigrant communities, Ali's and Aboulela's books narrate illegal activities and abuses of the female narrators at the hands of upper-class members of their own community. From the postcolonial critical stance that supports minority agency, it is very hard to critique such inequalities and unfair practices. The difficulty of responding to Duff's indictment of the culture of violence within the Maori community is here illustrative. In his unrelenting portrayal of Maori-on-Maori violence, Duff exposes a negative side to the positive support for Maori cultural rejuvenation in being reluctant or even unable to respond to his characterisation of the Maori as 'hard drinking men, and not a few women, who were appalling parents, who were wife beaters, child rapists, beer-sodden lowlifes' (1993, ix). Duff was criticised by Maori for exposing negative aspects of their culture; that he had 'hung out dirty Maori washing' (xi). From a social rather than cultural perspective, however, Duff's fiction asks readers to support the Maori by tackling the socio-economic conditions in New Zealand that make Maori violence and poverty a reality.

More serious than the paper wars of academic dissent surrounding writers who expose negative aspects of their cultural group, as Duff and Ali have experienced, many writers have been exiled or imprisoned for criticising their community. Examples only from those writers cited in this book are Ngũgĩ wa Thiong'o, Wole Soyinka, Ken Saro-Wiwa, and Pramoedya Ananta Toer. Neil Lazarus identifies the political sensitivity that led to Ngũgĩ's imprisonment and exile due to his criticism of Kenyan national neocolonialism in the 1970s: '[f]rom the point of view of officialdom, it would seem that what is required of African writers is that they continue to hurl abuse at colonialism while euphemizing the authoritarianism of different postcolonial regimes under the rubric of "nation building"' (1990, 214). To be seen as criticising one's culture appears to incite damaging emotional reactions that obfuscate the critique itself, which is, in the case of the texts cited here, arguably rooted in economic issues of inequality and financial disenfranchisement. In the era of identity politics that grew out of decolonial independence and minority rights in the mid-to-late-twentieth century, hyper-sensitivity to perceived cultural insults deflect attention away from urgent analysis of material inequalities and the negative socio-cultural repercussions of poverty and lack. An economic literary response to London's Bangladeshi majority in Tower Hamlets or to Auckland's Maori and Pacific Islander majority in council housing fictionalised in Duff's Pine Block reads the fiction for insights into the factors contributing to such inequality and the authors' suggestions for improvement and solutions.

Reading Duff and Ali outside of the frame that Kabeer identifies as 'the highly racialized discourse of difference' reveals multiple and complex economic considerations that constrain and shape the characters' daily lives and relationships. *Once Were Warriors* and *Brick Lane* remain, however, primarily texts about the cultural identity of indigenous and immigrant individuals and communities. On the contrary, in Wheatle's Brixton novels, Jamaican culture and heritage plays a minor role in the second- and third-generation young black British male characters' sense of self. The protagonists in each of Wheatle's novels are each principally concerned with achieving upward mobility out of the urban poverty they experience or see around them. In *East of Acre Lane*, *Brixton Rock*, and *The Dirty South*, the life ambitions expressed by most characters centre on visions of themselves in prestigious clothes and cars, admired by women, friends, and their families. Their financial savvy to meet these desires is impressive. In *The Dirty South*, the fourteen-year-old boys weigh up the relative merits of client group, risk, turnover, and profit to decide which type of drugs suit them as entry-level drug dealers (19–21). Describing the 'buzz' of shoplifting, twelve-year-old Dennis boasts, 'it's amazing the confidence new clothes can give you. We would hang out at Stockwell and New Park Road Youth Clubs, posing like we was [*sic*] in a hip hop video and tormenting those ghetto kids who were still wearing beat up trainers and cheap market clothes' (15). In Dennis's rare moments of reflection on the ethics of his muggings, stealing, beating, and drug dealing, the ends always justify the means—a euphoric 'buzz' and possessing things that others admire.

A group of young Auckland Samoans in Albert Wendt's short story 'Robocop in Long Bay' (2012) describe almost the same set of motivations as in Wheatle's story:

> 'We started pinching things cos our poor fucking parents were too bloody poor to get them for us,' offers Rube. 'We stole to help keep our 'āiga fed, mate.'
>
> 'Bullshit, mate,' Wait whispers. 'Only partly true. We also loved doing it, bro. Loved stickin' it to our teachers, the Man, the cops. Then we got to love the dough we made, especially that.' (17)

In both stories, these characters buy into the standard liberal dream of upward mobility, deemed accessible by ideologies of freedom and equality embodied in competitive entrepreneurship, rewarded risk-taking, meritocratic education, and fair employment. Faced with negative experiences in education and employment, however, they eschew those paths to success espoused by the mainstream to focus directly on the end product, the possession of money and goods by the most expedient means. Neither Jamaican nor Samoan cultural traditions are shown to offer alternative value systems with which the youths can feel content *not* to consume. On the contrary, the young men have internalised capitalism into their respective cultural frames, which for Samoans requires sharing resources and helping their elders. The colonial-era process by which colonised cultures adopted and adapted capitalist social relations, outlined in the analysis of postcolonial historical novels in Chap. 2, has here been completed, so that by the contemporary era the neoliberal capitalist societies of the UK and New Zealand are natural, normal, and unchallenged.

In the early postcolonial novel, *The Beautyful Ones Are Not Yet Born*, Ayi Kwei Armah's narrator is more articulate than Wheatle's and Wendt's teenagers about the desire that motivates consumption. The unnamed man expresses the attraction of money as 'the uncontrollable feeling of happiness and power … whenever he found himself able, no matter for how brief a spell, to do the heroic things that were expected all the time' (114–115). Unlike Dennis, however, Armah's narrator is troubled by his desire, and tries to resist its corrupting influence: '[h]ow was it possible for a man to control himself, when the admiration of the world, the pride of his family and his own secret happiness, at least for the moment, all demanded ... Money. Power' (115). This moral dilemma creates the novel's tension, between the narrator's socialist leanings and his idealism for the new nation-state, and the neocolonial money-grabbing which includes skimming, bribery, and corruption in order to share in the nation's profits. In narrating a mundane office joke that reveals the culture of bribery to complement the low civil-servant salary, the man laments:

> It is so normal, all of this, that the point of holding out against it escapes the unsettled mind. ... The foolish ones are those who cannot live life the way it is lived by all around them, those who will stand by the flowing river and disapprove of the current. *There is no other way*, and the refusal to take the leap will help absolutely no one at any time. (108, my italics)

Striking is this 1968 fictional articulation of Thatcher's infamous slogan, 'there is no alternative.' The maxim at once embodies the tenets of neoliberalism and justifies its perpetuation by decrying as foolish any resistance or alternative to the free-market political economy, which is considered common sense, and thus devoid of ideology. Whereas Armah awaits a later generation of 'beautyful ones' to replace the 'foolish,' in the post-Thatcher neoliberal world that Wheatle's and Wendt's characters inhabit,[9] no alternative is even offered, with Thatcher's saying internalised and accepted by the characters. The sadness expressed in Armah's narrative voice, which conveys the neocolonial-era mourning for what might have been, gives way in the neoliberal era to a matter-of-fact, business-like approach to making ends meet. In narratives written from the perspectives of youths born into the neoliberal era, they have neither seen nor heard of an alternative.

Far from offering a window on Jamaican, black British, or Samoan New Zealand immigrant *culture*, these works describe in considerable detail the functioning of an illegal, underground *economy*. Just as Armah portrays systemic corruption as an integral part of the political economy of neocolonial Ghana, Wheatle and Wendt offer readers a view into contemporary, developed-world political economies that have normalised the discourse of self-help and user pays. In both neocolonial and contemporary contexts, the characters' sense of self is closely related to the goods they possess, consume, and share with their families: in both, illegal activities are the means to achieve these desires. In *The Dirty South*, Noel's drug money tops up his mother's unemployment benefit and gives her money to join her friends at the local bingo, and in 'Robocop in Long Bay,' Mr Makiva is proud of his prestigious late-model truck, stolen by his sons, who gift it to him under the cultural exchange custom of *fa'alavelave*. In terms of Sen's capabilities approach, only through illegal activities can these characters fully participate in the cultural expectations of their respective societies.

The deeply material nature of the marginalisation that Wheatle suggests drives violence and criminality among South London youth confirms Zygmunt Bauman's analysis of the 2011 London riots as the poor claiming their right to be consumers (Bauman 2011), which Slavoj Žižek paraphrases as 'an ironic response to consumerist ideology: "You call on us to consume while simultaneously depriving us of the means to do it properly – so here we are doing it the only way we can!"'(2011, n.p.). Žižek's rhetorical question—'[c]an we even imagine what it means to be a young man in a poor, racially mixed area, a priori suspected and harassed by the police, not only unemployed but often unemployable, with no hope of a future?' (2011, n.p.)—has many literary answers, in a long history of London minority writing, of which Wheatle's is most contemporary. While Dennis thinks his dad's reminiscing about his involvement in the 1981 Brixton riots is boringly out of date and seriously uncool, Wheatle suggests resonant periodicity that makes the 2006 novel prefigure the 2011 UK riots just as the 1979 setting of *Brixton Rock* foreshadowed the 1981 Brixton riots. Indeed, interviewed in April 2011 to mark the thirty-year anniversary of the 1981 riots, only four months before the 2011 outbreak of street violence, Wheatle claims he 'can imagine a repeat of 1981' (Wheatle qtd in Walker 2011, n.p.). In comparing the two events, many commentators have outlined the similarities, which include high youth unemployment, overbearing police harassment, lack of adequate family and community funding, and an overarching mood of discontent and marginalisation.[10]

Žižek's summary of impoverished South London socio-economic conditions and socio-cultural expectations effectively paraphrases the settings of many of the novels discussed in this chapter, including by Lins, Duff, Ali, and Wheatle. In these novels, almost all interaction occurs within the community defined by the localised geographical area. The narrative focus on in-group power struggles, expressed alternately as between gangs (*City of God*; *Once Were Warriors*), religious and ethnic factions (*Brick Lane*), and drug dealers' turf wars (*Brixton Rock*; *The Dirty South*), concurs with Žižek's diagnosis of the 2011 riots:

> [T]he conflict was between two poles of the underprivileged: those who have succeeded in functioning within the system versus those who are too frustrated to go on trying. The rioters' violence was almost exclusively directed against their own. The cars burned and the shops looted were not in rich neighbourhoods, but in the rioters' own. The conflict is not between different parts of society; it is, at its most radical, the conflict between society and society, between those with everything, and those with nothing, to lose; between those with no stake in their community and those whose stakes are the highest. (n.p.)

The in-group tensions based on socio-economic inequality that Žižek sketches are contemporary expressions of the same structures of internal colonialism seen in previous chapters. The rise of neoliberalism without alternative and the concomitant shift from class to cultural identity as the main bearer of social registration means that 'the poor' are no longer recognised as a definable, bounded social category.

In their emphasis on the unintelligibility and inchoate drives and aims of the riots, Bauman, Žižek, and other commentators including Stuart Hall and Paul Gilroy, as well as politicians and mainstream media, confront the non-topic of the depoliticisation of social life. In appearing apolitical and unguided, the 2011 riots embody neoliberalism's driving ideology of the market's disconnect from politics, which made it impossible to interpret this protest against consumerism as a political act. In the inability to settle on a coherent explanation for the riots, the entanglement of the social and cultural with the economic and political is most evident precisely because it is impossible to separate them. Neoliberal ideological and state policy principles, however, emerge across all explanations. For example, the media portrayal of the rioters as greedy, morally corrupt, and 'feral,'[11] reinforced by police targeting black youths in impoverished areas such as South London (Laursen 2015, 312; London School of Economics 2011, 19), alludes to the criminalisation of poverty that puts the onus on the individual—construed under liberalism as free and equal—rather than on the state and capitalist economic system within which they function. Media bewilderment at the fact that around 50% of rioters were students or had higher education refuses to acknowledge the commercialisation of the education industry incommensurate with the jobs and salaries available—despite student protests against raises in tuition fees ongoing since 2010 and taking place concomitantly with the 2011 riots. The media's inability to connect the two protests again illuminates the difficulty of understanding the salience of economic inequality to social life, as the popular imaginary that construes tertiary students as successful in education, middle-class, or upwardly mobile is at odds with the perception of rioters as delinquent social failures.

The above ingredients, combined with the cutting of welfare expenditure under post-financial crisis austerity, has led low socio-economic youths, both black and white depending on the local demographics, to act in accordance with neoliberal expectations: undertaking their consumer duty to shop through violence and crime. As Stuart Hall puts it in regard to the riots, 'they've taken the message of Thatcherism and Blairism and the coalition: what you have to do is hustle. Because nobody's going to help you' (Hall qtd in Williams 2012, n.p.). Noel in *The Dirty South* concurs: 'I'm gonna hustle for what I can get in this fucked up racist world and *fuck* anybody who don't like it! Including *you*. Do you know how it feels to walk with your mum when she's carrying Lidl bags?' (44, italics in original). In the passages leading up to this quote, Noel describes the humiliation of seeing his mother work in a degrading job at a discount supermarket, where she is passed over for promotion: 'I'm not gonna struggle like that. I'm not gonna be a good nigger boy only for some white pussy to tell me I can't get a promotion. All for an extra fifty fucking p an hour!' (44). Noel's statements collapse racial discrimination and economic exploitation, or rather he sees no difference between these—both valid reasons he uses to justify his anger and his motivation to opt out of the mainstream standards of success in education and employment. While he labels the inequality he experiences as racist, it is the economic repercussion of that racism—shopping at Lidl, missing promotion—that upsets him most. Poverty, he suggests, is an integral and expected part of his ethnicity, an outward sign, like skin colour, of marginalisation. In the comments from such fictional characters, as in many of the interviews in the comprehensive and extensive London School of Economics study and report *Reading the Riots*, the entanglement of socio-cultural and economic factors render it difficult to tease apart racial, cultural, or economic forms of discrimination. Hall's diagnosis of the 2011 riots as '[r]ace segueing into consumerism—a classic neo-liberal descant' (2011, 726) encapsulates the interrelated cultural and economic elements portrayed in the fiction.

Wheatle's novels do not contain riots, and yet after the 2011 events they illuminate in retrospect many of the issues identified as factors leading to and catalysts of the civil unrest. The great number of interviews with rioters, including the *Reading the Riots* study and several television documentaries, speak to the public desire to understand why the riots happened, with personal narratives bringing eyewitness immediacy. At the same time, the polyphony of experiences made it difficult to pinpoint one easy cause or reason, resulting in confusion in popular opinion which in turn facilitated inaction from leaders. Riot participants' difficulty in articulating the sources of their anger and resentment chime with similar incoherence in fiction. In *Brick Lane*, friction between the Muslim immigrant Bengal Tigers and the right-wing, white nationalist Lion Hearts explodes in Bengali street riots, 'revenge for the revenge. ... It's not even about anything anymore. It's just about what it is. Put anything in front of them now and they'll fight it. A police car, a shop window, anything' (400). Ali's focus on ethnic identity and belonging throughout the novel does not appear to fit with the smash-and-grab violence of the riots that form its dramatic climax, and these short scenes jar with the intimate and domestic sphere of the main narrative. In the Maori context, Duff also struggles to identify what causes feelings of exclusion. His protagonist reflects:

> [Jake] can see things not equal, not balanced, that you can't put into words and so you do the only thing you can do—strike out. Swear and curse and get furious at not being able to do a damn thing to catch up. Maybe you just want some of their material action. (100)

Rather than co-ordinated rioting or stealing, Jake cruises the pubs looking for a fight. Although violence is an outlet for his aggression which makes him feel, momentarily, like a winner, it does nothing to help him 'catch up' and improve his 'material action.' Thus, the cycle of violence is set to perpetuate. Sherman Alexie similarly describes senseless acts of violence and vandalism on the Native American reservation in *Reservation Blues*, which his authorial overview diagnoses as stemming from the broken dreams of 'those who dreamed in childhood of fishing salmon but woke up as adults to shop at the Trading Post and stand in line for U.S.D.A. commodity food instead' (14). Across each of these examples, the characters can only vaguely gesture toward the source(s) of their anger, which thereby leads to an equally misdirected retaliation, usually in violence against their own property or people.

Such inarticulacy in both fiction and in society at large diagnoses a general inability to identify, define, and thereby address the impact of neoliberalism in the social sphere. This is the rage of US homeowners trashing their repossessed homes as a violent reaction against having a potent symbol of their financial success taken from them. It is also the high emotion, the indignity of injustice, of anger, and frustration at feeling unable to access the markers of success expected by society that underpin the 2011 riot participants' explanations. Across these diverse contexts, the financially marginalised rarely choose to opt out of the neoliberal dream; rather, they have been pushed out by the conditions of inequality that profit one sector of society at the expense of the other. Caught in the seemingly inescapable poverty trap, the losers of capitalism are victims of neoliberalism's slow violence, an insidious, invisible violence that Rob Nixon calls 'an attritional violence that is typically not viewed as violence at all' (2011, 2). In their aggressive responses to the corrosive pressures of alienation, the poor react with actual violence: spectacular, newsworthy, and condemnable.

EMOTIONAL AND BEHAVIOURAL RESPONSES TO INEQUALITY

The yo-yo of hope and despair that forms the narrative tension in much postcolonial fiction dealing with dreams of success confronting sobering realities mirrors the boom-and-bust cyclical rollercoaster that is intrinsic to capitalism. The difficulty for writers and their characters to locate and articulate the concrete reasons that cause their feelings of exclusion echoes the difficulty in broader social discourse of defining neoliberalism or unmasking the ideology behind the 'natural,' 'common sense' contemporary political economy. Due to the assumed split between literature and economics, it has been difficult to theorise the intersections between and relatedness of these correlations. Bringing together the two discourses, Akerlof and Shiller in *Animal Spirits* theorise the market as a direct result of emotion and behaviour. Thus, they claim that success breeds market confidence, failure leads to conservatism and market contraction, with dramatic fluctuations rather than a gentle upward trajectory being the norm. Analysis of the emotional impact of alienation from the neoliberal political economy fosters understanding of economically marginalised peoples' motivations and behaviour, and further helps account for social flare-ups commonly mediatised as random or surprising. On the contrary, everyday individual instances of petty theft, property damage, and acts of violence, which sporadically swell into larger group protests and riots, may be read as common symptoms of capitalism's crisis, merely occurring at the bottom end of the socio-economic scale and more visible than the veiled thefts and dispossessions carried out by the elite financiers and technocrats, only occasionally revealed in high-profile cases such as AIG Insurance and HSBC bank.

Emphasis on behavioural, cognitive, psychological, and identity economics brings this social science closest to the content of literary analysis. Their ambitions, however, remain quite opposite: economists extrapolate their analysis of individual affect into macro-economic variables such as debt and unemployment, while literary critics are wary of extending their findings too far outside of the text. Rita Felski's forms of recognition may help breach the disciplinary gap. Her phenomenological approach, attuned to 'moments when histories and cultures overlap' (40), validates the following analyses of recurrent patterns in fiction from diverse world spaces that portray responses to inequality. The recurrence of certain behaviours, such as physical violence as a response to frustration, or the uncanny echo of the same words or images appearing in several, unrelated novels, such as the term 'slum' and descriptions of dirt, shit, and rubbish in impoverished areas, draw attention to how 'accumulated experience [i]s distinctive yet far from unique' (39). When Pankaj Mishra's narrator of *The Romantics* (1999) recognises that in 1980s Benares 'the small, unnoticed tragedies of thwarted hopes and ideals Flaubert wrote about in *Sentimental Education* were all around us' (Mishra qtd in Felski, 40), Felski identifies the logic of self-extension, in which the reader may 'see aspects of oneself in what seems distant and strange' (39). Her argument that the specificities of fiction often highlight characters' and readers' blind spots and misrecognitions is corroborated in the inarticulacy of many writers to clearly diagnose competitive capitalism as underlying their characters' failures and disappointments. On the other hand, her claim that 'structures of recognition ensure that books will often function as lifelines for those deprived of other forms of public acknowledgement' (43) validates the drive to narrativise as a means of making sense of complex phenomena, such as the 2008 financial crisis and structures of inequality.

Akerlof and Shiller's privileging of the psychological motivations that inform economic practice foreground social and cultural responses to economic inequality and poverty. Their study reveals certain beliefs and behaviours common among the underprivileged that are consistent across different time periods and cultural groups. In particular, they find that the poor are averse to risk-taking for fear of falling further, and so they make self-defeating choices and express anti-social behaviour because they feel unfairly treated, excluded, and victimised. Further, they lack motivation to study, work, or save for the intangible future that has, in their experience, always delivered let-downs not rewards. Akerlof explores these psychological reasons for common economic phenomena further with Rachel Kranton in *Identity Economics* (2010). Here, they argue that economics must, belatedly in relation to other social sciences, accommodate identity issues into their calculations of financial behaviour in order to account for the clearly racialised trends in wealth participation. In relation to inequality between whites and African Americans, they claim, '[b]lack/white disparities are arguably the United States' worst social problem. Their persistence is difficult to explain with current economic theories. With an identity model, the facts fall into place' (97). The economic turn to identity, which is an aspect of the social body normally reserved for fields of cultural analysis, is indicative of the disciplinary *rapprochement* that encourages literary analysis also to widen its field and methodology. In particular, Akerlof, Kranton, and Shiller's specific work on intergenerational poverty among ethnic minorities in the USA is informative to the project of postcolonial economics.

In introducing their application of identity economics to poverty among minority groups in the USA, Akerlof and Kranton outline a long history of economic discrimination of minority groups. Victims of white-settler exclusion from free-market opportunities certainly include African Americans and Native Americans. At various historical moments, other groups have also been identified as the bottom of the socio-economic pile, including Catholics, the Irish, the Chinese, the Okies during the Depression-era dispossession of the Midwest, and Latinos, particularly since post-war economic migration. The trends these economists identify, of a close correlation between ethnic and economic marginalisation, and patterns of intergenerational poverty and chronic un- and underemployment, are common issues also present in postcolonial spaces. For example, Akerlof and Kranton (2000) cite the 2000 US census that found the percentage of African American child poverty, at 38%, is nearly four times higher than for whites (97), an inequality also found in relation to ethnic-minority children in the UK, and Maori and Pacific Island children in New Zealand.

The authors themselves argue for theoretical correspondence between the US and postcolonial spaces, suggesting that discrimination of African Americans in the US is similar to the colonial subject under empire—an argument that unwittingly supports the inclusion of the US in postcolonial studies. The writers further reference a group of thinkers central to postcolonial studies, including W.E.B. Du Bois, James Baldwin, bell hooks, Edward Said, and Frantz Fanon (101), and cite from fiction and journalism as case studies of attitudes to identity and belonging. For example, in explaining why people tend to give up trying to achieve in situations where the chances of succeeding are low, Akerlof and Kranton quote from the autobiography of African American journalist and novelist Jill Nelson. Her work illustrates that, '[i]n the trade-off between work and dignity, dignity wins out' (104): '[t]here is a thin line between Uncle-Tomming and Mau-Mauing. To fall off that line can mean disaster. On one side lies employment and self-hatred; on the other, the equally dubious honor of unemployment with integrity' (Nelson qtd in *Identity Economics*, 102). Nelson's biographical use of a nineteenth-century American novel and the decolonising-era Kenyan independence insurgency blurs the lines between past and present, First and Third World, self and other, reality and fiction. In their focus on identity economics and their choice of texts to illustrate their points, these behavioural economists are unwittingly doing the work of postcolonial economics. Certainly, Akerlof and Kranton are not literary theorists, yet their casual use of fiction and of postcolonial cultural contexts to illustrate their study of American inequality grasps a commonality of feeling that concurs with Felski's claims for recognition.

Within the dominant discourse rhetoric that upholds the idea of the efficiency of capitalism to encourage competition and to best ensure actors make rational decisions that will ensure the best financial outcomes, minority agents continually make 'bad' decisions and 'wrong' choices that are in economic terms self-destructive, and thus not understandable to the mainstream. Yet, Akerlof and Kranton's work on identity utility, which models how 'bad' economic decisions may have 'good' motivations and repercussions for a person's standing in their social and cultural groups (160–163), helps clarify the pervasiveness of activities deemed 'bad' from an economic standpoint. Their focus on in-group/out-group identity provides a socioeconomic perspective on the fictional portrayals of characters conflicted in their struggle simultaneously to belong in their minority community and to succeed according to mainstream (out-group) values of achievement. The common postcolonial personification of the 'brown Pakeha,' the 'coconut,' the 'Oreo cookie,' the Native American 'red apple,'and the 'black diamonds' of South Africa's 'cappuccino society'—derogatory terms used against their own members—all speak to this apparent conflict between minority identity and neoliberal norms construed as an emptying-out of identity, which is problematically construed as economic failure.

Immanuel Wallerstein argues that such self-positioning is part of the capitalist function of racism, as discussed in Chap. 2. For Wallerstein, racism not only justifies inequality but also maintains it from inside, in effect replicating in the cultural psyche colonialism's modus operandi that installed capitalism in the colonies as a self-perpetuating system:

> [Racism] has served to socialize groups into their own role in the economy. The attitudes inculcated (the prejudices, the overtly discriminatory behaviour in everyday life) served to establish the framework of appropriate and legitimate behaviour for oneself and for others in one's own household and ethnic group. Racism, just like sexism, functioned as a self-suppressive ideology, fashioning expectations and limiting them. (79)

Whereas the historical fiction discussed in Chap. 2 portrayed bigotry through racist comments made by colonial characters, the fiction analysed in this chapter testifies to the relevance of Wallerstein's statement about the negative judgements and low expectations these characters have of themselves and their peers, including choosing behaviour that fits stereotypes of poor, urban ethnic minorities, thereby perpetuating them. For example, rather than challenging the system within which they fail to achieve, or working harder within the neoliberal model in which they are likely to fail, Wheatle's and Wendt's characters rationalise drug dealing or stealing as optimal means to earn money or acquire the consumer goods their own society expects of them.

The portrayal of characters who give up on mainstream social norms in order to fit in with their own community—that which Wallerstein calls a 'self-suppressive ideology'—abounds in fiction, despite encouragement to escape the poverty trap through education and the personal discipline of holding down a job, such as Beth in *Once Were Warriors*, and Dennis's parents in *The Dirty South*. In *Once Were Warriors*, Jake responds to Beth's search for ways to move out of the state-housing 'slum' as part of her dream of upward mobility as only that—a childish dream:

> Even in his better moments he just looked at a woman, gave her one of those smiles. Of dismissal. Telling her she was kidding herself. And he'd ask her why she wanted to be different from everyone else, wasn't she satisfied and who'd she think she was anyway? (9)

In this passage, the reader is hard-pressed to disagree with Jake's evaluation. Narrated by Beth as she wanders through her house the morning after another drunken party, the reader discovers simultaneously with Beth broken bottles, vomit, mess, a passed-out drunk, and her own black eye in the mirror. Wheatle similarly describes low expectations of achievement according to mainstream standards that make gangs, drugs, crime, and violence seem normative and inevitable for young, black, urban males. Both *Brixton Rock* and *The Dirty South* begin with the protagonist in prison, placing himself within the norms: 'This was where all those bastards in the Home said I'd end up' (*Brixton Rock*, 1); 'They say there are more black men behind bars and in mental institutions than there is in universities in England' (*The Dirty South*, 1). Such comments are thinly disguised authorial input with a political critique, a reading that is reinforced by Duff's and Wheatle's open claims to have lived similar lives to their protagonists.[12] The retrospective narrative structure in *The Dirty South*, which begins where the novel ends, allows Wheatle to trace in close detail the living conditions, family situations, and peer pressure that lead his characters out of education and onto the streets, and into a culture of drug dealing, stealing, and violence. Knowing the end result at the beginning provides the reader with a context of economic and broader social failure through which to read the whole novel. These novels' insider perspectives that allow the writer to explore characters' psychological and emotional states effectively offer textbook examples of identity economics.

Duff's and Wheatle's novels are set in developed-world cities, which may be seen as sharing structures of economic inequality with the US context that gave rise to Akerlof and Kranton's theory of identity economics. The fact that novels from developing-world urban slums also capture the same contrast between characters feeling like losers according to mainstream expectations and winners in their chosen lives of crime also suggests the applicability of identity economics to radically different social and cultural contexts. Dionne Brand's *At the Full and Change of the Moon* (1999) portrays multiple generations of a black Trinidadian family. The cycle of poverty is constant, although the forms of economic oppression change through the eras of slavery, seasonal plantation work, and itinerant labouring in waves of migration across the Caribbean, the Americas, and, latterly, the UK. A contemporary character, Carlyle, offers a poignant description of his feeling of relief at committing his first crime, an armed robbery at age 16, at feeling 'a certain kind of power in shame and violation' (139):

He walked home, becoming more and more himself, becoming calmer and calmer but inside himself so excited he felt like jumping up, something like electricity running through him, something like water too, electricity and water, and he was burning in the middle of it, bright like something so hot it was white.

He no longer had to do anything inside the tight line of shame he had felt around his head, the waking up in the mornings ashamed, washing his feet and his face and his mouth ashamed, putting on his clothes ashamed, eating whatever little there was with his head bowed, ashamed, and walking up the street like a good boy going to school, ashamed. An enveloping sense of shame wrapped around them all, and there was no cause he could point to for all this shame, and he didn't understand it and he didn't want it. (139)

Through his restricted world view, constrained by this isolated community of descendants of Maroons in Trinidad, Carlyle is unable to identify what the reader interprets as markers of poverty in the rudimentary washing facilities and lack of food. The material reality in which he lives is so normal he is blind to it. Amid the fuzzy pall of shame he feels but cannot describe, the intensity and clarity of his rush of euphoria in the first paragraph is understandably attractive—the 'buzz' earlier described in Wheatle's *The Dirty South*. Without having the language to describe concepts of identity and belonging, Carlyle nevertheless recognises a sense that doing crime is somehow more true to himself than his other daily actions. Selfhood, in this passage, is not constructed of cultural markers at all; rather, the character claims his own agency, literally centring a narrative in which he 'burn[s] bright in the middle of it,' by replacing poverty and shame with consumerism and confidence earned from crime.

The choice of the buzz of crime rather than the humiliation of low-status jobs is also clearly spelt out in Lins's background sketches of many characters in *City of God*. The book relentlessly and somewhat didactically draws a causal link between deprived backgrounds and resultant anti-social behaviour, criminal acts, and violence, a connection which 'sparked an intense debate in Brazil about the relationship between violence, drug-dealing, social injustice, political action and the role of civil society' (Introduction, para 4). The job of day labourer on construction sites is described as particularly demoralising, made worse by the irregularity of the work, its easy dismissal, and long commutes by public transport or sleeping rough on the site:

Hellraiser decided he'd never be skint again. Work like a slave? Never. He wasn't going to eat packed lunches and take orders from white guys, always doing the donkey work with no chance of moving up in life, waking up really early to start work and earn peanuts. ... The idea of sweating it out on a construction site with the thirsty bastards from up north seemed more attractive, but like hell it was – the best gangsters have luck on their side. One day he'd hit the jackpot. (35)

Tellingly, Lins describes almost identical reasons as motivating another character, Hammer's turn to crime, with the repetition of several words and images reinforcing both the prevalence of these restricted options for favela inhabitants and their vivid reaction against it (118). In both examples, Hellraiser and Hammer prefer to feel dominant for a moment, as gangsters, than to suffer a lifetime of inferiority as workers, even though the criminal lifestyle choice is probably lethal.

In a female variation on the same theme in Lins's novel, women in a shoplifting gang describe stealing as preferable to working as cleaning women, a job that is 'bad for the body and soul' (225):

They hated working as domestics – truth be told it was a life of contempt, drudgery and little money. Nostalgic always said she wasn't going to be the world's whipping boy just because she hadn't had everything a human being needed to make a decent life for herself. She wasn't the one who'd invented racism, marginalisation or any other type of social injustice, and it wasn't her fault she'd given up her studies to polish the floors in rich bitches' houses. She wanted enough money to ensure a decent life for her kids, something she couldn't get by working, and so at the end of every month, like the other women, she hit supermarkets thirty to forty times, and was always successful. They had money to pay the doctor, the dentist, to buy food and their children's schoolbooks and stationery. All they wanted was a decent life. (225–226)

Whereas Marx theorised that worker alienation would result in solidarity and a proletarian revolution, these characters remain in and even accept the economic model that subjugates them. Instead of challenging the system, they challenge each other in a constant competition with their peers as well as with the wealthy from whom they steal.

Compelling across all the above examples from developing- and developed-world cities is the characters' sense of justification for their violence and crimes, a certain pride in identity buoyed by their belief that their chosen behaviour is the best way toward both personal and material wellbeing. All of these characters are motivated by the same materialist concerns as those expounded in the mainstream version of the neoliberal fantasy promised by Thatcher as the individual's right to own property and make one's own consumer choices. The power and seduction of consumerism that Žižek and Hall identify in relation to the 2011 UK riots applies across these multiple contexts of violence and crime. As fiction, these texts are each focalised through characters who experience economic injustice first hand so that the reader has direct access to their emotions and reasoning.

Identity economics, like Sen's capabilities approach, helps to understand the complex calculations behind decisions that at first glance look to condemn the poor to further poverty and thus to a life outside of the neoliberal economy. Linking economic satisfaction to emotional wellbeing makes sense of the attractiveness of violence and crime as outcomes of deprivation and ostracism from the expected social norms. To consider decision-making as socio-economic in motivation provides a frame for postcolonial literary analysis to deal with behaviours and actions with an eye to commensurability over and above the absolute differences of cultural specificity and scales of material wealth and welfare. Efforts in social and behavioural economics to factor identity, emotion, and ethics into their discipline, in work such as that by Akerlof, Shiller, and Kranton, all take Sen's capabilities approach as foundational. Following in this mould, in *The Spirit Level: Why Equality is Better for Everyone* (2010), British social epidemiologists Richard Wilkinson and Kate Pickett analyse the social rather than individual or behavioural costs of inequality. Whereas Piketty uses longitudinal and international data to focus on the mechanisms that create, maintain, and change levels of inequality without engaging with the social issues that result from inequality, address the ethical issue of why such inequality is undesirable. Basing their research on economic data[13] similar to Piketty's provides a way out of the often-inflammatory discourse of identity issues of immigration, ethnicity, race, and religion.

Wilkinson and Pickett's demonstration of the negative impact of inequality on all parts of society, including those who are comfortably off and wealthy, rejects the mainstream assumption that poverty and precarity are relevant only to those directly affected (12–13). The book's evidence of how rising inequality increases the overall national occurrence of social and health problems sets up a national discussion on inequality based on mutual benefit for all. The importance of encompassing all of society in their study, from rich to poor, is that it actively asks the winners of capitalism to see their fate as linked to rather than separate from the poor. *The Spirit Level* supports the post-2008 turn of attention to internal inequality within nations, while the strongly similar trends of social outcomes found in its international comparative data argue for the collapsed split between the developing and the developed world. Their evidence of the link between material equality (301–309), health, and social behaviour provides statistical backing to the causal relation between poverty and underachievement explored in fiction.

Impoverished characters subjected to violence, a common representation in postcolonial novels, benefit from economic analysis of the impact of inequality on behaviour. Sen, Akerlof, Shiller, Kranton, Wilkinson, and Pickett suggest that reasons for violence include low levels of trust within a community, responses to feelings of shame, injured pride, and humiliation, and responses to a perceived challenge to one's status. One such structure of violence that recurs in fiction is a chain by which the strong hurt the weak, who in turn hurt the weaker, a syndrome Wilkinson and Pickett define by the psychological term 'displaced aggression' (166). Abani provides a simple explanation of the phenomenon in *GraceLand*. In answer to Elvis's question about why the poor bully the poor, an elderly beggar answers: 'Look, Elvis, dese are poor people. Poor people are hungry people, and like Bob Marley talk, a hungry man is an angry man' (226). Displaced aggression is one of the many ways in which the poor jeopardise their own economic success through detrimental behaviour, and reinforce negative stereotypes and low expectations by reducing motivation to succeed. Furthermore, the concept of displaced violence accounts for the internal colonialism that has been a focus throughout this book; the great majority of harm is done to one's own family and community rather than to the elite outsiders who are the instigators of injustice.

Displaced aggression recurs frequently in postcolonial fiction, often in the form of incomprehensible violence done to the protagonist or narrator. Such powerful illustrations of unfairness, powerlessness, and victimhood generate the reader's emotional engagement in the narrative, by creating empathy that cuts across the distance of time and space to render familiar otherwise foreign contexts. Pramoedya provides a succinct example of displaced aggression in *House of Glass*, in a trickle-down of power from the Dutch civil servant to the native clerk, women, and children, and finally to an illiterate, Muslim native worker: 'I came in for more insults from my boss. I took it out on my subordinate. He no doubt went home and took it out on his wife, who in turn took it out on the children, and the children took it out on the servant' (20). Kiana Davenport, in *Shark Dialogues*, similarly describes violence in the hierarchical work environment of sugar plantations, from the white owners down to the Hawai'ian and immigrant Filipino labourers: 'the *luna* [foreman] pushed them, pressured by the manager, the manager in turn pressured by plantation owners, rich, missionary descendants' (120). In one among many fictional examples of incest, in *Q&A*, Ram is powerless to stop Gudiya being raped by her own father (Swarup 2006, 83), whose humiliation at his come-down in life from a top astronomer to shop assistant living in a Mumbai chawl leads him to drunkenness and domestic abuse (72–84). In each of these examples, the concept of violence is relative and cumulative, cascading in a multilinked chain from the top to the bottom of the economic hierarchy, from the latent violence and ethical crime of economic inequality in the profit-driven capitalist workplace, to the actualised violence and real crimes committed on the victimised body of servants, labourers, women, and children.

This direct structure of cause and effect contains damning critique of economic inequality as a source of violence. However, this original catalyst is easily overlooked due to the narrative positioning typical in postcolonial fiction that focuses on the local and specific rather than the general; on the poor rather than on the rich. The focus on the intimate level of actual violence done to the victim often establishes a narrative of victimhood in which it is difficult to apportion blame or suggest solutions to these underlying inequalities. While the drives to maximise profit and reap rewards and accolades for himself motivate, respectively, Pramoedya's Dutch colonial administrator, Davenport's white plantation owner, and Swarup's director of the Space Research Institute, the lack of narrative focus on the immoral and unethical behaviour of these rich figures makes it difficult to indict the rich. Instead, the common notion of the poor as criminal is reinforced.

In another cluster of fictional representations of displaced aggression that does not directly locate the origin of violence in economic inequality, the poor take out their frustration on their peers. As argued earlier in this chapter, the reasons for such violence tend to remain sketchy or unvoiced, which suggests the difficulty of identifying capitalism's injustice as a structure of modern-day society. In Alexie's *The Absolutely*

True Diary of a Part-Time Indian, Junior's teacher can only interpret the chain of violence in facile terms of generic low self-esteem: '"You know that Rowdy's dad hit him, don't you?" "Yeah," I said. Whenever he came to school with a black eye, Rowdy made sure to give black eyes to two kids picked at random' (52); '"your friend Rowdy, he's given up. That's why he likes to hurt people. He wants them to feel as bad as he does"' (53). In Wheatle's *Brenton Brown*, Brenton's girlfriend reports on a similar cycle of violence. Rather than critiquing the causes of violence or even indicting the perpetrators, however, the narrator aims her critique at the inefficacy of the state social services:

> 'Cos I was the oldest my mom beat the living shit out of me when things went wrong in our house. If Dad came home drunk and shouted at her I would get it in the neck in the morning. On some mornings I got it all over my fucking body. I spent my eleventh birthday in some battered woman's home. The crazy thing about it was that Mum was in there for Dad battering her but the social workers never even realised she was beating the living shit out of me! (Chap. 8, para 67)

The narrator of this passage works hard to keep her tone neutral, in order not to blame either of her parents for their violence. While this strategy usefully muddies reader's expectations of victimhood, Wheatle does not go on to explore the many, interlinking layers of victim and offender.

In *Once Were Warriors*, a novel centred around multiple forms of violence, Duff's relentlessly negative characterisation of Maori makes it difficult for the reader familiar with the culturalist paradigm to romanticise Maori as a culture in touch with cultural traditions. In one of many examples in the text, Jake Heke 'woke, almost invariably, with a desire to punch someone, which grew quickly to vivid imaginings of wrongs done him, slights, looks, and so he feeling hurt and then – naturally enough, as he saw it – wanting to right things by the only way he knew how: with his fists' (50). Jake turns his rage indiscriminately on men and women, his own family, friends, and total strangers, and he has a particularly strong hatred of the Chinese takeaway owners, immigrants he finds threatening because they have figured out how to succeed where he has failed (173–175). Jake's misplaced rage against the Chinese minority, also seen in Chap. 2 with the Maori children bullying their Moriori cousin in Makereti's *Where the Rekohu Bone Sings*, exemplifies Wilkinson and Pickett's suggestion that displaced violence is also the root of the perceived threat some minorities express as racism or exclusion toward other foreign immigrants (167). Neither Duff nor Makereti openly pinpoint the structural inequality of pre-contact Maori society. Instead, they allow the issue to remain implicit—Duff by reminding readers of the negative aspects of pre-contact Maori society, with its rigid class hierarchy from slaves to chiefs, and Makereti through the Maori–Moriori relationship of conqueror and conquered, landowner and slave.

The above examples all closely map local environments of threat that culminate in characters taking out violence out on the closest people around them, usually within family and community. In each of these examples, privilege and punishment is marked by age, race, or gender: women and children are typically victims, but also perpetrators in turn. As one particular form of the same hierarchical structure of internal colonisation outlined in historical contexts in the preceding chapters, displaced violence argues for an economic basis of inequality as underpinning the perpetuation of injustice that on the surface looks to be culturally motivated. Not only is this violence carried out by one generation on the next, leading to a cycle that repeats across time, but also by one ethnicity, race, gender, religion, and social status on another, in a confusion of targets that emphasises the entanglement of the economic in the social and cultural fabrics of which the nation, and indeed the world-system, consist.

Notes

1. See The Poverty Site, 'Low Income and Ethnicity' and London's Poverty Profile.
2. The common yet simplistic view of the informal economy as negative for the national economy because it is untaxed and unregulated is being overturned in development economics and international policy studies. Examples of positive contributions include the highly specialised and skilled production from within slum communities, and the number of alternative economic models they provide, including circular economics, inclusive economics, social banking, and bottom-up industrial practices.
3. The event is still of political relevance in Nigeria, particularly as ex-residents continue to agitate for legal reparations. The slum was again forcibly cleared in 2012.
4. The South African management group specialises in building airports and hotel chains in South and East Asia, and also owns coal mines in Australia. See GVK website.

5. See the 'Seaside and Country Homes' section of the Housing Moves website.
6. Used in measures including the Gini coefficient, the Consumer Price Index, and the Purchasing Power Parity exchange rate. For critical analysis of relative poverty measures, see Angus Deaton 1997; Branko Milanovic 2005; and Shaohua Chen and Martin Ravallion, 'More Relatively-Poor People in a Less Absolutely-Poor World.'
7. See, in particular, the character of the Chief, *Once Were Warriors*, 182; 191.
8. Around 95% of Bangladeshis in London come from the region of Sylhet. See Naila Kabeer, *The Power to Choose: Bangladeshi Women and Labour Market Decisions in London and Dhaka*, 193–216. For materialist critiques of *Brick Lane*, see Rehana Ahmed 2010, and Darragh P. Hall (Unpublished Manuscript).
9. Wheatle mentions Thatcher in several of his books: in *Brenton Brown*, which takes an overt class-based line on London inequality, the eponymous protagonist links his own delinquent youth of the 1980s to Thatcher's police-led clamp-down on protests, including against the mining unions and leading up to the Brixton riots (Chap. 10, para 4); in *The Dirty South*, Dennis's father also contextualises the 1980s in terms of Thatcher's economic policy influencing the Brixton riots, high black unemployment, and the demise of the British working class (4).
10. For a more detailed enumeration of the similarities between the 1981 Brixton riots and those of August 2011, see Ole Birk Laursen 2015.
11. While the most common explanations for the riots given in the media were poor parenting, gangs, criminality, moral decline, and greed, the top responses by the 270 riot participants interviewed were poverty, policing, government policy, and unemployment. See *Reading the Riots: Investigating England's summer of disorder*, 11.
12. Both writers claim their fiction is strongly motivated by and based on their life experiences. Wheatle acknowledges his personal experience of broken homes, borstal, and prison in the Afterword of *Brixton Rock*. Duff describes *Once Were Warriors* as his attempt to understand the cycle of poverty and his own problems with drinking and violence as related to his upbringing in *Maori: The Crisis and the Challenge*, xi–xiii.
13. Wilkinson and Pickett draw their statistics predominantly from the World Bank, United Nations groups, and national bureaus. The data sets do not differentiate, as Piketty does, between income and capital forms of inequality.

Works Cited

Primary

Abani, Chris. *GraceLand*. New York: Farrar, Straus and Giroux, 2004.
Aboulela, Leila. *Minaret*. London: Bloomsbury, 2006.
Adiga, Aravind. *The White Tiger*. London and New York: Free Press, 2008.
Alexie, Sherman. *Reservation Blues*. New York: Grove Press, 1995.
Ali, Monica. *Brick Lane*. London: Doubleday, 2003.
Auster, Paul. *Sunset Park*. New York: Henry Holt, 2010, Kindle Edition.
Begag, Azouz. *Le Gone du Chaâba*. Paris: Éditions du Seuil, 1986.
Blumenfeld, Simon. *Jew Boy*. London: London Books, 2011 [1935].
Boo, Katherine. *Behind the Beautiful Forevers*. London: Portobello, 2012.
Brand, Dionne. *At the Full and Change of the Moon*. New York: Grove Press, 1999.
Chamoiseau, Patrick. *Texaco*. Trans. Rose-Myriam Réjouis and Val Vinokurov, New York: Vintage, 1997 [Gallimard, 1992].
Dickens, Charles. *Bleak House*. London: Penguin Classics, 2003 [1853].
Disraeli, Benjamin. *Sybil, or the Two Nations*. Public Domain Books, 2010 [1845], Kindle Edition.
Duff, Alan. *Maori: The Crisis and the Challenge*. Auckland: Harper Collins, 1993.
———. *Once Were Warriors*. Auckland: Tandem, 1990.
Duiker, K. Sello. *Thirteen Cents*. Cape Town: David Philip, 2000.
Gbadamosi, Gabriel. *Vauxhall*. London: Telegram, 2013.
Greenwood, James. *Unsentimental Journeys*. London: Ward, Lock & Tyler, 1867.
Hamid, Mohsin. *How to Get Filthy Rich in Rising Asia*. London: Hamish Hamilton, 2013.
Lins, Paulo. *City of God*. Trans. Alison Entrekin. London: Bloomsbury, 2006 [1997], Kindle Edition.
London, Jack. *The People of the Abyss* [1903], http://www.gutenberg.org/ebooks/1688. 3 January, 2017.
Magona, Sindiwe. *Mother to Mother*. Claremont: David Philip, 1998.
Milanovic, Branko. *Worlds Apart. Measuring International and Global Inequality*. Princeton, NJ: Princeton University Press, 2005.
Mishra, Pankaj. *The Romantics*. London: Picador, 1999.
Mulligan, Andy. *Trash*. New York: Ember, 2011.
Naipaul, V.S. *A Bend in the River*. London: Vintage, 1989 [1979].
Orwell, George. *Down and Out in Paris and London*. London: Penguin Classics, 2001 [1933].
Rowling, J.K. *The Casual Vacancy*. London: Little Brown, 2012, Kindle Edition.
Sinclair, Iain. *Downriver*. London: Penguin, 2004 [1991].
Suri, Manil. *The Death of Vishnu*. London: Bloomsbury, 2001.
Swarup, Vikas. *Q and A*. London: Black Swan, 2006 [2005].

Wendt, Albert. 'Robocop in Long Bay' in *Ancestry*. Wellington: Huia, 2012, 1–22.
Wheatle, Alex. *Brixton Rock*. London: Arcadia, 1999.
———. *East of Acre Lane*. London: Harper Collins, 2001.
———. *The Dirty South*. London: Serpent's Tail, 2008.
———. *Brenton Brown*. BlackAmber Books, 2011, Kindle Edition.
Wilde, Oscar. *The Picture of Dorian Gray*. London: Dover, 1993 [1890].

Secondary

Ahmed, Rehana. 'Brick Lane: A Materialist Reading of the Novel and Its Reception,' *Race and Class* 52(2), 2010, 25–42.
Akerlof, George A., and Rachel E. Kranton. 'Economics and Identity,' *Quarterly Journal of Economics* 65(3), August 2000, 715–753.
Akerlof, George A., and Rachel E. Kranton. *Identity Economics: How Our Identities Shape Our Work, Wages, and Well-Being*. Princeton: Princeton University Press, 2010.
Bauman, Zygmunt. 'The London Riots—On Consumerism Coming Home to Roost' in *Social Europe Journal*, 9 August, 2011, http://www.social-europe.eu/2011/08/the-london-riots-on-consumerism-coming-home-to-roost/. 3 January, 2017.
Booth, Charles. Descriptive Maps of London Poverty [1898]. London School of Economics Digital Archive, http://booth.lse.ac.uk/static/a/4.html. 3 January, 2017.
Brown, Phillip, Hugh Lauder, and David Ashton, *The Global Auction: The Broken Promises of Education, Jobs and Incomes*. Oxford: Oxford University Press, 2011.
Chang, Ha-Joon. 'Why Developing Countries Need Tariffs,' Oxfam and The South Centre, 2005.
———. *Bad Samaritans: The Guilty Secrets of the Rich Nations and the Threat to Global Prosperity*. London: Random House, 2007.
Davis, Mike. *Planet of Slums*. London and New York: Verso, 2006.
Deaton, Angus. *The Analysis of Household Surveys: A Microeconometric Approach to Development Policy*. Baltimore: Johns Hopkins University Press, 1997.
Dorling, Danny. *The 32 Stops: Lives on London's Circle Line*. London: Penguin, 2013, Kindle Edition.
Engels, Frederick. *The Conditions of the Working Class in England*. Public Domain Books 2011 [1845], Kindle Edition.
Engels, Friedrich. *The Housing Question*. New York: International, 1935 [1872].
Eurostat, *Trafficking in Human Beings*. 2015 Edition. Luxembourg: Publications Office of the European Union, 2014, http://ec.europa.eu/antitrafficking/sites/antitrafficking/files/eurostat_report_on_trafficking_in_human_beings_-_2015_edition.pdf. 3 January, 2017.

Hall, Darragh P. 'Success and the City: Working in the World's Capital in Monica Ali's *Brick Lane*,' Unpublished Manuscript.
Hall, Stuart. 'Old and New Identities, Old and New Ethnicities,' in *Culture, Globalization and the World--System: Contemporary Conditions for the Representation of Identity*. Ed. Anthony D. King. Basingstoke, London: Macmillan, 1997, 41–68.
———. 'The Neo-liberal Revolution,' *Cultural Studies*, Vol. 25, No. 6 (Nov 2011), 705–728.
Harvey, David. *Rebel Cities*. London and New York: Verso, 2012.
Harvey, David. *Spaces of Hope*. Berkeley and Los Angeles: California University Press, 2000.
Hechter, Michael. *Internal Colonialism: The Celtic Fringe in British National Development*. New Brunswick, NJ: Transaction, 1999 [1975].
Hyman, Prue. 'Unplugging the Machine,' in *The Piketty Phenomenon: New Zealand Perspectives*. Wellington: Bridget Williams, 2014, Kindle Edition.
Kabeer, Naila. *The Power to Choose: Bangladeshi Women and Labour Market Decisions in London and Dhaka*. London: Verso, 2000.
Keynes, John Maynard. 'National Self-Sufficiency,' *The Yale Review*, Vol. 22, no. 4 (June 1933), 755–769.
Latouche, Serge. *In the Wake of the Affluent Society: An Exploration of Post-development*. Trans. Martin O'Connor and Rosemary Arnoux. London and New Jersey: Zed Books, 1993 [1991].
Laursen, Ole Birk. 'Reading the Riots: Precarity, Racial Injustice and Rights in the Novels of Alex Wheatle', in *Reworking Postcolonialism: Globalization, Labour, and Rights*. Eds. Pavan Malreddy, Birte Heidemann, Ole Birk Laursen, and Janet Wilson. London: Palgrave Macmillan, 2015, 214–228.
Lazarus, Neil. *Resistance in Postcolonial African Fiction*. New Haven and London: Yale University Press, 1990.
London School of Economics. *Reading the Riots: Investigating England's Summer of Disorder*. London: LSE and *The Guardian*, 2011, http://eprints.lse.ac.uk/46297/. 3 January, 2017.
Massey, Doreen. *World City*. Cambridge, UK: Polity Press, 2007.
Nixon, Rob. *Slow Violence and the Environmentalism of the Poor*. Cambridge, MA and London: Harvard University Press, 2011.
Peck, Jamie. *Constructions of Neoliberal Reason*. Oxford: Oxford University Press, 2010.
Phillips, Michael M. 'Buyers' Revenge: Trash the House After Foreclosure,' *Wall Street Journal*, 28 March, 2008, http://online.wsj.com/articles/SB120665586667569881. 3 January, 2017.
Rinehart, Gina. Sydney Mining Club Speech, August 2012, https://www.youtube.com/watch?v=OUCbWfJSw5g. 3 January, 2017.

Robins, Nick. 'Loot: In search of the East India Company,' *Open Democracy*, 22 January, 2003, https://www.opendemocracy.net/theme_7-corporations/article_904.jsp. 3 January, 2017.

Sen, Amartya. *Inequality Reexamined*. Cambridge, MA: Harvard University Press, 1992.

Smith, Adam. *The Wealth of Nations*. London: Penguin Classics, 1999 Edition [1776].

Walker, Peter. 'Brixton: Could It Happen Again? 30 Years After the Riots,' *The Guardian*, 2 April, 2011, http://www.theguardian.com/theguardian/2011/apr/02/brixton-riots-anniversary. 3 January, 2017.

Wilkinson, Richard and Kate Pickett. *The Spirit Level: Why Equality is Better for Everyone*. Harmondsworth and New York: Penguin, 2010.

———. 'A Divided Britain?: Inequality Within and Between the Regions,' *The Inequality Trust*, 2014, http://www.equalitytrust.org.uk. 3 January, 2017.

Williams, Zoe. 'The Saturday Interview: Stuart Hall,' *The Guardian*, 11 February, 2012, https://www.theguardian.com/theguardian/2012/feb/11/saturday-interview-stuart-hall. 3 January, 2017.

Žižek, Slavoj. 'Shoplifters of the World Unite' in *London Review of Books*, 19 August 2011, http://www.lrb.co.uk/2011/08/19/slavoj-zizek/shoplifters-of-the-world-unite. 3 January, 2017.

Websites

GVK: http://www.gvk.com/.

Housing Moves: http://www.housingmoves.org/. 3 January, 2017.

London's Poverty Profile: http://www.londonspovertyprofile.org.uk. 3 January, 2017.

The Poverty Site UK: http://www.poverty.org.uk/06/index.shtml. 3 January, 2017.

CHAPTER 5

Conclusion

The similarities across fictional portrayals of poverty and inequality analysed in this study belie the expectation that experiences of immiseration in a contemporary, developed welfare state have nothing in common with those of 150 years earlier, or that people classified by national measures as poor in a developed country do not share material circumstances with the poor in developing nations of the Global South. Within developed white-settler nations today, the colonial legacy continues in deep-rooted inequality which marks indigenous peoples and more recent migrants as significantly worse off than their white compatriots. The extent to which these communities were hardest hit by the 2008 financial crisis and ensuing recession puts paid to earlier multiculturalist celebrations of cultural difference and the end of racism. In the USA, 53% of African American homebuyers and 47% of Hispanics, compared to 26% of white homebuyers, were issued high-interest sub-prime mortgages in 2006 (Dodd 2014, 2), with the incidence or risk of foreclosure among these minorities double that of white homeowners.[1] Although such evidence strongly suggests, as Nigel Dodd puts it, that 'society's poorest are paying for the misjudgements of its wealthiest' (2), financial experts at the 2010 Financial Crisis Inquiry Committee argued that the sub-prime meltdown was caused by government promotion of home ownership to those who could not afford it, rather than due to their aggressive lending campaigns and dubious packaging of risk and debt. Matt Taibbi paraphrases the tone of banking experts: 'what sank the economy was poor black people who were pushed into buying homes they couldn't afford by the government. ... the financial crisis was caused by lazy poor people living in too much house' (244). As with the official inquiry into the Lonmin shootings, the US Financial Crisis Inquiry Committee attributed no fault for the sub-prime collapse, and financial institutions bailed out by the government were not persecuted, while those 'lazy poor people' at the bottom of the wealth distribution scale lost their homes. Within the national scale of wealth distribution in the developed world, in which Piketty's statistics show that the bottom 50% own less than 5% of the wealth (261), indigenous peoples and ethnic minorities are disproportionately represented.

The US government's response to the financial crisis focused on resuscitating the economy, which included investing trillions of dollars to bail out the banks and big corporations that had caused the crash. At the same time, police and the legal infrastructure evicted recalcitrant residents from foreclosed homes and persecuted demonstrators at the Occupy protests that sprang up around the country. The heavy-handed British response to the 2011 riots, including incarceration of rioters, was analogous in its intolerance of civic resistance. The response to the Lonmin strike in South Africa similarly supported the British company, its investors, and its important role in the South African mining industry, while coming down heavily on those directly impacted by the company's employment and housing conditions. Thirty-four miners were killed for protesting against the inequality of business practices that condemn the workers to impoverished livelihoods and lifestyles which they find degrading and humiliating because they see the comparative wealth and privilege of their union leaders and company directors.

Over 170 years earlier, the Chinese Emperor wrote to Queen Victoria of the similarly transparent iniquities and glaring hypocrisies of the British opium trade, which reaped enormous profit for Britain while weakening the Chinese with addiction and debt. The British response to the Emperor's ban on the trade was a succession of wars and the loss of Hong Kong, in defence of the global mobility of free trade. These historically and geographically different events are brought into dialogue by shared structures and mechanisms of global capitalism and the human response to them. Each demonstrates the impact of international trade and finance on the nation, influencing the political economy that governs, legislates, and polices in favour of the global, often at the expense of the local, and of the wealthy at the expense of the poor. In each case, on-the-ground local and even national interests (such as Greece's 2015 failed push for debt amnesty) are subordinate to the macro-level importance of global trade and geopolitical influence.

The anecdotes at the beginning of each chapter throughout this book also register the impact of global trade on the individual psyche and body. Each incident or event reveals a physical dependence on the functioning capitalist economy, for the commodity itself, in the case of opium growers and users, for the job and salary derived from the global price of platinum, for Marikana workers, and for the speculative global derivatives trade that funded sub-prime mortgages. These industries impacted on the individual's body and psychology as much as on their financial wellbeing, generating the conditions for positive emotions (the addict's hit, the pay-day euphoria, the pride of home ownership) and for negative repercussions (the ruin of addiction, the working poor, the newly homeless or bankrupt). Although the power structures, income levels, and lifestyle expectations are not comparable across these examples, in each case the economically disadvantaged reacted with rage against inequality they vividly perceived: the Chinese against the British, the Marikana workers against the company, and dispossessed homeowners following the 2008 sub-prime collapse. In each case, the government response was a condemnation of protest, criminalising the poorest in each society as a failure of the individual to succeed rather than the logical outcome of a system that produces winners and losers. In its infiltration into all parts of political, social, and cultural life, capitalism's inherent inequality is manifested in hierarchy at every level, from the individual's place in the nation's wealth and income tally to the nation's global ranking by competitive measures such as Gross Domestic Product.

The history of capitalism is also the history of violence, both to enforce the social conditions required for constant expansion and in resistance to it, as the anecdotes and literary examples from colonial, neocolonial, and neoliberal periods attest. The regular occurrence of violence in colonial and postcolonial spaces, including wars, pogroms, military coups, massacres, riots, strike breaks, slum demolitions, forced housing evictions, and theft, share a common denominator in the wresting of control over resources. These material grounds for violence are, however, frequently masked by civilisationalist and culturalist arguments. In capitalism's colonial era, Britain's invasion of Burma and Canton, the US annexation of Hawai'i, and the incursion of settlement gave way to neocolonial instability under the capitalist imperialism of new independence. Although the violence of bad governance in instable states is cast alternately as racial (Burma, Fiji), ethnic (Nigeria, Rwanda), religious (South Sudan), or class-based (Cambodia), each war, takeover, or political ouster has been ultimately concerned with ownership and control of the means of profiting from land, resources, and labour power. In more recent history, the 1994 Rwandan Hutu pogrom against the Tutsi, the 2014 breakdown of the post-war Iraqi government set up by the USA and led by the minority Sunni, and the Syrian Civil War provide contemporary examples of internal conflict of which the origins are entangled in economic privileges distributed under colonial or neoimperial regimes. The geopolitics of contemporary global governance have deep roots in historical financial interests, such as France's uranium mines in Mali, British oil extraction in Nigeria, and US oil interests in Iraq.

The focus on internal colonialism in each of the chapters has also illuminated repeating patterns of injustice and inequality within cultural groups and national communities that replicate the power imbalance between rich and poor on local levels. Zamindar tax collectors in Bengal and comprador middlemen in the Cantonese opium *Hongs* and in Sub-Saharan neocolonial business make the crossover from traditional and colonial to contemporary hierarchies of caste, class, and ethnicity. The black South African policemen who opened fire on their compatriots at Marikana, and London East End violence, theft, and the 2011 looting of local shops across the UK, demonstrate violence and crime among and between the poor within their own communities. Violence within economically, socially, and culturally marginalised groups contradicts expectations of compassion and solidarity among the persecuted and subjugated, and illuminates their belief in and struggle for a part in the mainstream society that is deeply founded on the capitalist ideology of individual competitiveness and the right to consume. The literary and historical examples in this book demonstrate capitalist relations shot through with coercion and violent interactions on every level. Crimes are perpetrated by the elite in the name of enforcing capitalism as much as by the poor and disenfranchised in the time-honoured way of accessing the capitalist order when other avenues appear exhausted. Siding with the critics of neoliberalism from other disciplines, a postcolonial economic perspective argues against the historical criminalisation of poverty to instead claim that the presence of poverty is itself the crime, and that the capitalist world-system that creates and perpetuates inequality is unjust and unethical.

The end of absolute poverty and the reduction of relative poverty in the developed world to around 25% today, despite the significant contributions of the post-war welfare state, are often claimed as major achievements of the modern political economy. The existence of any poverty, however, might rather be read as an indictment of the uneven distribution of the benefits of economic growth and development, which neoliberalism promised but has failed to deliver. Instead, in an irony of globalisation, precisely the fact of world-level interconnectivity has enabled the rigorous documentation of long-term and global trends in inequality, convincingly argued in work such as that by Piketty, that shows the periodicity of today's growing wealth gap with those of the past. Equally importantly, the pervasive global media recorded the synchronicity of the 2008 financial crisis and its fallout, creating a global-level awareness of the individual's and the nation's place in the world-system. Communications technology made possible real-time tracking of the flow of international finance through the rolling, domino-like effect of the US sub-prime collapse into global banking, the collapse of national economies, and the worldwide private-sector recession. Media further fostered global connectivity through documenting waves of protest that transcended the individual city and nation, such as the Occupy movement, the Arab Spring, and anti-austerity protests.

The most recent of the cyclical, periodic crises of capitalism, the 2008 crash demonstrated to citizens of the richest countries in the world that financial hardship is not only felt by a small minority that has opted out or dropped out of the capitalist mainstream. People who considered themselvesmiddle class lost their homes to foreclosures and their jobs to company austerity at the same time as privatisation rolled back services in education, healthcare, and pensions. The rage of evicted homeowners is mirrored in demonstrations and protests throughout the developed world, including the participation of students and tertiary educated youths in the 2011 UK riots: indebted, diploma-ed, under- and unemployed. Home ownership and a tertiary education no longer signify an individual's success in neoliberalism's celebrated competitive meritocracy. Certainly, the notion of development in capitalism's core is synonymous with ever-more sophisticated financial, industrial, logistical, and technological progress, while the social side of the concept has been all but forgotten.

More clearly than in capitalist core countries, the countries of the Global South demonstrate the dubiousness of the discourse of development that assumes a nation's improvement and progress through economic growth. It is difficult to ascertain how much reduction in global poverty has occurred in response to the work of international institutions such as the World Bank, the International Monetary Fund, and the United Nations, and through the bilateral and regional trade deals that mark the era of neoliberal globalisation, most recently exemplified by the Trans-Pacific Partnership. Claims of reduction in absolute poverty, of fewer people living below the $1.25 poverty line, fail to deal with the increasing number of people who earn just above that threshold (Chen and Ravallion 2012), who, by Amartya Sen's capabilities schema, have made little material gain in terms of life outcomes and even less in comparison with the increasing concentration of wealth in the hands of the few in some of the world's poorest countries. Among the statistics of global inequality expressed in the percentile schema Piketty popularised, the wealthiest 10% in China take home 60% of the nation's income, a level of income inequality only matched by South Africa. The Forbes list of world billionaires includes those from China, Indonesia, Mexico, India, Kazakhstan, and Russia—the nation with the highest concentration of billionaires (Harvey 2014, 165; 169).

The desire to change the unfair and unequal economic structures at the root of extreme wealth and poverty necessarily entails tackling cultural values entrenched in Western society and many individuals' understandings of ambition and success. The cultural packaging of failure as the individual's personal weakness, the celebration of success in terms of financial wellbeing, and the hero-worship of the super-rich encourage the poor to buy into the promises of consumerism. In each of the colonial, neocolonial, and neoliberal eras, expectations of revolution expounded by, respectively, Karl Marx, Frantz Fanon, and David Harvey have been disappointed. The geopolitical situation in 2017 looks equally unpromising. Nearly a decade after the 2008 financial collapse, austerity measures rather than banking reforms have effaced the energies of the Occupy movement in the USA and across Europe, and resoundingly defeated Greece's efforts to infuse the political left with its socialist origins and voice of conscience. Conservative populism has gained sway—most markedly evident in Brexit and the US election of Donald Trump—by masking systemic unevenness in the economic world-system with recourse to nationalist and racist cultural arguments that still fail to engage with increasing inequality between rich and poor.

More optimistically, the increasing currency of the term 'neoliberalism' in mainstream media since 2008 indicates the turn of focus from cultural to economic issues of selfhood, identity, and belonging. As Stuart argues in a late paper reflecting on the aftermath of the financial crisis and the 2011 UK riots, naming capitalism as the underlying system of inequality may be a necessary precursor to change: 'naming neo-liberalism is *politically* necessary to give the resistance to its onward march content, focus and a cutting edge' (2011, 706, italics in original). Recent politics bear out the growing familiarity with the vocabulary of economic inequality. In 2015, the Greek Syriza government challenged EU politics by underlining the inefficacy of the debt repayment structure and calling austerity inhumane and unethical. Both excitement from the left and theatrical predictions of catastrophe from the right have followed Jeremy Corbyn's leadership of the UK Labour party on a platform of a rejuvenated socialism that is unashamed of its Marxist origins and twentieth-century history. In the USA, an equally grey-haired veteran socialist, Bernie Sanders, attracted enormous support, particularly from young voters, in his 2016 run for the Democratic presidential campaign.

Narratives of Inequality offers a rubric for studying economics in literature by tracing the history of capitalism in colonial and postcolonial spaces. It therefore remains outside the present scope to address the resistance and alternatives to global neoliberalism that are offered in fiction. Postcolonial studies has made a significant contribution to the recognition of and respect for the complex, rich, and valuable differences of indigenous, ethnic, and minority cultures that have been sidelined by modernity's—and thus capitalism's—grand narratives. The strength of postcolonial literary analysis is in showing how the imaginary reveals difference, resilience, resistance, and new potentialities. In comparison with the other social science and humanities fields that are anchored in the real, finite, and particular, fiction has the creative freedom to postulate, hypothesise, and explore alternative communities, societies, and life-worlds.

Postcolonial studies, founded on promoting minority resistance to the Western hegemony of colonial imperialism, which is also the imperialism of capitalism, is a natural ally of neoliberal critique. The postcolonial sense of justice in registering dissent from the under-represented, the marginalised, and the oppressed, is closely aligned with the anti-neoliberal condemnation of inequality. Both postcolonial studies and critiques of global neoliberalism are deconstructive methodologies that expose the man-made and self-interested underpinnings of hegemonic state apparatuses encoded in socio-cultural norms. Both anti-establishment positions are indebted to Marx's early formulations of capitalism and its local and specific formations of political economy, and both engage to varying degrees with the political, revolutionary, and utopian ideals of Marxism. Just as the discipline of economics is no longer embarrassed to explore its own subjective truths, literary critique must also reject the neoliberal construction of the university that condescendingly considers the arts as useless. Rather than act as apologists for the very fictionality of its subject, as if it were untethered from actuality and superfluous to everyday material reality, literary critics have a role to play in challenging the hegemony of the capitalist world system.

To refuse to take seriously the potential of the imaginary in challenging the hegemony of the capitalist world-system is to bow to the neoliberal dogma of 'there is no alternative' thinking. The difficulty of accounting for inequality *in our own societies* signals the pervasiveness of the no-alternative belief in neoliberalism that makes it difficult to think of viable alternative models, or even to question the political economy, which we imagine too difficult to understand and too solid to challenge. From this perspective, the reluctance of postcolonial studies to analyse the material impoverishment that is so present in the fiction is not only squeamishness about speaking for a cultural Other, but also an inability to think past the strictures of our own socio-economic frame.

Near the beginning of his chapter on utopian city architecture in *Spaces of Hope*, Harvey sets out the challenge of the imaginary to bridge the gap with the real:

> Why is it, in Roberto Unger's (1987a, 37) words, that 'we often seem to be (such) helpless puppets of the institutional and imaginative worlds we inhabit.' Is it simply that we lack the will, the courage, and the perspicacity to open up alternatives and actively pursue them? ... In the humanities a fascination with what is called 'the imaginary' is everywhere apparent. And the media world that is now available to us has never before been so replete with fantasies and possibilities for collective communication about alternative worlds. Yet none of this seems to impinge upon the terrible trajectory that daily life assumes in the material world around us. We seem, as Unger (1987a, 331) puts it, to be 'torn between dreams that seem unrealizable and prospects that hardly seem to matter.' Is it really a choice between 'Dreamworks' or nothing? (2000, 155)

As a geographer, Harvey can only gesture toward the humanities' focus on the imaginary, which, in his vagueness, is almost disparaging about its relevance to neoliberal critique. Unfortunately, literary theorists and critics hardly seem more convincing or convinced of the ability of the imaginary to cross the divide into the feasible and the real. The writers discussed in this present study are openly engaged in critiques of capitalism, offering dreams that come true and prospects that do matter, at least within the narrative frame. Literary critics have a duty to match the authors' extensive knowledge of and interest in the political economy with equally informed and rigorous analysis. Approaching the social engagement of literature through understanding of global and historical world capitalism brings the discipline to the table of neoliberal critique, to add its vast body of work and unique perspectives to the pressing debate of economic inequality and its solutions.

Note

1. See Debbie Gruenstein Bocian, Wei Li, and Keith S. Ernst, 'Foreclosures by Race and Ethnicity: The Demographics of a Crisis' (2010): in the period 2007–2009, 8% of African Americans and Hispanics and 4.5% of whites lost their homes to foreclosures (2); the risk of foreclosure is estimated at around 21.5% for African American and Hispanic homeowners, and 14.8% for whites (3).

Works Cited

Secondary

Chen, Shaohua and Martin Ravallion. 'More Relatively-Poor People in a Less Absolutely-Poor World,' World Bank Development Research Group Working Paper 6114, July 2012.

Dodd, Nigel. *The Social Life of Money*. Princeton, NJ: Princeton University Press, 2014.

Gruenstein Bocian, Debbie, Wei Li, and Keith S. Ernst, 'Foreclosures by Race and Ethnicity: The Demographics of a Crisis,' Center for Responsible LearningReport, June 2010, http://www.responsiblelending.org/mortgage-lending/research-analysis/foreclosures-by-race-and-ethnicity.pdf. 3 January, 2017.

Hall, Stuart. 'The Neo-liberal Revolution,' *Cultural Studies*, Vol. 25, No. 6 (Nov 2011), 705–728.

Harvey, David. *Seventeen Contradictions and the End of Capitalism*. Oxford: Oxford University Press, 2014.

INDEX

A
Abani, Chris
  Graceland, 168, 170, 175, 176, 202
Aborigines, 16, 63, 65, 68, 69, 83, 87, 90
Aboulela, Leila
  Minaret, 17, 127, 135, 183
Abrahams, Peter
  Mine Boy, 102
Achebe, Chinua
  A Man of the People, 17, 126, 130, 136
  No Longer at Ease, 126
  The Trouble with Nigeria, 135, 144
Adichie, Chimamanda Ngozi
  Half of a Yellow Sun, 118, 127, 135
Adiga, Aravind
  The White Tiger, 171, 175
African Americans, 4, 5, 116, 195, 219
Akare, Thomas
  The Slums, 116, 117
Akerlof, George A.
  and Rachel E. Kranton, 195, 196, 198, 201, 202
  and Robert J. Shiller, *Animal Spirits*, 7, 9, 136, 149, 156, 193–195, 201, 202
Alexie, Sherman
  Absolutely True Diary of a Part-Time Indian, 203
  Reservation Blues, 168, 192
Ali, Monica
  Brick Lane, 161, 162, 181, 182, 186, 189, 192, 206
Amin, Samir
  Maldevelopment, 108, 139, 149
Armah, Ayi Kwei
  The Beautyful Ones Are Not Yet Born, 126, 136, 140, 187
Auster, Paul
  Sunset Park, 155
Austerity, 1, 6, 15, 81, 82, 129, 191, 215–217
Australia
  colonial history of, 62
  inequality in, 60, 63, 65, 66, 68, 93, 102, 149

B
Bahadur, Sanjay
  Hul: Cry Rebel!, 41, 92
  The Sound of Water, 104
Bandung Conference, 111
Banking, 1, 2, 8, 48, 54, 73, 128, 144, 155, 205, 211, 215, 216
Barratt Brown, Michael
  The Economics of Imperialism, 106, 149
Bauman, Zygmunt, 189, 190
Belfort, Jordan
  Wolf of Wall Street, The, book, 2, 147
Bello, Walden, 107, 149
  Dark Victory, 107
Boo, Katherine
  Behind the Beautiful Forevers, 168, 171, 176
Brand, Dionne
  At the Full and Change of the Moon, 198
Brazil
  inequality in, 111, 173
Brecht, Bertolt
  The Threepenny Opera, 143
Brennan, Timothy
  Salman Rushdie and the Third World, 107
Bretton Woods Agreement, 108, 149
Brown, Nicholas
  The Political Horizon of Twentieth-Century Literature, 141
Brown, Phillip, and Hugh Lauder and David Ashton
  The Global Auction, 130, 166
Buckley, Ken, and Ted Wheelwright, 62–67, 78, 90, 93
Burma (Myanmar)
  colonial history of, 77, 213
  inequality in, 77, 90, 213, 218
Bush, George W., 45, 53, 59

C
Cameron, David, 35
  speech at Peking University, 36, 45
Capitalism, 1, 2, 5–7, 9, 11, 12, 17, 19, 21–30, 35–38, 40–42, 44–47, 49, 51, 52, 54–56, 58–66, 69–73, 75, 77, 79, 80, 83, 85, 87, 89–91, 93, 99–101, 106–108, 110–112, 118, 121, 123–125, 128, 133, 135–137, 139, 141, 142, 146, 147, 149, 156–158, 160, 162, 164, 166, 175, 187, 193, 194, 196, 197, 202, 212–217, 219
  alternatives to, 11, 28, 111, 217
  colonialism and, 26, 29, 38, 59, 77, 93, 100, 108, 111
  consumerism, 187, 190, 191, 201, 216
  contradictions in, 135, 143, 146, 156
  corruption and, 2, 136, 137, 169, 170, 176
  debt, 194, 211, 217
  employment, 165, 175, 179, 180, 182, 183, 187
  history of, 9, 12, 19, 21, 25, 28, 44, 128, 137, 213, 217
  indigenous peoples and, 71, 73, 80, 83, 211
  Industrial Revolution and, 23
  labour and, 66, 84, 89, 175
  land ownership and, 43, 75, 175
  primitive accumulation, 62, 75, 101.
    See also Marx, Karl
  psychology of, 29, 147, 177, 193
  racism and, 29, 79, 80, 83, 136
Carey, Peter
  True History of the Kelly Gang, 67, 68
Cash crops, 107
Chamoiseau, Patrick

Texaco, 167, 177
Chang, Ha-Joon, 9, 44, 47, 81, 136–138, 137, 159
 23 Things They Don't Tell You about Capitalism, 9, 146, 175
 Bad Samaritans, 44, 80, 92, 159
 Economics: The User's Guide, 10
 Why Developing Countries Need Tariffs, 92, 159
China
 colonial history in, 23, 59
 Hong Kong, 36, 42, 44, 49, 92, 212
 inequality in, 216
 opium trade in. *See* OpiumChomsky, Noam
 Profit over People, 43, 44, 50, 62, 105
 World Orders Old and New, 46, 149
Class. *See* Social class
 Middle-class, 12, 115, 121, 142, 155, 156, 166, 171, 174, 175, 191, 215
 Upward mobility, 18, 66–68, 80, 93, 130, 157, 177, 186, 187, 197
 working-class, 65, 70, 101, 115, 123
Clayton, Hamish
 Wulf, 71, 73, 74
Colonialism
 British Empire, 23, 49, 51, 55
 capitalism, 12. *See also* Capitalism
 critiques of, 27, 43, 46
 Dutch colonialism, 55–57, 203
 French colonialism, 61, 131, 160
 internal, 42. *See also* Internal colonialism
 mandates, 112
 private investment in, 47
 settler, 36, 60, 61, 64–66, 89, 110, 159

 strategic territories, 55
Combined and uneven development, 25, 39, 115, 141, 161
Communism, 26, 107, 111, 113, 120, 121, 123
Corruption, 2, 17, 49, 92, 126, 130, 131, 135–139, 143, 145, 171, 176, 177, 188. *See also* Capitalism

D
Davenport, Kiana
 Shark Dialogues, 16, 36, 71, 76, 84, 203
Davis, Mike
 Late-Victorian Holocausts, 41, 108
 Planet of Slums, 90, 160, 167, 170, 176
Debt, 8, 9, 20, 29, 55, 102, 107, 108, 124, 131, 147, 157, 194, 211, 212, 217. *See also* Capitalism
Defoe, Daniel, 9, 19, 61, 143
Derrida, Jacques
 Specters of Marx, 25
Development loans, 107, 109, 131
Dickens, Charles, 3, 4, 12, 19, 161, 165, 178, 179
Dorling, Danny
 Injustice: Why Social Inequality Persists, 3
 The 32 Stops, 162
Dubois, W.E.B., 25, 122, 196
Duff, Alan
 Maori: The Crisis and the Challenge, 185, 206
 Once Were Warriors, 166, 178, 180, 181, 186, 189, 197, 204, 206
Dutch East Indies, 28, 36, 55, 56, 76, 92, 112. *See also* Indonesia

E

Eagleton, Terry
  Why Marx Was Right, 26, 146
East End, 161, 162, 165, 173, 214
East India Company, 38–41, 44, 46–50, 54–56, 60, 61, 100, 163
Economics
  behavioural, 6, 28, 156, 194, 201
  classical, 41, 51, 59, 61, 80, 81, 158
  discipline of, 48, 85, 217
  historical, 3, 6, 44, 65
  identity, 27, 194–196, 198, 201
Egypt
  colonial history of, 60, 114
  inequality in, 28, 111, 114
  Suez Crisis, 112–114, 122
Engels, Friedrich, 3, 4, 162, 166
Environment, 7, 17, 27, 42, 55, 78, 84, 94, 104, 179, 203

F

Famine, 40, 77, 91, 108, 131
Fanon, Frantz, 25, 87, 107, 126, 130, 196, 216
  The Wretched of the Earth, 87, 126
Fellaheen, 114, 115, 135
Felski, Rita
  Uses of Literature, 8, 11–14, 52, 103, 194, 196
Financial crisis
  bailouts of, 53, 212
  films about, 2
  in 1929, 2, 5
  in 2008, 1–4, 6–8, 25, 29, 52–54, 128, 129, 136, 143, 147, 157, 181, 194, 211, 215
  popular-economics books about, 2
First World, 5, 6, 124, 141, 155
Fitzgerald, F. Scott
  The Great Gatsby, 2, 4

Free market, 1, 36, 37, 39, 41, 44–47, 50–53, 79, 93, 109, 146, 157, 170, 184, 188, 195. *See also* Market

G

Gay, John
  The Beggar's Opera and Polly, 10, 143
Geopolitics, 20, 22, 55, 57, 79, 104, 112, 118, 141, 214
Ghali, Waguih
  Beer in the Snooker Club, 112, 113, 121, 123, 127, 149
Ghazipur opium factory, 46, 47, 99
Ghosh, Amitav
  interview with, 37, 46
  River of Smoke, 38, 47, 48, 50, 52, 85, 146
  Sea of Poppies, 38, 41, 46, 78
  The Glass Palace, 54, 58, 76, 78, 84
Globalisation, 1, 6, 12, 21, 24, 25, 37, 43, 45, 55, 73, 103, 110, 120, 168. *See also* Capitalism
Grace, Patricia
  'Ngati Kangaru', 145
Great Depression, the, 2, 4, 45, 64, 160
The Great Gatsby, film. *See* Luhrmann, Baz
The Great Gatsby, book. *See* Fitzgerald, F. Scott
Great Recession, the, 4
Gross Domestic Product, 5, 81, 213

H

Hall, Stuart, 123, 158, 164, 190, 216
  'The Neo-liberal Revolution', 123, 164
Hamid, Mohsin
  How to Get Filthy Rich in Rising Asia, 168, 171

The Reluctant Fundamentalist, 120
Harvey, David
  Rebel Cities, 42, 172
  Seventeen Contradictions and the End of Capitalism, 9, 146, 216
  Spaces of Hope, 172, 218
Hawai'i, 71
  colonial history of, 72, 73
  inequality in, 72, 94, 203
Homelessness, 13, 29, 172, 176
In fiction, 134, 146, 171, 175, 176
Hong Kong, 36, 42, 44, 49, 60, 92, 212. *See also* China
Housing foreclosures, 6, 211, 215
Hugo, Victor, 19

I
India
  colonial history of, 36
  inequality in, 61, 90, 111, 125, 167, 171, 172, 216
  Mumbai, 167, 172, 175; Annawadi, 168, 171, 176
Indonesia
  Dutch East Indies, 36, 55
Industrial Revolution, 23, 38, 47, 88, 92, 161. *See also* Capitalism
Inequality
  measures of, 3, 6, 177–178
  of income, 216
  of wealth, 110
  patterns of, 55, 73, 156, 178, 179, 194
  wellbeing and, 76, 179, 201, 202
Injustice, 4, 12, 14, 15, 18–20, 52, 64, 77, 80, 100, 116, 120, 122, 134, 135, 144, 170, 174, 193, 200, 203, 214
Internal colonialism, 42, 60, 66, 67, 116, 129, 133, 135, 161, 190, 202, 214

in colonial era, 83
in neocolonial era, 29, 143
in neoliberal era, 24, 25, 28, 65, 188, 202
International Monetary Fund (IMF), 45, 107, 158, 170, 215
Invisible hand, 157

J
Jameson, Fredric
  The Political Unconscious, 13
  'Third-World Literature in the Era of MultinationalCapitalism', 142
Japan, 56, 58, 93
  imperialism, 56
Jones, Gavin
  American Hungers, 27, 91
Judd, Denis
  Empire, 21

K
Kabeer, Naila
  The Power to Choose, 182–183, 185–186, 206
Keynes, John Maynard, 7, 160, 162, 177

L
Lazarus, Neil
  The Postcolonial Unconscious, 13, 30
  Resistance in Postcolonial African Fiction, 125, 185
  Mind the Gap, 140–142
  The Postcolonial Unconscious, 13
Lenin, Vladimir Ilyich
  Imperialism, the Highest Stage of Capitalism, 58, 61

Lins, Paulo
  City of God, 173, 175, 189, 199
Lloyd, Sarah
  poverty, 88
London
  Canary Wharf, 163, 164
  city of, 46, 160
  colonial history of, 163, 173, 189
  East End, 161, 181
  fiction, 161, 162, 183
  finance in, 215
  inequality in, 18, 160, 161, 182, 206
  Tower Hamlets, 161, 163
  2011 London riots, 161
Lonmin, 99–101, 104, 106, 115, 148, 163, 212
Luhrmann, Baz
  Australia, film, 68
  The Great Gatsby, film, 2
Lumumba, Patrice, 25, 126, 139–140
Luxemburg, Rosa
  The Accumulation of Capital, 91, 149
  The Junius Pamphlet, 58

M
Magona, Sindiwe
  Mother to Mother, 173
Makereti, Tina
  Where the Rekohu Bone Sings, 74, 85, 204
Malthus, Thomas, 61, 89, 92, 94
Maori, 63, 70, 71, 74, 75, 85, 86, 145, 166, 180, 181, 185, 204
Marikana, 100, 102, 214. *See also* Lonmin
Market
  free market, 37, 109, 170, 184
  instability of, 1, 157
  protectionism and, 45–48, 70, 113, 137, 159

Marx, Karl, 3, 6, 19, 22, 117, 200, 216
  In postcolonial studies, 13, 25–26, 110, 124, 217
  on colonialism, 25, 46, 61–62
  primitive accumulation, 62, 75, 82
Massey, Doreen
  World City, 73, 160, 163–166
Materialism, 21, 24, 25, 91, 147
Mau Mau, 102, 117, 122, 196
Michaels, Walter Benn
  The Trouble with Diversity, 82
Military intervention, 44, 87, 113, 119
Mills, John Stuart, 49, 51, 61
Mining, 15, 16, 20, 56, 100, 103, 104, 115, 148, 206, 212
Moriori, 74, 75, 85–87, 204, 205
Myanmar. *See* Burma

N
Naipaul, V.S.
  A Bend in the River, 183, 184
Nasser, Gamal Abdel, 107, 112, 121
Native Americans, 71, 192, 195
Neocolonialism
  comprador elite. *See* Social class
  critique of, 110, 142, 188
  foreign-ownership in, 109, 124
Neoliberalism
  critiques of, 64, 142, 143, 146, 156, 214, 217
  deregulation and, 105
  ideology of, 106, 156, 174, 188, 190, 214
  the neoliberal city, 159, 167, 172
New Zealand
  colonial history of, 63, 74, 145, 178
  inequality in, 63, 70, 74, 85, 86, 102, 149, 180, 181

Ngũgĩ wa Thiong'o, 18, 102, 103, 120, 122, 124, 125, 131–133, 135, 136, 141, 185
Devil on the Cross, 102, 125, 131, 132, 136
Globalectics, 18
Weep Not, Child, 102
Nigeria, 17, 113, 119, 136, 145, 169, 205
inequality in, 133, 134, 143, 168, 170, 214
Lagos, 167, 169
Nixon, Rob, 14, 18, 193
Nkrumah, Kwame, 25, 107, 122
Non-Alignment Movement, 111

O
Opium, 16, 35–40, 42, 44, 46, 48–53, 55, 56, 59, 63, 72, 78, 85, 87, 100, 106, 109, 110, 146, 158, 161, 212–214
trade, 36–38, 40, 42, 44, 49, 51, 53, 72, 85
traders, 53, 63
Wars, 35–37, 49, 72
Orwell, George
Down and Out in Paris and London, 3, 121, 161, 162

P
Phenomenological reading, 11
Philippines, 56, 57, 94, 109, 184
Piketty, Thomas
Capital in the Twenty-first Century, 2, 5, 6, 9, 10, 14, 38, 53, 64, 106, 201, 212
Political economy, 1, 4, 8, 14, 20, 27, 44, 51, 55, 73, 81, 92, 110, 125, 133, 149, 158, 159, 169, 170, 174, 180, 188, 212, 218, 219

Porter, Bernard
The Lion's Share, 21, 63, 64, 70, 100
Postcolonial studies
discipline of, 12, 14, 15, 22, 24–28, 121
critique of, 36, 54, 57, 59, 75, 76, 90, 111, 112, 179, 217, 218
Marxism and, 25, 26, 110, 124, 217
Poverty
criminalisation of, 29, 43, 80, 89, 190, 203, 213, 214
features of, 166, 173, 179, 195
history of, 88
measures of, 6, 178, 179, 216
the poor, 5, 68, 174, 179, 190, 194
Pramoedya Ananta Toer, 36, 55, 185, 202
This Earth of Mankind quartet, 55
Protest, 1, 72, 82, 99, 105, 190, 213, 215

R
Racism, 29, 83, 175, 191, 197, 205, 211. *See also* Capitalism
Rhodesia, 63, 64, 100, 102, 115, 119
Rinehart, Gina, 104–106, 163
Riots UK 2011, 88, 189–191, 201, 206, 214, 216
Robins, Nick
East India Company, 54
Loot, 38, 163
The Corporation that Changed the World, 54
Romanticism, 22

S
Said, Edward, 196
Culture and Imperialism, 14, 22, 23, 119
Orientalism, 14, 87

Saro-Wiwa, Ken, 143, 144, 185
  'Africa Kills Her Sun', 143
Sartre, Jean-Paul
  Colonialism and Neocolonialism, 61, 87, 93, 126, 139–142
Satire, 29, 133, 139, 142, 143, 145, 147, 148
Scott, Kim
  That Dead Man Dance, 15, 16, 65, 67–70, 83, 93
Sedláček, Tomáš, 7, 30
  The Economics of Good and Evil, 9
Sembène, Ousmane
  The Last of the Empire, 130, 131
  Xala, 126, 131
Sen, Amartya, 91, 189, 202
  Imperial Illusions, 21
  on India, 48
  Inequality Reexamined, 25, 177, 178
  The Argumentative Indian, 9
Slow violence, 15
Slums, 17, 19, 90, 101, 159, 167, 168, 171, 176, 178
Smith, Adam, 23, 51, 94, 157, 158
Social class
  class structure, 64, 68, 69, 166, 184
  comprador elite, 17, 60, 103, 114, 135
  middle–class, 12, 115, 121, 142, 155, 156, 166, 171, 174, 175, 191, 215
  'the one per cent', 130, 163
  upward mobility, 18, 66–68, 80, 93, 130, 157, 177, 186, 187, 197
  working–class, 65, 70, 101, 115, 123
South Africa
  inequality in, 99, 102, 115, 125, 173, 216
Soyinka, Wole, 171, 185
  Opera Wonyosi, 143, 145
Stiglitz, Joseph
  The Great Divide, 130, 144

The Price of Inequality, 131, 143
Structural Adjustment Programmes, 81, 117, 170
Sukarno, 107, 112
Suri, Manil
  The Death of Vishnu, 171, 175, 176
Swarup, Vikas
  Q&A, 171, 175, 203

T
Taibbi, Matt
  Griftopia, 147, 212, 213
Tax rates, 123
Thatcher, Margaret, 157, 158, 163, 188, 206
Third Way, 107, 111, 112, 125, 126
Third World, 5, 6, 17, 107, 111, 119, 123, 124, 139, 142, 147, 149, 163, 166, 167, 172, 196
Trade tariffs, 45, 137, 159

U
Underdevelopment, 17, 107, 111, 139, 148, 170
USA
  colonial history of, 6
  imperialism, 14, 94, 109, 111, 115, 119, 158
  inequality in, 93, 111, 116

V
Violence
  by police, 87, 99, 102, 190
  displaced aggression, 202, 203
  dispossession and, 41, 43, 68, 75, 160
  domestic, 39, 203
  psychological, 80, 179, 181, 194, 198, 202

W

Wakefield, Edward Gibbon, 61
  A View of the Art of Colonization, 61, 62
Wallerstein, Immanuel, 65, 87
  Historical Capitalism, 24, 65, 83, 87, 197
Warwick Research Collective
  Combined and Uneven Development, 13
Wealth, 3, 5, 6, 9, 14, 17, 24, 37, 42, 50, 65, 168. *See also* Inequality
Wendt, Albert
  'Robocop in Long Bay', 187, 189
Wheatle, Alex
  Brenton Brown, 165, 204, 206
  Brixton Rock, 165, 186, 189, 198, 206
  The Dirty South, 165, 178, 186, 188, 189, 191, 197–199, 206
Wilkinson, Richard, and Kate Pickett
  The Spirit Level, 201, 202
Wolf of Wall Street, The, book. *See* Belfort, Jordan
Wolf of Wall Street, The, film, 2
Wood, Ellen Meiksins
  Empire of Capital, 23, 24, 66, 112
Woodmansee and Osteen
  The New Economic Criticism, 8, 28, 30
World Bank, 45, 101, 107, 117, 128, 131, 137, 149, 170, 177, 206, 215
World-system, 5, 20, 23, 24–26, 37, 44, 54, 59, 109, 112, 143, 156, 161, 163, 178, 182, 214–216, 218
World War One, 35, 58, 59, 93
World War Two, 81, 92, 94, 107, 172
Wright, Alexis
  Carpentaria, 15, 16, 103, 104

Z

Zahedieh, Nuala
  The Capital and the Colonies, 23
  'Overseas Trade and Empire', 24
Zamindars, 40, 41, 50, 76, 214
Žižek, Slavoj
  'Shoplifters of the World Unite', 186
  'The Need to Censor Our Dreams', 26

CPSIA information can be obtained
at www.ICGtesting.com
Printed in the USA
LVHW081518281119
638279LV00012BA/1333/P